The EXTREME SEARCHER'S Internet Handbook

3rd Edition

Raves for *The Extreme Searcher's Internet Handbook*

"[Hock's] clear and useful guide will help anyone interested in going beyond Google, explaining when, why, and how best to use various search tools and other web resources."

—Library Journal

"A treasure trove of tips and tricks for finding information online. ... Despite being aimed at serious searchers, this is an excellent book for people of any skill level."

—Chris Sherman
SearchDay

"Buying this book has to be the quickest way you can access year's of hard-won web searching experience. Invaluable."

—William Hann
FreePint

"A phenomenal resource for both extreme and not-so-extreme researchers. Great tips, clear explanations, and years of expertise distilled into 250 pages of clear, engaging text. This book should be on every searcher's desk."

—Mary Ellen Bates
author, *Building & Running a Successful Research Business*
and co-author, *Researching Online for Dummies*

"Here is a great how-to guide by one of the world's foremost search trainers."

—Greg Notess
Search Engine Showdown

"Clearly laid out and easy to read. Screenshots supplement the written information and a full index ensures that readers will be able to find content quickly and easily. ... a very useful book to have."

—Phil Bradley
Program: Electronic Library and Information Systems

"When a search fails, check this book for new approaches. When a source doesn't behave as it did before, check this book for alternatives. When you're confronted with an entirely new type of request or a topic area with which you are totally unfamiliar, check this book for a qualified resource."

—Marydee Ojala
editor, *ONLINE*
From the Foreword to the 3rd Edition

"The author retains his clear writing style, nice glossary, and handy surfing tips ... should be required reading for librarians, online professionals, and anyone else who wants to get the most out of the Internet. Recommended."

—CHOICE

The EXTREME SEARCHER'S Internet Handbook
3rd Edition

A Guide for the Serious Searcher

Randolph Hock

Foreword by Marydee Ojala

CyberAge Books

Medford, New Jersey

First printing, 2010

**The Extreme Searcher's Internet Handbook:
A Guide for the Serious Searcher, 3rd Edition**

Copyright © 2010 by Randolph E. Hock

Library of Congress Cataloging-in-Publication Data

Hock, Randolph, 1944-
   The extreme searcher's Internet handbook : a guide for the serious searcher / Randolph Hock. -- 3rd ed.
      p. cm.
   Includes index.
   ISBN 978-0-910965-84-2
1. Internet searching--Handbooks, manuals, etc. 2. Web search engines--Handbooks, manuals, etc. 3. Computer network resources--Handbooks, manuals, etc. 4. Web sites--Directories. 5. Internet addresses--Directories. I. Title.
   ZA4230.H63 2009
   025.0425--dc22

2009039927

Printed and bound in the United States of America.

President and CEO: Thomas H. Hogan, Sr.
Editor-in-Chief and Publisher: John B. Bryans
Managing Editor: Amy M. Reeve
VP Graphics and Production: M. Heide Dengler
Book Designer: Kara Mia Jalkowski
Cover Design: Laura Hegyi
Copyeditor: Beverly Michaels
Indexer: Candace Hyatt

www.infotoday.com

To Pamela

CONTENTS

Chapter 7   Sights and Sounds: Finding Images, Audio, and Video 195

Chapter 8   News Resources 225

FIGURES AND TABLES

FOREWORD

The continual evolution of the internet as a vehicle for the serious researcher requires searchers to match their behavior to the web terrain. "Tried and true" is a phrase that holds little value for extreme searchers. What worked last year or even six months ago could now be ineffective. Lessons learned are not committed to memory, as they become obsolete overnight. New search features, changes in databases, alternative search engines, algorithmic alterations, enhanced search capabilities, deactivation of key elements, and other modifications to search engines necessitate instant modifications to the course of research endeavors.

The Extreme Searcher's Internet Handbook not only introduces you to the basic information you need to know to become a serious searcher, but it also exposes you to the nuances, advanced techniques, and attitude of extreme searchers.

When I first heard the term "extreme searcher," I wondered how the notion of extreme sports applied to web search. Searchers don't generally practice their trade outside. They're not competing with the elements as ice climbers do or going for a snowboarder's big air. They don't travel with surfboards, racing bicycles, or other sports paraphernalia. They don't compete in the X Games.

Extreme searchers don't necessarily look the part. They could wear a suit and tie or jeans and a T-shirt. They could prefer high heels to flip-flops or vice versa. They could be neatly coifed or sport a Mohawk. They are found with fingers on a laptop or a mobile device rather than paragliding over the ocean or skiing off a cliff. They are not muddy from a motocross race. What do extreme searchers have in common with those who practice extreme sports? Adventure. The thrill of the chase. Knowing they're pitting themselves against an ever-changing environment. Striving for their personal best. A winning attitude.

Searching is a personal pursuit. Although there has been some movement toward collaborative searching, for most online researchers, it's you against the machine. It's the individual searcher who needs to be cognizant of the realities of databases, search engines, and information sources. It's you who will be able to turn a source upside down to shake out the answer; you who will expertly manipulate the search engine to reveal hidden information.

To be really good at searching means keeping up with all the changes. And no one is better qualified to help you do this than Ran Hock. He started out when online searching did not equate to internet searching. Online was a rarefied place, where only librarians and other information professionals plied their trade and honed their skills. Ran guided us through that version of extreme search, teaching about Boolean logic, structured databases, and arcane search command languages.

Easily making the transition from those early days, when online research was kept within a gated community, Ran embraced the wilder, less defined arena of internet searching. His fierce determination to spread his knowledge of search techniques resulted in this book. His understanding of the fluidity of internet research resulted in a third edition.

One thing you'll notice in this edition is a decreased emphasis on directories. Although directories were a driving force in the early days of internet search, the search engine companies have moved on. Instead of concentrating on directories and specialized portals, they've turned their attention to tweaking search algorithms and creating new types of search experiences.

We still have the "big three" when it comes to major search engines: Google, Yahoo!, and Bing (the new name for Microsoft Live). Basic search in these engines has remained relatively static, although they offer some new services and a few cosmetic alterations to their websites.

The newest idea to strike the web search world is social media. Whether you think of this as social networking, Web 2.0, social search, or consumer generated content, it's becoming an important component of real-time search and another search skill to master.

I've taught with Ran—and listened to him speak—at many educational events, such as WebSearch University, Internet Librarian, Internet Librarian International, and Computers in Libraries. Every time, even if the events are only weeks apart, I learn something new. His ability to keep himself updated is a boon for the rest of us. When a search fails, check this book for new approaches. When a source doesn't behave as it did before, check this book for alternatives. When you're confronted with an entirely new type of request or a topic area with which you are totally unfamiliar, check this book for a qualified resource.

Your reading experience, however, goes beyond the printed book. At The Extreme Searcher's Web Page (www.extremesearcher.com), you'll find updates to the websites mentioned here, notifications when URLs change, and warnings when companies go out of business or radically change their content.

Want to become an extreme searcher? Want to impress your friends, colleagues, and employers with your search expertise, your ability to find information others can't, and your knowledge of the latest in search? Want to experience the joy that comes from mastering difficult search situations and wrestling a thorny search problem to a successful conclusion?

Read this book. You'll be "extremely" glad you did.

—Marydee Ojala

Marydee Ojala edits *ONLINE: Exploring Technology & Resources for Information Professionals* and writes its business research column (The Dollar Sign). She contributes feature articles and news stories to *Information Today*, *Searcher*, *EContent*, *Intranets*, *Business Information Review*, and Information Today's *NewsBreaks*. Her blog is ONLINEInsider.net. She plans conference programs for Internet Librarian International, WebSearch University, and Search Engine Meeting. She has been co-chair of the Buying & Selling eContent conference. A long-time observer of the information industry, Marydee speaks frequently at library and information science conferences.

ACKNOWLEDGMENTS

The third edition of this book owes its existence to a large degree to the support of the readers of the first two editions. I sincerely appreciate the many comments that I have received, and I am also grateful to the increasing number of instructors who have chosen to use the book as a text in their courses.

As with my other books, I extend my thanks and appreciation to the exceptional, hard working, generous, and downright nice group of people at Information Today, Inc. I particularly thank Amy Reeve, Managing Editor (who is great to work with for many reasons, not the least of which is her tolerance for my sometimes wanting to do things "my way"); John Bryans, Editor-in-Chief and Publisher (who is not just always supportive, but always enthusiastic); Heide Dengler, VP of Graphics and Production; Kara Mia Jalkowski, Book Designer; Laura Hegyi, Cover Designer; Rob Colding, Marketing Coordinator; Beverly Michaels, Copyeditor; and Candace Hyatt, Indexer. I continue to be immensely grateful to their leader, Information Today, Inc. President and CEO, Tom Hogan, Sr., for all the extraordinary things that he has done and continues to do, both for me and for the information community at large.

On the home front, I thank my wonderful wife, Pamela, who deals lovingly and well with the vicissitudes of having a writer in the house.

INTRODUCTION

For many years, Thomas' English Muffins has had a slogan proclaiming that the tastiness of its muffins is due to the presence of myriad "nooks and crannies." The same may be said of the internet. It is in the internet's nooks and crannies that the true "tastiness" often lies. Almost every internet user has used Google and probably Yahoo!, and any group of experienced searchers could probably come up with another dozen or so sites that every one of them had used. But even for experienced searchers, time and task constraints have meant that some nooks and crannies have not been explored and exploited. These unexplored areas may be broad internet resources (discussion groups), specific types of resources (multimedia), or the nooks and crannies of a specific site (even Google). This book is intended to be an aid in that exploration.

Back on the culinary scene, I am told that some people don't take the few extra seconds needed to maximize tastiness by splitting their English muffins with a fork, but, driven by their busy schedules, just grab a knife and slice them. This book is written for those who seek to savor the extra tastiness from the internet. It will hopefully tempt you to discover what the nooks and crannies have to offer, and how to split the internet muffin with a fork almost as quickly as you can slice it with a knife.

Less metaphorically, this book is written as a guide for researchers, students, writers, librarians, teachers, and others, covering what serious users need to know to take full advantage of internet tools and resources. It focuses on what the serious searcher "has to know" but, for flavor, a dash of the "nice-to-know" is occasionally thrown in. It assumes that you already know the basics, you frequently use the internet, and you know how to use your browser. For those who are less experienced online searchers, my aim is to provide a lot that is new and useful. For those with more experience, I hope to reinforce what you know while introducing some new perspectives and new content.

If you are among those who find themselves not just using the internet but *teaching* it, the book should help you address an extensive range of students' questions. Much of what is included here is based on my experience training thousands of internet users from a wide range of professions, across a broad age range, and from more than 40 countries.

BRIEF OVERVIEW OF THE CHAPTERS

The chapter topics reflect congruence between the types of things that experienced internet users most frequently inquire about and a categorization of the kinds of resources available on the internet. An argument could certainly be made for dividing the content differently. While there is a chapter on finding products online, for example, you may wonder why there is not one specifically on finding "company information." This is because company information pervades almost every chapter. Not every chapter will be of utmost interest to every reader, but it's worth giving each chapter at least a quick glimpse. You may be surprised what some nooks (and crannies, of course) contain.

Although the nature of each chapter means that each has its own organization, they all share some common elements. Typically, each chapter includes these aspects:

- Useful background information, along with suggestions, tips, and strategies for finding and making the most effective use of sites in that area.
- Resource guides that will lead you to collections of links to major sites on the topic.
- Selected sites, which were chosen because (1) they are *valuable* resources that many if not most readers should be aware of, and (2) they are *representative* of the types of sites that are most useful for the topic. Deciding which sites to include was often difficult. Many of the sites included in this book are considered to be "the best" in their area, but space limitations meant that hundreds of great sites had to be excluded. These difficult decisions were made more palatable, however, because the resource guides included in the chapters will lead you quickly to those other great sites—you're only one or two clicks away.

Following is a quick rundown of what each chapter covers.

Chapter 1: Basics for the Serious Searcher

This chapter covers background information that serious searchers need to know in order to be conversant with internet content and issues. The background it includes helps users understand more fully the characteristics, content, and searchability of the internet. For those who teach others how to use the internet, it provides answers to some of the more frequently asked questions. Among the things included in Chapter 1 are a brief history of the internet, a look at the kinds of "finding tools" available, issues such as retrospective coverage and copyright, resources regarding citing internet sources, and suggestions for keeping up-to-date.

Chapter 2: Directories and Portals

For finding precisely what we need on the web, there are a variety of tools, including search engines, general directories, specialized directories, and portal sites. This chapter discusses the two categories of directories (general and specialized) and general, but customizable, portals. The directories offer a good look at what kinds of resources are available and can provide insight and help in focusing on a topic and identifying the most valuable resources. Portals pull together selected news, weather, and other frequently needed information, and can add greatly to the efficiency of getting what you need.

Chapter 3: Search Engines: The Basics

This chapter provides background and details about search engines that the serious searcher needs to know in order to get the best results. It also presents a case for not getting too excited about metasearch engines.

Chapter 4: Search Engines: The Specifics

This chapter examines the major search engines in detail, identifying their strengths, weaknesses, and special features, and also includes an overview of other engines. It also describes "visualization" engines (for a very different and fruitful "look" at search engine results).

Chapter 5: Discussion Groups, Forums, Newsgroups, and Their Relatives

Newsgroups, discussion groups, mailing lists, and other interactive forums form a class of internet resources that too few researchers take advantage of. These tools, which can be useful for a broad range of applications from solving a software problem to competitive intelligence, can be gold mines. This chapter outlines what they are, why they are useful, and how to locate the ones you need.

Chapter 6: An Internet Reference Shelf

All serious searchers have a collection of tools they use for quick answers—the web equivalent of a personal reference shelf. This chapter emphasizes the variety of resources available for finding quick facts, offers some direction on finding the right site for a specific need, and suggests several dozen sites of which most serious searchers should be aware.

Chapter 7: Sights and Sounds: Finding Images, Audio, and Video

Not only are there billions of images, audio files, and video files available on the web, but they are searchable (and, even better, they are findable). Whether you are looking for photos of world leaders or rare birds, a famous speech, the sound of an elephant seal, or your favorite song, this chapter provides a look at what resources and tools are available for finding the needed file and discusses techniques for doing so effectively.

Chapter 8: News Resources

This chapter covers the range of news resources available on the internet—news services and newswires, newspapers, news aggregation services, and more—and explains how to find what you are looking for effectively and efficiently. The chapter not only emphasizes the searchability of these resources, but it also calls attention to the limitations the researcher faces, particularly with regard to archival and exhaustivity issues.

Chapter 9: Finding Products Online

Whether for one's own purchase, an organization's purchase, or competitive analysis purposes, many searchers find themselves tracking and comparing products online. This chapter shows where to look and how to do it efficiently and effectively.

Chapter 10: Your Own Place on the Web: Participating and Publishing

The web has become a much more interactive, participatory, collaborative, and sharing place than it was a few years ago. Millions of people are "'publishing" on the web, perhaps without even realizing it. This chapter discusses the various options that are available for becoming a part of the web, ranging from Twittering to having a full-blown website.

SOME INTRODUCTORY ODDS AND ENDS

Most of the sites I discuss in the book do not charge for access. Occasionally, reference is made to sites that require a paid subscription or offer information for a fee; these are included here in part as a reminder that (as the serious searcher is already aware) not all of the good stuff is available for free on the internet. Commercial services such as LexisNexis, Factiva, and Dialog contain proprietary information that is critical for many kinds of research and is not available on the free web.

All sites included here were chosen because they have useful content. Except for association, government, and academic sites, most of the sites mentioned are supported by ads. On the internet, just as with television and radio, if the ratio of advertisements to useful content is too high, we can switch to another channel or another website. Some of us have come to appreciate the ads to some extent, aware as we are that advertising is what makes many valuable sites possible.

A Word on Usage

Although *internet* and *web* are not synonymous, most users do not distinguish between them. When it makes a difference, I use the appropriate term. Where I refer to resources that are generally on the web part of the internet, web is used. Where the terms are interchangeable, either term may be used.

About the Third Edition

I continue to be very gratified by the warm reception the first two editions of this book have received, which is the major impetus for the third edition. I have been particularly pleased that, in addition to its use by individuals interested in becoming more capable internet users, the book has also gained increased use as a textbook and is now being used both for graduate courses and at the undergraduate level for research and information literacy courses. Since the second edition, much of the content of the book has changed, but much has also stayed the same. Almost all of the "old standby" websites are still there, though in many cases they have been enhanced and occasionally their names have been changed. The descriptions of practically all of the sites that were in the second edition required at least some updating, and many sites, especially the search engines, required very substantial updating to reflect changes in content and changes in the interfaces. A few sites (very few) from the second edition have gone away completely, and several new sites have been added for this edition, primarily "Web 2.0" sites such as Twitter, Facebook, and LinkedIn.

Some Final Basic Advice Before You Proceed

As we have encountered the internet over the last decade or so, most of us have learned much of what we know about it in a rather piecemeal fashion, for instance, having been told about a great site, having bumped into it, or having read about it. Although this is, in many ways, an effective approach to exploring the internet, it can leave gaps in our knowledge. Because each user has individual needs, no single book can fill all of the gaps, but this one attempts to help by providing a better understanding of what is out there—as well as offering some starting points and suggestions for getting what you need—to help you find your way to the most useful nooks and crannies.

As you explore, keep in mind the following three guidelines to help you get the most value from the internet:

> One: Click everywhere.
>
> Two: Click where you have never clicked before.
>
> Three: Split your muffins with a fork.

ABOUT THE EXTREME SEARCHER'S WEB PAGE

As a supplement to this book (and his other books), the author maintains The Extreme Searcher's Web Page at www.extremesearcher.com. There you will find information about the author's books and links to sites included in this and his other books. A list of links for all of the websites included in this book can be found at that site. URLs for sites covered in this book occasionally change, and once in a while (we hope not very often), a website covered may just disappear. The Extreme Searcher's Web Page is updated on a continuing basis to account for those changes, and you will sometimes also find new sites added there. (If you should find a "dead link" on the site before the author does, you are encouraged to report it to him at the email address below.)

Since links to all websites in the book are on The Extreme Searcher's Web Page, if you bookmark that site (and use it), you will not have to type in any of the URLs included in the book. You should find the site particularly helpful for browsing through the sites covered here.

Enjoy your visit and please send any feedback to ran@extremesearcher.com.

Disclaimer

Neither the publisher nor the author makes any claim as to the results that may be obtained through the use of The Extreme Searcher's Web Page or of any of the internet resources it references or links to. Neither publisher nor author will be held liable for any results, or lack thereof, obtained by the use of this page or any of its links; for any third-party charges; or for any hardware, software, or other problems that may occur as the result of using it. The Extreme Searcher's Web Page is subject to change or discontinuation without notice at the discretion of the publisher and author.

CHAPTER 1

BASICS FOR THE SERIOUS SEARCHER

In writing this book, I have made the assumption that the reader knows the internet basics—what it is, how to get connected, and so forth. The "basics" covered in this chapter involve background information that serious searchers need to know to be fully conversant with internet content and issues, as well as general ways of approaching internet resources to find just what you need. I go over some details already familiar to many readers, but I include this background material for two purposes: (1) to allow readers to understand more fully the characteristics, content, utility, and nuances of the internet in order to use it more effectively, and (2) to help those who find themselves teaching others how to use the internet, by providing answers to some of the more frequently asked questions.

As for general approaches to finding the right resources, this chapter provides an overview and comparison of the kinds of "finding tools" available and a set of strategies that can be applied. The coverage of strategies goes into some detail on topics (such as Boolean logic) that will also be encountered elsewhere in the book. Integral to all of this are some aspects and issues regarding the *content* that is found on the internet. These aspects include the questions of retrospective coverage, quality of content, and general accessibility of content, particularly the issue of the "Deep Web" (aka, the "Invisible Web," the "Hidden Web"). Woven into this content fabric are issues, such as copyright, that affect how information found on the internet can be used. Although only lightly touched upon, it is important that every serious user have an awareness of these issues. Lastly, the chapter provides some useful resources for keeping up with the latest internet tools, content, and issues.

THE PIECES OF THE INTERNET

First, the *internet* and the *web* are not synonymous, although the terms are frequently used interchangeably. As late as the mid-1990s, the internet had some clearly distinguishable parts, as defined by their functions. Much internet usage could be thought of as internet *sans* content. It was simply a communications channel that allowed easy transfer of information. Typically, a user at one university could use the internet to send or request a file from someone at another university using FTP (File Transfer Protocol). Sending email via the internet was becoming tremendously popular at that time. A user of a commercial search service such as Dialog or LexisNexis could harness the internet as an alternative to proprietary telecommunications networks, basically sending and receiving proprietary information. "Content" parts of the internet could indeed be found, such as Usenet newsgroups, where anyone with a connection could access a body of publicly available information. Gophers (menu-based directories allowing access to files, mainly at universities) were also beginning to provide access to content.

The world changed, and content was destined to become king, when Tim Berners-Lee at CERN (Conseil Européen pour la Recherche Nucléaire) in Geneva created the World Wide Web in 1991. The web provided an easy-to-use interface for both potential content providers and users, with a GUI (Graphical User Interface) incorporating hypertext point-and-click navigation of text, graphics, and sounds, and created what was for most of us at that time an unimaginable potential for access to information.

Within less than five years, the web had overtaken email and FTP in terms of internet traffic. By 2000, usage of the other parts of the internet was becoming fused into the web. Usenet newsgroups were being accessed through a web interface, and web-based email was becoming the main—or only—form of email for millions. FTP was typically being managed through a web interface. Gophers were replaced by web directories and search engines, and any gophers you find now are likely to be in your backyard.

A VERY BRIEF HISTORY

The following selection of historical highlights provides a perspective for better understanding the nature of the internet. It should be emphasized that the internet is the result of many technologies (computing, time-sharing of computers, packet-switching, etc.) and many visionaries and great technical thinkers coming together over a period of a few decades. In addition, what they were able to accomplish was dependent upon minds and technologies of preceding decades. This selection of highlights is merely a sampling and leaves out many essential technical achievements and notable contributors. The points here are drawn primarily from the resources listed at the end of this timeline.

1957   The USSR launches *Sputnik*.

1958   Largely as a result of the *Sputnik* launch, ARPA (Advanced Research Projects Agency) is established to push the U.S. ahead in science and technology. High among its interests is computer technology.

1962   J. C. R. Licklider writes about his vision of a globally interconnected group of computers providing widespread access to data and programs; the RAND Corporation begins research on distributed communications networks for military purposes.

Early 1960s   Packet-switching moves from theory to practice.

Mid- to Late- 1960s   ARPA develops ARPANET to promote the "cooperative networking of time-sharing computers" with four host computers connected by the end of 1969 (Stanford Research Institute, UCLA, UC Santa Barbara, and University of Utah).

1965   The term "hypertext" is coined by Ted Nelson.

1968   The Tymnet nationwide time-sharing network is built.

1971   ARPANET grows to 23 hosts, including universities and government research centers.

1972   The International Network Working Group (INWG) is established to advance and set standards for networking technologies; the first chairman is Vinton (Vint) Cerf, who is later often referred to as the "Father of the Internet."

1972– 1974   Commercial database services—Dialog, SDC Orbit, Lexis, The New York Times DataBank, and others—begin making their subscription services available through dial-up networks.

1973   ARPANET makes its first international connections at the University College of London (England) and the Royal Radar Establishment (Norway).

1974   "A Protocol for Packet Network Interconnection," which specifies the details of TCP (Transmission Control Protocol), is published by Vint Cerf and Bob Kahn.

1974 Bolt, Beranek & Newman, contractor for ARPANET, opens a commercial version of the ARPANET called Telenet, the first public packet-data service.

1977 There are 111 hosts on the internet.

1978 TCP is split into TCP and IP (Internet Protocol).

1979 The first Usenet discussion groups are created by Tom Truscott, Jim Ellis, and Steve Bellovin, graduate students at Duke University and the University of North Carolina, and Usenet quickly spreads worldwide.

The first emoticons (smileys) are suggested by Kevin McKenzie.

1980s The personal computer becomes a part of millions of people's lives. There are 213 hosts on ARPANET.

BITNET (Because It's Time Network) is started, providing email, electronic mailing lists, and FTP service.

CSNET (Computer Science Network) is created by computer scientists at Purdue University, University of Washington, RAND Corporation, and BBN, with National Science Foundation (NSF) support. It provides email and other networking services to researchers without access to ARPANET.

1982 The term "internet" is first used.

TCP/IP is adopted as the universal protocol for the internet.

Name servers are developed, allowing a user to get to a computer without specifying the exact path.

There are 562 hosts on the internet.

France Telecom begins distributing Minitel terminals to subscribers free of charge, providing videotext access to the Teletel system. Initially providing telephone directory lookups, then chat and other services, Teletel is the first widespread home implementation of these types of network services.

1984 Orwell's vision, fortunately, is not fulfilled, but computers are soon to be in almost every home.

There are more than 1,000 hosts on the internet.

1985 The WELL (Whole Earth 'Lectronic Link) is started. Individual users, outside universities, can now easily participate on the internet.

There are more than 5,000 hosts on the internet.

1986   NSFNET (National Science Foundation Network) is created. The backbone speed is 56K. (Yes, as in the total transmission capability of a 56K dial-up modem.)

1987   There are more than 10,000 hosts on the internet.

1988   The NSFNET backbone is upgraded to a T1 at 1.544 Mbps (megabits per second).

1989   There are more than 100,000 hosts on the internet.
ARPANET fades away.
There are more than 300,000 hosts on the internet.

1991   Tim Berners-Lee at CERN (Conseil Européen pour la Recherche Nucléaire) in Geneva introduces the World Wide Web.
NSF removes the restriction on commercial use of the internet.
The University of Minnesota releases the first gopher, which allows point-and-click access to files on remote computers.
The NSFNET backbone is upgraded to a T3 (44.736 Mbps).

1992   There are more than 1,000,000 hosts on the internet.
Jean Armour Polly coins the phrase "surfing the internet."

1994   The first graphics-based browser, Mosaic, is released.
Internet talk radio begins.
WebCrawler, the first successful web search engine, is introduced.
A law firm introduces internet "spam."
Netscape Navigator, the commercial version of Mosaic, is shipped.

1995   NSFNET reverts to being a research network; internet infrastructure is now primarily provided by commercial firms.
RealAudio is introduced, meaning that you no longer have to wait for sound files to download completely before you begin hearing them, allowing for continued ("streaming") downloads.
Consumer services such as CompuServe, America Online, and Prodigy begin to provide access through the internet instead of only through their private dial-up networks.

1996   There are more than 10,000,000 hosts on the internet.

1999   Microsoft's Internet Explorer overtakes Netscape as the most popular browser.

1999   Testing of the registration of domain names in Chinese, Japanese, and Korean languages begins, reflecting the internationalization of internet usage.

2001   Mysterious monolith does not emerge from the Earth and no evil computers take over any spaceships (as far as we know).

2002   Google is indexing more than 3 billion webpages.

2003   There are more than 200,000,000 IP hosts on the internet.

2004   Weblogs (blogs), which started in the mid-1990s, gain widespread popularity and attention.

2005   More than 50 percent of Americans who access the internet at home have a high-speed connection.

2006   Developmental focus is on a more interactive, personalized web, with collaboration, sharing, desktop-type programs, social networking, and use of APIs (Application Program Interfaces) to integrate data from multiple sources over the web. This shift is tagged "Web 2.0."

2009   Worldwide, there are more than 1.5 billion internet users, with the largest number of users in Asia (more than 650 million users).

Internet History Resources

Anyone interested in information on the history of the internet beyond this selective list is encouraged to consult the following resources.

A Brief History of the Internet, version 3.1

www.isoc.org/internet/history/brief.shtml

Compiled by Barry M. Leiner, Vinton G. Cerf, David D. Clark, Robert E. Kahn, Leonard Kleinrock, Daniel C. Lynch, Jon Postel, Larry G. Roberts, and Stephen Wolff, this site provides historical commentary from many of the people who were actually involved in the internet's creation.

Internet History and Growth

www.isoc.org/internet/history/2002_0918_Internet_History_and_Growth.ppt

This PowerPoint presentation by William F. Slater provides a good look at the internet's pioneers and provides an excellent collection of statistics on internet growth.

Hobbes' Internet Timeline

www.zakon.org/robert/internet/timeline

This detailed timeline emphasizes technical developments and who was behind them.

Internet World Stats

www.internetworldstats.com/stats.htm

This website provides a compilation of statistics, with graphs, for internet usage worldwide.

The "New" Web: Web 2.0

By 2006, most heavy-duty internet users had begun to hear the term Web 2.0 fairly frequently—a term coined (and trademarked) in conjunction with a series of web development conferences that began in 2004. Web 2.0 refers to a "second generation" of the web that provides a much greater focus on—and use of—desktop applications made available on the web and on collaboration and sharing by users. Forerunners of this include wikis, blogs, RSS, folksonomies (tagging), and podcasts. Though Web 2.0 has no precise definition, some people also define this new generation of the web in terms of the kinds of programs and techniques used, including APIs, social software, and Ajax (Asynchronous JavaScript And XML). The glossary of this book has brief definitions of those terms. From one perspective, what the new web is really about is the *user*, with a focus on areas of user interaction such as participation, publication, social software, sharing, and "the web as platform."

Though individual websites are not usually labeled as Web 2.0, if you look closely, you will have seen these elements in more and more websites. You are seeing manifestations of it when you encounter sites that allow for user-applied "tags" (such as Flickr), in the way a search engine might "suggest" search phrases as you type in your terms, in the ability to zoom and drag maps, and in the instant windows that open on pages in response to moving your cursor or clicking (such as some of the tabs on Yahoo!'s main page). This flexible interactivity with webpages and with the web carries over into increased interactivity with others on the web and can also make web-based software (such as Google Docs) flow as smoothly as similar programs on your desktop.

SEARCHING THE INTERNET: WEB "FINDING TOOLS"

Whether your hobby or profession is cooking, carpentry, chemistry, or anything in between, the right tools can make all the difference. The same is true for searching the web. A variety of tools are available to help you find what you need, and each tool does things a little differently, sometimes with a different purpose or different emphasis, as well as different coverage and different search features.

To understand the variety of tools, it can be helpful to think of most finding tools as falling into one of three categories (although many tools will be hybrids): (1) general directories, (2) search engines, and (3) specialized directories. The third category could indeed be lumped in with the first because both are directories, but for a couple of reasons discussed later, it is worthwhile to treat them separately.

All three categories may also incorporate another function, that of a "portal," which is a website that provides a gateway not only to links but also to a number of other information resources that go beyond just the searching or browsing function. These resources may include news headlines, weather, stock market information, alerts, yellow pages, and other kinds of handy information. A portal can be general, as in the case of My Yahoo! or iGoogle, or it can be specific for a particular discipline, region, or country.

Other finding tools provide identification of other kinds of internet content, such as discussion groups (forums), images, and audio. These tools may exist either on their own sites, or they may be incorporated into any of the three main categories of tools. These specialized tools will be covered in later chapters.

General Web Directories

The general web directories, such as the Yahoo! Directory and Open Directory, are websites that provide a large collection of links arranged in categories to enable browsing by subject area (see Figure 1.1). Interestingly, general directories, though once the major web "finding tool," are now almost an historical artifact, displaced very largely by search engines.

The advantages of general directories had been the categorization and the selectivity. The categories provide easy browsing of topics, and the selectivity provides a focus on sites that are generally highly regarded for

Figure 1.1

Open Directory main page

their content and usefulness. However, with the greatly improved relevance ranking provided by search engines (particularly with respect to the much greater role in ranking that "popularity" of sites plays), the selectivity provided by directories has become much less needed and much less used. The prominence of the Yahoo! Directory on Yahoo!'s main page has rapidly diminished—as late as 2002, the directory was Yahoo!'s most prominent feature, whereas today it is not even a link on Yahoo!'s main page.

The Role of General Directories

General web directories can be a good starting place when you have a very general question (museums in Paris, dyslexia), or when you don't quite know where to go with a broad topic and would like to browse down through a category to get some guidance.

General web directories are discussed in detail in Chapter 2.

Web Search Engines

Whereas a directory may be a good start when you want to be directed to just a few selected items on a fairly general topic, search engines are the place to go when you want something on a fairly specific topic (ethics of human cloning, Italian paintings of William Stanley Haseltine). Instead of searching brief descriptions of, at most, a few million websites, as with directories, search engine services allow you to search virtually every word from several billion webpages. In addition, web search engines allow you to use much more sophisticated techniques, so you can focus on your topic more effectively (Figure 1.2). The pages included in web search engines are not placed in categories (hence, you cannot browse a hierarchy), and no prior human selectivity was involved in determining what is included in the search engine's database. As the searcher, you provide the selectivity, by the search terms you choose and by the further narrowing techniques you apply.

The Role of Search Engines

If your topic is very specific or you expect that very little is written on it, a search engine will be a much better starting place than a directory. If your search needs to be exhaustive, use a search engine. If your topic is a combination of three or more concepts (e.g., *"Italian" "paintings" "Haseltine"*), use a search engine. Find out more about search engines in Chapters 3 and 4.

Figure 1.2

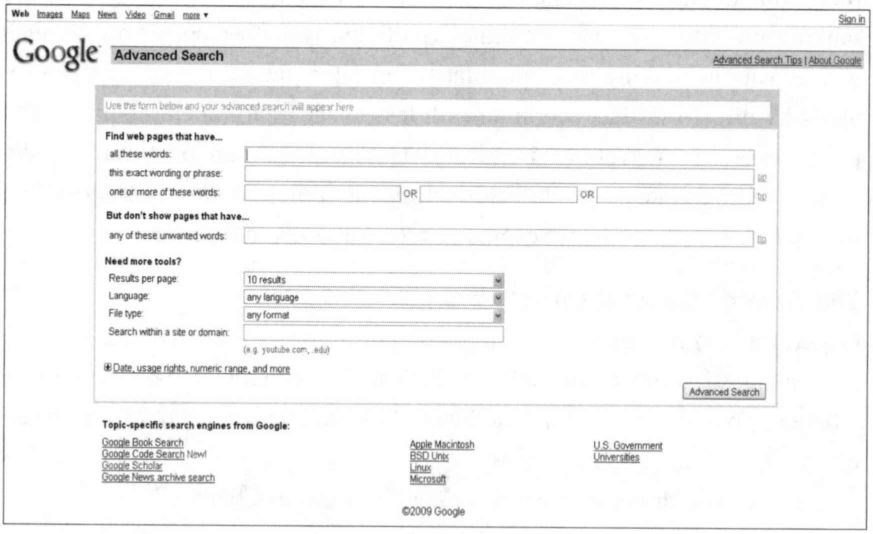

Google advanced search page

Specialized Directories (Resource Guides, Research Guides, and Metasites)

Specialized web directories are collections of selected internet resources (collections of links) on a particular topic. The topic could range from something as broad as medicine to something as specific as biomechanics. These sites go by a variety of names such as resource guides, research guides, metasites, cyberguides, and webliographies. Although their main function is to provide links to resources, they may also incorporate some additional portal features such as news headlines.

Indeed, this category could have been lumped in with the general web directories, but it is kept separate for two main reasons. First, the large general directories, such as the Yahoo! Directory and Open Directory, have several things in common besides being general: They provide categories you can browse, they have a search feature, and when you get to know them, they tend to have the same look and feel in other ways as well. The second main reason for keeping the specialized directories as a separate category is that they deserve greater attention than they often get. More searchers need to tap into their extensive utility.

The Role of Specialized Directories

Use specialized directories when you need to get to know the web literature on a topic, in other words, when you need a general familiarity with the major resources for a particular discipline or area of study. These sites can be thought of as providing some immediate expertise in using web resources in the area of interest. When you are not sure of how to narrow your topic and would like to browse, these sites can also often be better starting places than a general directory because they reflect a greater expertise in the choice of resources for a particular area than would a general directory, and they often include more sites on the specific topic than are found in the corresponding section of a general directory.

Specialized directories are discussed in detail in Chapter 2.

GENERAL STRATEGIES

For starters, there is no right or wrong way to search the internet. If you find what you need and find it quickly, your strategy is good. Keep in mind, though, that finding what you need involves other issues: Was it really the correct answer? Was it the best answer? Was it the complete answer?

At the broadest level, assuming that your question is one for which the internet is the best starting place, one approach to finding what you need on the internet is to start by answering the following three questions:

1. Exactly what is my question? (Identify what you need to know and how exhaustive or precise your answer needs to be.)
2. What is the most appropriate tool to start with? (See the previous sections on the categories of finding tools.)
3. What search strategy should I start with?

Answering these questions often takes place without much conscious effort and may take a matter of seconds. For instance, if you wanted to find out who General Carl Schurz was, you could go to your favorite search engine and type in those three words. The quick-and-easy, keep-it-simple approach is often the best.

Even with a more complicated question, it is often worthwhile to start with a very simple approach to get a sense of what is out there, then develop a more sophisticated strategy based on an analysis of your topic into concepts.

Organizing Your Search by Concepts

Thinking in terms of concepts is both a natural way of organizing the world around us and a way of organizing your thoughts about a search. Thinking in concepts is a central part of most searches. The concepts are the ideas that must be present in order for a resultant answer to be relevant, each concept corresponding to a required criterion. Sometimes a search is so specific that only a single concept may be involved, but most searches involve a combination of two, three, or four concepts. For instance, if our search is for *hotels in Albuquerque*, our two concepts are *hotels* and *Albuquerque*. If we are trying to identify webpages on this topic, any webpage that includes both concepts possibly contains what we are looking for, and any page that is missing either of those concepts is not going to be relevant.

The experienced searcher knows that for any concept, there will often be more than one term (*cars* as well as *automobiles*) that may indicate the presence of the concept, and these alternate terms also need to be considered. Alternate terms may include, among other things, (1) grammatical variations (e.g., *electricity, electrical*), (2) synonyms, near-synonyms, or closely related terms (e.g., *culture, traditions*), and (3) a term and its narrower terms. For an exhaustive search on the concept *Baltic states*, you may also want to search for *Latvia, Lithuania,* and *Estonia.* In an exhaustive search for information on the production of electricity in the Baltic states, you would not want to miss the webpage that dealt specifically with "Production of Electricity in Latvia."

When the idea of thinking in concepts is expanded further, it naturally leads to a discussion of Boolean logic, which will be covered in Chapter 4. In the meantime, the major point here is that, in preparing your search strategy, you need to think about what concepts are involved, and remember that, for most concepts, looking for alternate terms may be important.

A Basic Collection of Strategies

Just as there is no one right or wrong way to search the internet, there can be no list of definitive steps or one specific strategy to follow in preparing and performing every search. Rather, it is useful to think in terms of a toolbox of strategies and select whichever tool or combination of tools seems most appropriate for the search at hand. Among the more common strategies, strategic tools, or approaches for searching the internet are the following:

1. Identify your basic ideas (concepts) and *rely on the built-in relevance ranking* provided by search engines. When you enter terms in the major search engines and many other search sites, only those records (webpages) that contain all those terms will be retrieved, and the engine will automatically rank the order of output based on various criteria (Figure 1.3).

2. Use simple *narrowing techniques* if your results need narrowing:
   - Add another concept to narrow your search (instead of *hotels Albuquerque*, try *inexpensive hotels Albuquerque*).
   - Use quotation marks to indicate phrases when a phrase defines your concept(s) more exactly than if the words occur in different places on the page, for example, *"foreign policy."* Most websites that have a search function allow you to specify a phrase (a combination of two or more adjacent words in the order written) by the use of quotation marks.
   - Use a more specific term for one or more of your concepts (i.e., instead of *intelligence*, try *military intelligence*).
   - Narrow your results to include only those pages that contain your most important terms in the title of the page. (These kinds of techniques will be discussed in Chapter 4.)

3. *Examine your first results* and look for, and then use, relevant terms you might not have thought of at first.

4. *If you do not seem to be getting enough relevant items, use the Boolean OR operation* to allow for alternate terms; for example, *electrical OR electricity* would find all items that have either the term *electrical* or the term *electricity*. How you express the OR operation varies a bit with the finding tool, but in most cases, it is the word OR, in capital letters.

5. *Use a combination of Boolean operations* (AND, OR, NOT, or their equivalents) to identify those pages that contain a specific combination of concepts and alternate terms for those concepts (for example, to get all pages that contain either the term *cloth* or the term *fabric* and also contain the words *flax* and *shrinkage*). As will be discussed later, Boolean is not necessarily complicated and is often implied without you doing anything; it can be as simple as choosing between "all of these words" or "any of these words" options.

6. *Look at what else the finding tools (particularly search engines) can do* to allow you to get as much as you need—and only what you need. Advanced search pages are probably the first place you should look.

Ask five different experienced searchers and you will get five different lists of strategies. The most important thing is to have an awareness of the

Figure 1.3

Ranked output from Yahoo! (note "Sponsor Results")

kinds of techniques that are available to you for getting everything you need and, at the same time, only what you need.

CONTENT ON THE INTERNET

Not only the amount of information but also the kinds of information available and searchable on the internet continue to increase rapidly. In understanding what you are getting—and not getting—as a result of a search of the internet requires consideration of a number of factors, such as the time frames covered, quality of content, and a recognition that various kinds of material exist on the internet that are not readily accessible by search engines. In *using* the content found on the internet, other issues must also be considered, such as copyright.

Assessing Quality of Content

A favorite complaint of those remaining people who are still a bit shy of the internet is that the quality of information they find is often low. The same could be said about information available from a lot of other resources. A newsstand may have both the *Economist* and the *National Enquirer* on its shelves. On television, you will find both The History Channel and infomercials. Experience has taught us how, in most cases, to make a quick determination of the relative quality of the information we encounter in our daily lives. In using the internet, many of the same criteria can be successfully applied, particularly those criteria we are accustomed to applying to traditional print resources, both popular and academic.

These traditional evaluation techniques and criteria that can be applied in the internet context include:

1. Consider the source.

From what organization does the content originate? Look for the name of the organization both on the webpage itself and in the URL. Is the content identified as coming from a known source such as a news organization, a government, an academic journal, a professional association, or a major investment firm? Just because the information does not come from such a source is certainly not cause enough to reject it outright. On the other hand, even if it does come from such a source, don't bet the farm on this criterion alone.

TIP:

If you don't immediately see a link to get back to the home page of a site, try clicking on the site's logo. It usually works.

Look at the URL. Often you will immediately be able to identify the owner. Peel back the URL to the domain name. If that does not adequately identify its origins, you can check details of the domain ownership on sites that provide access to a Whois database, such as Network Solutions' WHOIS Search (www.networksolutions.com/whois) or DomainTools (www.domain tools.com). For most countries, Whois-type sites are available. The Internet Assigned Numbers Authority provides a list of Whois sites by country (www.iana.org/domains/root/db).

Be aware that some look-alike domain names are intended to fool the reader as to the origin of the site. The top-level domain (.edu, .com, etc.) may provide some clues about the source of the information, but do not make too many assumptions here. An .edu or .ac domain does not necessarily assure scholarly content, given that students as well as faculty can often easily get a space on the university server.

A tilde [~] in a directory name is often an indication of a personal page. Again, don't reject something on such a criterion alone. There are some very valuable personal pages out there.

Is the actual author identified? Is there an indication of the author's credentials? The author's organization? Search for other things by the same author. Does she or he publish a lot on spontaneous human combustion or extraterrestrial origins of life on Earth? If you recognize an author's name and the work does not seem consistent with other works from the same author, question it. It is easy to impersonate someone on the internet.

2. Consider the motivation.

What seems to be the purpose of the site—academic, political, consumer protection, sales, entertainment (don't be taken in by a spoof!)? There is nothing inherently bad (or for that matter necessarily inherently good) in any of those purposes, of course, but identifying the motivation can be helpful in assessing the degree of objectivity. Is any advertising on the page clearly identified, or is advertising disguised as something else?

3. Look at the quality of the writing.

If there are spelling and grammatical errors, assume that the same level of attention to detail probably went into the gathering and reporting of the "facts" given on the site.

4. Look at the quality of the documentation of sources cited.

First, remember that even in academic circles, the number of footnotes is not a true measure of a work's quality. On the other hand, and more importantly, if facts are cited, does the page identify the origin of the facts? If a lot rests on the information you are gathering, check out a few of the cited sources to be sure they really do give the facts that were quoted.

5. Is the site and its contents as current as it should be?

If a site is reporting on current events, the need for currency and the answer to the question of currency will be apparent. If the content is something that should be up-to-date, look for indications of timeliness, such as a "last updated" date on the page or telling examples of outdated material. For example, if it is a site that recommends which search engines to use, and WebCrawler is still listed, don't trust the currency (or for that matter, accuracy) of other things on the page. What is the most recent material that is referred to? If you find a number of dead links, assume the author of the page is not giving it much attention.

6. For facts you are going to use, verify using multiple sources, or choose the most authoritative source.

Unfortunately, many "facts" given on webpages are simply wrong, whether from carelessness, exaggeration, guessing, or other reasons. Often facts are wrong because the person creating that page's content did not bother to check the facts. If you need a specific fact, such as the date of a historic event, look for more than one webpage that gives the date and see if they agree. Also remember that some websites are more authoritative than others. If you have a quotation in hand and want to find who said it, you might want to go to a source such as Bartleby.com (which includes very respected quotations sources), instead of taking the answer from a webpage of lesser-known origins.

For more details and other ideas about evaluating quality of information found on the internet, the following two resources will be useful.

The Virtual Chase: Evaluating the Quality of Information on the Internet
www.virtualchase.com/quality

Created by Genie Tyburski and now maintained by Justia.com, this site provides an excellent overview of the factors and issues to consider when evaluating the quality of information found on a website. The site provides checklists and examples of sites that demonstrate both good and bad qualities.

Evaluating the Quality of WWW Resources
www.valpo.edu/library/user/evaluation.html

This site from Valparaiso University provides a detailed set of criteria and also about three dozen links to other sites that address the topic of evaluating web resources. Links to exercises and worksheets on the topic are also included.

Retrospective Coverage of Content

It is tempting to say that a major weakness of internet content is lack of retrospective coverage. This is certainly an issue for which the serious user should have a high level of awareness. It is also an issue that should be put into perspective. The importance and amount of relevant retrospective coverage available depends on the kind of information you are seeking at any particular moment and on your particular question. It is safe to say that no webpages on the internet were created before 1991.

Books, Ancient Writings, and Historical Documents

The lack of pre-1991 webpages does not mean that earlier *content* is not available. Indeed, if a published work is moderately well-known and was written before 1922 or so, you are at least as likely to find it on the internet as in a small local public library. Take a look at the list of works included in the Project Gutenberg site and The Online Books Page (see Chapter 6) where you will find works of Cicero, Balzac, Heine, Disraeli, Einstein, and thousands of other authors. Also look at some of the other websites discussed in Chapter 6 for sources of historical documents.

Scholarly and Technical Journals and Popular Magazines

If you are looking for full-text articles from journals or magazines written several years ago, you are not likely to find them free on the internet (and, for most journal articles, you are not even very likely to find the ones written this week, last month, or last year). This lack of content is more a function of copyright and requirements for paid subscriptions than a matter of the retrospective aspect. The distinction also needs to be made here between free material and "for fee" material on the internet. On a number of internet sources (such as IngentaConnect and Google Scholar), you can find references to scholarly and other material going back several years. Most likely you will need to pay to see the full text, but fees tend to be very reasonable. Whatever source you use for serious research, whether it's the internet or other, examine the source to see how far back it goes.

Newspapers and Other News Sources

If, when you speak of news, you think of "new news," retrospective coverage is not an issue. But if you are looking for newspaper articles or other news reports dating back more than a few days, the time span of available content on any particular site is crucial. In 2000, many newspaper websites contained only the current day's stories, with a few having up to a year or two of stories. Fortunately, more and more newspaper and other news sites are now archiving their material, and you may find several years of content on the site. Look closely at the site to see exactly how far back the site goes.

Old Web Pages

A different aspect of the retrospective issue centers on the fact that many webpages change frequently and many simply disappear altogether. Pages that existed in the early 1990s are likely either to be gone or to have different content than they did then. This becomes a significant problem when trying to track down early content or citing early content. Fortunately, there are at least partial solutions to the problem. For very recent pages that may have disappeared or changed in the last few days or weeks, a search engine's "cache" option may help. For webpages in their databases, major search engines have stored a copy. If you find the reference to the page in search results, but when you try to go to it, either the page is completely gone or the content that you expected to find on the page is no longer there, click on the "cached" option and you will get to a copy of the page as it was when the search engine last indexed it. Even if you found the page elsewhere initially, search for it using a search engine, and if you find it there, try the cache.

For locating earlier pages and their content, try the Wayback Machine.

Wayback Machine—Internet Archive

www.archive.org

The Wayback Machine provides access to the Internet Archive, which has the purpose of "offering permanent access for researchers, historians, and scholars to historical collections that exist in digital format." It allows you to search more than 150 billion pages and see what a particular page looked like at various periods in internet time. A search yields a list of what pages are available for what dates as far back as 1996 (Figure 1.4). As well as web-pages, it archives moving images, texts, music, and other audio. Its produc-ers claim it is the largest database ever built.

Figure 1.4

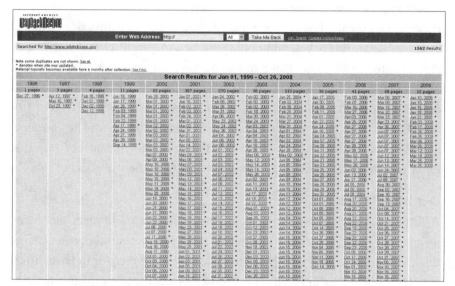

Wayback Machine search results showing pages available for whitehouse.gov

CONTENT—THE DEEP WEB

No matter how good you are at using web search engines, there are valuable resources on the web that search engines will not find for you. You can *get to* most of them if you know the URL, but a search engine search will probably not find them for you. These resources, often referred to as the Deep Web, the Hidden Web, or the Invisible Web, contain a variety of content, including—and most importantly—databases of articles, data, statistics, and government documents. The term *invisible* here refers to "invisible to search engines." There is nothing mysterious or mystical involved.

Knowing about the Deep Web is important because it contains a lot of tremendously useful information—and it is large. Various estimates put the size of the Deep Web at from 200 to 500 times the content of the visible web. Before that number sinks in and alarms you, keep in mind the following:

1. The Deep Web contains very important material.
2. For the information there that you are likely to have a need for and the right to access, there are ways of finding out about it and getting to it.
3. While the sheer volume seems overwhelming, most of the material may be meaningless except to those who already know about it, or to the producer's immediate relatives. Much of the material that can't be found is probably not worth finding.

To adequately understand what the Deep Web is all about, one must know why certain kinds of content are not visible to search engine searches. Note the use of the word *content* instead of the word *sites*. The main page of a Deep Web site is usually easy to find and is covered by search engines. It is the rest of the site (webpages and other content within the site) that may be hidden. Search engines do not index certain web content mainly for the following reasons:

1. The search engine *does not know about the page*. No one has submitted the URL to the search engine, and no pages currently covered by the search engine have linked to it. (This falls in the category, "Hardly anyone cares about this page, you probably don't need to either.")
2. The search engines have *decided not to index* the content because it is too deep in the site (and probably less useful), the page changes so frequently that indexing the content would be somewhat meaningless (as, for example, in the case of some news pages), or the page is generated dynamically and likewise is not amenable to indexing. (Think in terms of "Even if you searched and found the page, the content you searched for would probably be gone.")
3. The search engine has been *asked not to index* the content by the presence of a robots.txt file on the site that asks engines not to index the site or not to index specific pages or particular parts of the site. (A lot of this content could be placed in the "It's nobody else's business" category.)
4. The search engine *does not have or use the technology required* to index non-HTML content. This applies to files such as images and a few other file types. Until 2001, this category included file types such as PDF (Portable Document Format) files, Excel files, Word files, and

others that began to be indexed by the major search engines in 2001 and 2002. Audio and video content, such as "flash" movies, have been difficult to index, but with an increased amount of readable data attached to such files, the files are much more searchable and retrievable than they were just a few years ago. Because of this increased coverage, the Deep Web may actually be shrinking in proportion to the size of the total web.

5. The search engine cannot get to the pages to index them because *it encounters a request for a password or the site has a search box* that must be filled out in order to get to the content.

It is the last part of the last category that holds the most interest for searchers—sites that hold their information in databases. Prime examples of such sites would be phone directories, literature databases (such as Medline), newspaper sites, and patents databases. As you can see, if you can find out that the site exists, then you can search its contents (without going through a search engine). This leads to the obvious question of where one finds out about sites that contain unindexed (Deep Web) content.

The best way to find out about these sites is to find a good specialized directory (resource guide) that covers your area of interest. In such a directory, you will find reference to the major websites in that subject area, including websites that contain databases (see Chapter 2 for the discussion of specialized directories).

In the past, there were multiple sites that contained collections of links to major Deep Web websites. Some of the best known have now been discontinued or have not been updated because of the difficulty of adequately keeping up. The following site, however, is a directory of searchable databases that provides another way of finding Deep Web websites for a broad variety of subject areas. For more information on what the Deep Web is, why things are invisible to search engines, etc., you may also want to check out the excellent (though now somewhat dated) book by Chris Sherman and Gary Price, *The Invisible Web: Uncovering Information Sources Search Engines Can't See* (CyberAge Books, Medford, NJ, 2001).

CompletePlanet
completeplanet.com

The site claims to cover "70,000 searchable databases and specialty search engines," but a significant number of the sites are such things as company website searches, university catalogs, and art gallery catalogs, and many are not necessarily "invisible." It does list a lot of useful resources, but the content on the CompletePlanet site also brings home the point of how trivial much Deep Web material can be.

COPYRIGHT

Because of the serious implications of this topic, this section could extend for thousands of words. Because this chapter is about basics, however, a few general points will be made here, and the reader is encouraged to go for more detail to the sources listed next, which are much more authoritative and extensive on the copyright issue. For those in large organizations, particularly an educational institution, you may want to check your organization's website for local guidelines regarding copyright.

Copyright—Some Basic Points

Here are some basic points about copyright:

1. For the U.S., "Copyright is a form of protection provided by the laws of the United States (title 17, U.S. Code) to the authors of 'original works of authorship,' including literary, dramatic, musical, artistic, and certain other intellectual works" (www.copyright.gov/circs/circ1.pdf). As stated on the official U.K. Intellectual Property site, "Copyright gives the creators of a wide range of material, such as literature, art, music, sound recordings, films and broadcasts, economic rights enabling them to control use of their material in a number of ways, such as by making copies, issuing copies to the public, performing in public, broadcasting and use online. It also gives moral rights to be identified as the creator of certain kinds of material, and to object to distortion or mutilation of it" (www.ipo.gov.uk/types/copy/c-about/c-about-faq/c-about-faq-whatis.htm). Other countries will have similar definitions and descriptions according to their own legal definition of copyright. Regardless of the country, copyright (and any failure to acknowledge it appropriately) has legal, moral, and economic implications and repercussions.

TIP:

On virtually every site, look for a site index and a search box. They are often more useful for navigating a site than the graphics and links on its home page.

2. Assume that what you find on a website is copyrighted, unless the site states otherwise or you know otherwise, based, for example, on the age of the item. See the site for the copyright office in your own country for details about the time frames for copyrights. (In the U.S., of considerable use for webpage creators is the fact that "Works by the U.S. Government are not eligible for U.S. copyright protection" (www.copyright.gov/circs/circ1.pdf). You should still identify the source when quoting something from a site, even if the material is not under copyright.

3. The same basic rules that apply to using printed material apply to using material you get from the internet, the most important being: For any work you write for someone else to read, cite the sources you use.

For more information on copyright and the internet, see the following sources.

U.S. Copyright Office

www.copyright.gov

The official U.S. Copyright Office site has copyright information (for the U.S.) directly from the horse's mouth.

The U.K. Intellectual Property Office—Copyright

www.ipo.gov.uk/copy

The copyright section of the U.K. Patent Office site describes in detail, but also in a very readable fashion, what both the creators and users of copyrighted material need to know.

Canadian Intellectual Property Office—A Guide to Copyrights

www.cipo.ic.gc.ca/eic/site/cipointernet-internetopic.nsf/eng/wr00037.html

This is, as the site says, a "guide," not a legal document. Look particularly at the "Twenty Common Questions About Copyright" section. (For other countries, do a search for analogous sites.)

Copyright Website

www.benedict.com

This site is particularly good for addressing, in laypersons' language, the issues involved in the copyright of digital materials. It also provides background and discussion on some well-known legal cases on the topic.

**Copyright and Fair Use in the Classroom, on the Internet,
and the World Wide Web**

www.umuc.edu/library/copy.shtml

This page, from the University of Maryland, is an example of an institutional site that provides practical guidelines—in this case, in the educational context—for use of copyrighted material on websites and elsewhere.

CITING INTERNET RESOURCES

The biggest problem with citing a source you find on the internet is identifying the author, the publication date, and so forth. In many cases, the information just isn't there, or you have to really dig to find it. Basically, when citing internet sources, you need to give as much of the typical citation information as you would for a printed source (author, title, publication, date, etc.), add the URL, and include a comment such as "Retrieved from the World Wide Web, October 15, 2009" or "Internet, accessed October 15, 2009." If your reader isn't particularly picky, you can just give the information about who wrote it, the title (of the webpage), a date of publication if you can find it, the URL, and when you found the material on the internet. If you are submitting a paper to a journal for publication, to a professor, or including it in a book, you need to be more careful and follow whatever style guide is recommended. Since the details of exactly how you will write the latter kind of citation will vary both with the particular style (MLA, APA, Chicago, etc.) and with the type of publication (articles, books, newsletters, standalone website page, etc.), it is not feasible to provide examples here. Fortunately, many style guides are available online. The following two sites provide links to popular style guides online.

Journalism Resources—Guide to Citation Style Guides

bailiwick.lib.uiowa.edu/journalism/cite.html

Karla Tonella provides links to more than a dozen online style guides.

Citation Styles, Style Guides, and Avoiding Plagiarism: Citing Your Sources
www.lib.berkeley.edu/instruct/guides/citations.html

This site provides a compilation of guidelines based on the following well-known style guides: MLA, APA, Chicago, and Turabian.

KEEPING UP-TO-DATE ON INTERNET RESOURCES AND TOOLS

For those who want to be alerted to the more valuable resources that become available online, the following sites will be useful. Also, numerous specialized sites that cover specific areas (such as science) or tools (such as search engines) will be mentioned throughout the following chapters. All the sites listed here provide free email alert services and also provide archives of past content.

ResourceShelf

www.resourceshelf.com

This site, compiled and edited by Gary Price and Shirl Kennedy and updated daily, provides extensive updates on new resources. The site also provides a blog newsletter that is extremely useful for being alerted to new sites, particularly those in the Deep Web.

FreePint

www.freepint.com

This U.K.-based site, created by William Hann, provides:

- A free email newsletter with tips on internet searching and reviews of websites
- FreePint Bar (forums where subscribers can post internet-related research questions and comments)
- Resources including book reviews and event listings, and the FreePint Portal that brings together current and archived FreePint articles and book reviews, etc.

ResearchBuzz

www.researchbuzz.org/wp

This site, maintained by Tara Calishain, covers news on a broad spectrum of internet research tools and provides articles, archives, and a weekly newsletter.

Internet Resources Newsletter

www.hw.ac.uk/libwww/irn

Produced by the Heriot-Watt University Library, "the free, monthly newsletter for academics, students, engineers, scientists and social scientists" contains descriptions and reviews of new, useful websites, and other internet-related news, reviews, press releases, etc.

The Internet Scout Project

scout.wisc.edu

The Internet Scout Project produces the Scout Report, published since 1994, which provides well-annotated reviews of new sites, with a weekly report on websites for research, education, general interest, and network tools.

CHAPTER 2

DIRECTORIES AND PORTALS

Though we may seldom consciously think about it, when we are on a quest for anything (*quest* as in *quest*ion), we usually take one of two routes: browsing or asking. Using a department store analogy, if I am looking for men's suits, I can browse the store directory, find that menswear is on the third floor, go there, and browse there for the signs that lead to men's suits, then follow other signs that lead to the right style, price, and size. Along the way, I may gain information about what else is available. If I am looking for digital picture frames, I could take the same approach, but I might not be sure whether to look in the home furnishings department with other frames or in the electronics section. In either case, I also have the option of just asking a sales associate, who, with a little bit of luck, will tell me precisely where to go. There are benefits to both approaches, which present the temptation here to go into a long (perhaps risky) soliloquy on hunters versus gatherers, gender differences (men's archetypal antipathy toward asking directions), etc. Finding things on the internet is similar. We can browse through labels (categories), or we can ask directly, using a search engine. Even for individual websites, we often have the choice of just asking, using a search box, or browsing categories. Each approach has its advantages and disadvantages, bringing up issues such as terminology, serendipity, efficiency, reliability, etc. In this chapter, we look at tools for browsing: directories and portals. General directories try to organize selected sites from across all subject areas, specialized directories focus more precisely on a specific subject or content type, and portals bring together (usually on a single page) a collection of selected content (links or actual information) relevant to a specific subject area or an individual's needs. The common themes of all of these tools are *selectivity* and *organization* of information.

GENERAL WEB DIRECTORIES

General web directories are websites that selectively catalog and categorize the broad range of sites available on the web and usually include only sites that are likely to be of interest to a large number of users. Although general web directories, such as the Yahoo! Directory, have quite a bit in common with web search engines, they also differ tremendously from search engines, particularly in size, purpose, and, of course, selectivity and organization.

General web directories serve unique research purposes and in some cases may be the best starting point, even though their databases include far less than 1 percent of what search engine databases cover.

The content of general directories is (usually) handpicked by people who ask, "Is this site of enough interest to enough people that it should be included in the directory?" If the answer is yes (and in some cases, if the owner of the site has paid a fee), the site is added to the directory's database (catalog) and is listed in one or more of the subject categories. The result is a collection of sites that is selective (sites have to meet the selection criteria) and categorized (all sites are arranged in categories; see Figure 1.1). Because of the selectivity, the directory user is working, theoretically, with higher quality sites—the wheat and not the chaff. Because the sites are arranged in categories, the user has the option of starting at the top of the category hierarchy and browsing down until the appropriate level of specificity is reached. In further contrast to search engines, directories (both general and specialized) usually have only one entry for each site, instead of including many pages from the same site. For search purposes, the directories may index a site only under the words in the category, the name of the site, and a brief description, in contrast to search engines, which may index every word on a page.

The databases of general web directories are much smaller than those created and used by web search engines, the former containing at most a few million sites and the latter billions of pages. Web directories are designed primarily for browsing and for answering general questions. Sites on very specific topics, such as "UV-enhanced dry stripping of silicon nitride films" or "social security retirement program reform in Croatia," are generally not included. As a result, directories are most successfully used for *general* rather than *specific* questions, for example, "types of chemical reactions" or "social security." Although browsing through the categories is the major idea behind the design of general web directories, directories do provide a search box to allow you to bypass the browsing and go directly to the sites in the database.

As stated in Chapter 1, though they were once (circa early 1990s) the major web "finding tool," general web directories are now almost an historical artifact, having been replaced in most circumstances by search engines. The advantages of general directories had been their categorization and selectivity. They still provide categories for easy browsing of topics, but the selectivity function has become much less relevant. The greatly improved ranking of results now offered by search engines has resulted in "high quality" sites now much more likely to appear near the top of the list of search engine results. Interest in general directories has plummeted, reflected in the fact that the prominence of the Yahoo! Directory on Yahoo!'s main page has diminished: As late as 2002, the directory was Yahoo!'s most prominent feature, while today it does not even have a link on Yahoo!'s main page. Yahoo! has quietly been pulling the plug on its directory. The other major general directory, Open Directory, is still alive, but it receives little attention from the general web user.

STRENGTHS AND WEAKNESSES OF GENERAL WEB DIRECTORIES

Strengths

✔ Selective

✔ Classified (categorized)

✔ Easily browsed

✔ Good for general questions

✔ Most have some searchability

Weaknesses

✔ Relatively small database compared to web search engines

✔ May not have sites addressing very specific topics

✔ Typically less search functionality than most search engines

✔ Paid inclusion may affect quality

✔ Tend to index only the main pages of sites

CLASSIFICATION OF SITES IN GENERAL WEB DIRECTORIES

General web directories typically organize sites into about a dozen broad categories, with each of those categories broken down into additional levels of hierarchy. This categorization can be the most important reason to go to a directory. It allows browsing down through the levels of the classification hierarchy and can provide valuable direction for a searcher who is not quite sure how to narrow down a broad topic.

Different directories use different classification schemes, which may influence a user to choose one over another. Yahoo! has a major category for Government, but in Open Directory, government sites are scattered among other categories. Both directories, however, do use cross-references (indicated by an @ sign), which means that you do not have to rely entirely on choosing exactly the correct category in which to begin your browsing.

SEARCHABILITY OF GENERAL WEB DIRECTORIES

Most general web directories have a search box on their main page, which can cause confusion with web search engines. (Technically, almost any website that has a search box does indeed have a search engine behind it, but that's not what is generally meant by *web search engine*.) By entering a term in a directory's search box, you will usually be searching the directory's database. Both the Yahoo! Directory and Open Directory automatically AND all of the terms you enter, and allow you to use quotation marks to search for phrases and a minus sign to exclude a term. Both also have an advanced search page that enables you to search within a specific category.

Size of Web Directory Databases

Whereas major web search engines can contain as many as several *billion* records (webpages), directories typically have a few *million* or a few thousand records (sites). This is good news and bad news: good because it is reflective of the high degree of selectivity, bad because you are missing out on the vast majority of web content that is out there.

When to Use a General Web Directory

When all of these factors are combined, they point to some fairly obvious situations in which starting with a directory may be your best bet:

1. For a general question—in other words, when you don't have something very specific in mind—a general web directory can be the place to go. What defines "general" vs. "specific"? As a rule of thumb, you might think in terms of the number of concepts involved. Let's say you're headed to Tblisi for the first time, and you just want to look around on the web to see what information is available about the city. One or two concepts such as *Tblisi* or *Tblisi museums* is fairly general, and you might want to head for a directory rather than a search engine. A search involving three concepts is getting more specific than a general directory is able to support, for example, *Tblisi art museums*. Similarly, if a single term itself is very specific, such as *cyclopentanecarbaldehyde*, don't count on a directory.

2. This is basically a corollary of the previous point: Start with a general web directory when you know you need to get more specific than what you have in mind at the moment, and you need to browse to help narrow your search.

The Major General Web Directories

Two very large general web directories and a few directories that are smaller and more selective but not subject-specific make up the major general web directories category. We'll look here at the two largest and some additional representative, well-known, more selective sites. Following that is a discussion of specialized directories that focus on particular subject areas.

Yahoo! Directory

dir.yahoo.com

The Yahoo! Directory is the best-known general web directory, although it is probably smaller than Open Directory. For Yahoo! users, it is important to clearly distinguish the Yahoo! Directory from the Yahoo! web search. Yahoo!

started as a directory rather than as a search engine, and in its first years, the main Yahoo! page was primarily a directory, with the list of categories dominating the page. By 2001, the emphasis on the main page had moved in the direction of a web portal, with a lot more resources besides just the directory. In 2004, Yahoo!'s marketing emphasis moved to the search function, as Yahoo! began offering its own general web search databases in order to compete with Google. By mid-2006, the directory function was, to say the least, "downplayed," with the directory categories not shown at all on the main page or even directly linked to it. (Hopefully, Yahoo! will continue to at least maintain the directory, but as with many other internet companies, the user's fate rests in the hands of whichever Silicon Valley marketing whiz is currently in charge.) To get to the Yahoo! Directory, the easiest way is to go directly to dir.yahoo.com.

Browsing Yahoo!

Yahoo! has categorized the sites in its directory into more than a dozen major categories on the Directory home page, each typically with three to six sublevels, for example:

Home > Science > Mathematics > Geometry >
Computational Geometry > Trigonometry

You can get a fairly full understanding of the capabilities Yahoo! provides for browsing through a close examination of a directory page. Figure 2.1 shows a page that resulted from clicking on the Social Science category, and from there, on Anthropology and Archaeology.

Note the following points:

1. There is a search box that allows you to search the web, the Directory, or just within the current category. The Categories choice is a very powerful tool. If you are looking for graphics sites (from the "graphic arts" side rather than from the computer and web side), you might start by browsing from "Arts and Humanities" to "Design Arts" to "Graphic Design." At that point, because more than 1,000 Yahoo! listings are available from that level, you might use the search box to search just in the current category to avoid encountering many irrelevant sites.

2. Near the top of each page, Yahoo! reminds you where you are in the directory (Directory > Social Science > Anthropology and Archaeology).

Figure 2.1

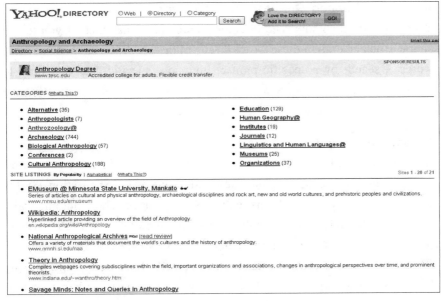

Yahoo! Directory page

(In the web design world, these kinds of links are known as "bread-crumbs.") The preceding levels are clickable here, allowing you to go back up the hierarchy one or more steps.

3. The Categories section of each page shows what additional subcate-gories are available and how many listings are in each. The @ sign indi-cates that this is a cross-reference to a category primarily found elsewhere in the hierarchy. In this example, on the Anthropology and Archaeology page, if you click on Anthrozoology, you will be taken to a page from the Biology category.

4. Site Listings lists the sites classified at this current level of specificity. Clicking on an entry will take you to the actual site. In some cases, the list can be broken down by popularity or in alphabetical order. The Sponsor Results found here are ads.

5. Inside Yahoo! listings (not shown in Figure 2.1) takes you to poten-tially relevant Yahoo! resources such as News, Finance, and country information.

Yahoo!'s Advanced Directory Search Page

Yahoo! provides an advanced directory search page that enables you to use simple Boolean ("all of these words," "any of these words," or "none of these words"), search by a specific phrase, limit to a specific category, limit to when updated, apply the SafeSearch limit (to avoid "adult content"), and specify how many results are shown per page.

Yahoo! Directory RSS Feeds

If you would like to be alerted to new entries in Yahoo! Directory categories, you can take advantage of the New Additions via RSS section on the Directory's main page. With this feature, you can have Yahoo! automatically notify you, through your personalized My Yahoo! portal or other RSS reader, of new additions in any of more than 30 directory categories/subcategories. (RSS feeds are discussed in detail in Chapter 8, but briefly, RSS [Really Simple Syndication] is an HTML format by which news providers, websites, blogs, and others can easily distribute their content to other sites.)

Yahoo! Kids

Yahoo! Kids (kids.yahoo.com) is the version of Yahoo! built for kids ages 7 to 12. The directory portion of the site contains age- and content-appropriate sites, along with a number of other references and other features to use at home and in the classroom.

Open Directory Project

dmoz.org

Open Directory Project (Open Directory) is the largest of the general web directories (with more than 4 million sites) and differs from Yahoo!'s directory in several significant ways: (1) Instead of paid editors, Open Directory uses volunteers (more than 80,000 of them); (2) it is a pure "directory" and does not position itself as a portal or general web search engine; and (3) there are no paid listings. The Open Directory database is used for the directories that you will find on many other sites, including Google (at directory.google.com).

Browsing Open Directory

Open Directory divides its site into 16 top-level categories, and each is further categorized into several additional levels, such as:

TIP:

Browsing a general web directory can be a great way to get ideas for term papers.

Top: Society: Government: Finance: Central Banks: Supranational

The World category is unique in that it provides directory access to web-sites in 80 languages. The subcategories found there will differ.

A look at a sample directory page (as with Yahoo!) can identify some of Open Directory's most important aspects (Figure 2.2). The most significant features are:

1. A search box gives the option of searching the entire directory or just the current category.

2. A reminder, under the search box, is given of where you are in the subject hierarchy. Each level is clickable, allowing you to move back up the hierarchy easily.

3. The subject hierarchy is followed by a list of the subcategories and usually a "See also" list of additional categories. The latter points to other sections in the Open Directory, as does the @ sign that occurs after some of the subcategories.

4. Following the subcategories will be the listings of the sites themselves, with brief annotations.

5. If the directory database contains articles on this topic in languages other than English, you will see a listing for "This category in other languages."

6. Unique to Open Directory is the Descriptions link in the upper right-hand corner of the page. Clicking on this will take you to a "scope note" defining what kinds of things are placed in this category.

7. At the bottom of the pages are links to several search engines and even to Yahoo!. Clicking the links will execute a search on the name of the current category using these tools.

Searching Open Directory

The Open Directory database can be searched using the search box found on the main page, at the top of directory pages, and at the bottom of search results pages. Search syntax is a bit more sophisticated than that offered by Yahoo!:

- Multiple terms are automatically ANDed. *Eastern Europe* will get only those items containing both terms (capitalization is ignored).

Figure 2.2

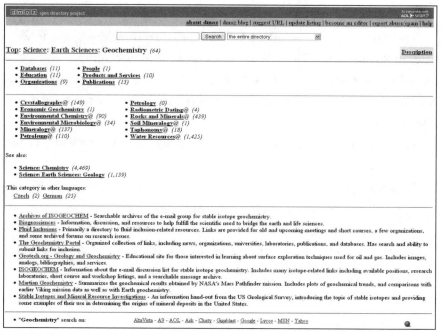

Open Directory directory page

- The automatic AND can be overridden by use of an OR (capitalization not required), e.g., *cycling OR bicycling.*

- You can specify a phrase by using quotation marks, e.g., *"Native American."*

- A minus sign or *andnot* will exclude a term; e.g., *vienna -virginia* will eliminate records containing the term *virginia* from the listing of websites (but not from categories).

- Prefixes can be used to limit results to records that have a particular term in the title, URL, or description, e.g., *t:austria, u:cam, u:cam.ac.uk or d:gardening.*

- You can use right-hand truncation. *german** will retrieve variants such as *german, germany,* and *germanic.*

- Various combinations of these functions can be used in combination. However, if you are looking for that degree of specificity, consider using a search engine instead of a directory.

Open Directory search results pages contain the following details (Figure 2.3):

- Category headings containing the term you searched for or headings that were identified through the websites identified by the search. The number of sites in the category is also shown.
- Sites where the title of the site or the annotation contained your term(s). The category in which the term occurred is also shown and is clickable so it can take you to that category.
- As when browsing through categories, links to search engines are given at the bottom of search results pages. Clicking on any of these links will cause you to be switched to that engine, and your search will be executed there. Another Open Directory search box will also be found at the bottom of search results pages.

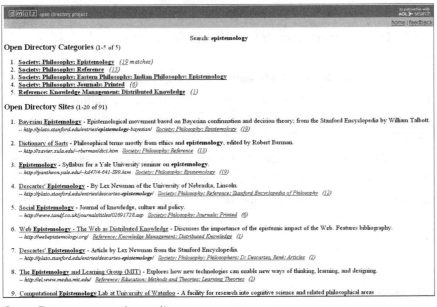

Figure 2.3

Open Directory search results page

Open Directory's Advanced Search Page

The link to the advanced search page, found on Open Directory's main page beside the search box, takes you to a page where you can limit your search to a particular category, to Categories Only or Sites Only, or to sites that fall in the categories of Kids, Teens, or Mature Teens.

OTHER GENERAL WEB DIRECTORIES

Other general web directories are available, although none as large as the two just discussed. Most of the others specialize in some way, and the dividing line between general and specialized is a bit hazy. Some directories are general with regard to subjects covered but specialized with regard to geographic coverage, such as the numerous country-specific directories. Those directories that are specialized by subject are covered later in this chapter. Here, though, we will look at two more directories that are general with regard to subject coverage but are much more selective and, hence, much smaller. Others fall in this category, but these two are certainly among the best and are representative of the genre. Additional directories that are general in terms of subject area but specialized in that they focus on academic material (INFOMINE, Intute, and BUBL LINK) are discussed later in this chapter.

ipl²: Information You Can Trust

www.ipl.org

ipl² is the result of a 2009 merger of two highly respected directories, Librarians' Internet Index and Internet Public Library, resulting in a collection of more than 40,000 well-organized, annotated, "librarian-approved resources," including ready reference resources, books, magazines, newspapers, and other special collections (for topics such as blogs, science fairs, and Native American authors). There is also a special emphasis on resources for children, teens, and teachers. ipl² offers a free "ask a question" reference service and a free regular newsletter that provides email updates on new sites added.

Browsing ipl²

ipl² provides 10-plus subject areas for browsing (each with from six to 30 subcategories), plus sections of links for Ready Reference, Reading Room (magazines and newspapers online), KidSpace, TeenSpace, Special Collections, and Searching Tools. Annotations are provided for each item.

Searching ipl²

A search box appears on most pages. The search automatically ANDs your terms, but you can use an OR between terms, and you can truncate using an asterisk (e.g., *transport**). The advanced search page provides for searching by simple Boolean, limiting to specific domains/sites, limiting to date range (when the site first appeared in the directory), and the ability to match search terms either exactly or in a fuzzy (approximate) mode.

Where to Find Other General Directories

Unfortunately, most lists of searching tools do not adequately distinguish between search engines and directories and simply lump the two species together. Keeping that in mind, one place to go for a list of regional (continent- or country-specific) tools is Search Engine Colossus (www.search enginecolossus.com).

Most Important Things to Remember About Directories

1. Web directories are most useful when you have a general rather than a specific question.
2. The content of directories is selected by humans who evaluate the usefulness and appropriateness of sites considered for inclusion.
3. Directories *tend* to have one listing per website and do not index individual pages.

SPECIALIZED DIRECTORIES

For some immediate expertise in web resources on a specific topic, there is no better starting point than the right specialized directory, or portal. Also known as resource guides, metasites, cyberguides, webliographies, or just plain "collections of links," these sites bring together selected internet resources on specific topics. They provide not only a good starting place for effectively utilizing internet resources in a particular area, but also, very importantly, a confidence in knowing that no really important tools in that area are being missed. The variety of these sites is endless. They can be discipline-oriented or industry-oriented; they may focus on a specific kind of document (e.g., newspapers or historical documents) or take virtually any other slant toward identifying a useful category of resources.

If the producer of the site adds some valuable content to the collection of links, such as news headlines or lists of events, you not only have a specialized directory, but a specialized portal or gateway, making it even more useful as a starting point.

STRENGTHS AND WEAKNESSES VS. OTHER KINDS OF FINDING TOOLS

Strengths

✔ Specialized
✔ Very selective
✔ Provides some immediate "web expertise"

Weaknesses

✔ Relatively small
✔ Variable quality and consistency

HOW TO FIND SPECIALIZED DIRECTORIES

There are at least a couple of ways to identify systematically a specialized directory for a particular area of interest. Some easy and reasonably effective ways include: using Yahoo!'s Web Directories subcategory; searching for them in search engines; keeping an eye out for them in professional journal articles and books; and using directories of directories.

Using Yahoo!

Yahoo! lists thousands of specialized directories. As a matter of fact, it lists one or more specialized directories for almost 800 categories, ranging from semiconductors to storytelling to sumo. The trick to finding them in Yahoo! is simple: Just look for the Web Directories subcategory, either by browsing through the Yahoo! categories list or by putting your subject and the phrase *"web directories"* in Yahoo!'s Directories search box. You may actually get more complete results by using the regular Yahoo! search box and searching for something like: *sumo "web directories" site:dir.yahoo.com*. (This syntax will be explained in Chapter 3.)

Using Professional Publications

Keep an eye out for articles that discuss internet resources for specific areas in professional publications (printed and online): journals such as *ONLINE* and *Searcher*, and websites for searchers such as FreePint (freepint.com).

Using Directories of Directories

Directories of directories are valuable resources for locating topic-specific information. The following two sites contain collections of specialized directories (and may contain other content as well).

The WWW Virtual Library

www.vlib.org

Perhaps the best-known catalog of web directories, The WWW Virtual Library, started by none other than Tim Berners-Lee, founder of the web, contains an excellent selection of specialized directories arranged by category. In essence, it is one large directory with individual sections maintained by a large number of volunteers, but because the format of each section is also very independently done, The WWW Virtual Library is indeed a collection of individual directories. The quality of the individual directories tends to be quite high.

Search Engine Guide—Search Engines Directory

www.searchengineguide.com/searchengines.html

Although this site does not adequately distinguish between search engines and directories, if you use the search box or browse the categories listed there, you will find a useful collection of specialized directories.

Using Search Engines

You may be successful in finding a specialized directory in your subject area by searching a term for your area AND the word *resources*, for example, *geology resources*. You may want to be more specific by using the phrase, "*internet resources*," for example, *geology "internet resources."* You can also try using *metasite* in addition to or instead of *resources*. For industry portals, search for the industry plus the word *portal*, for example, *"electronics industry" portal*. If you would like to get a site that provides a list of printed resources for a subject as well as internet resources, use the word *pathfinder*.

Many libraries provide pathfinders that are guides to both the literature and internet resources in their libraries. Even if you don't have access to the library that produced it, the guide can provide reminders of print sources you might want to track down.

WHAT TO LOOK FOR IN SPECIALIZED DIRECTORIES AND HOW THEY DIFFER

Many areas have a variety of directories. If you want to find the best, several factors must be considered. An excellent specialized directory does not have to be strong in all of these facets, but, depending on your needs, you might want to focus on a few particular aspects. Directories tend to differ mainly in these terms:

- Size – Sometimes large is good; sometimes having fewer sites to focus on is good.
- Categorization/Classification – Especially if the number of sites included is large, it is helpful to have them divided into useful categories.
- Annotations – A large portion of specialized directories (including many very good ones) do not have annotations describing the sites they list. Annotations, however, can be very useful, as they provide a quick overview of what the sites cover and any special characteristics of the sites.
- Searchability – A fairly small portion of specialized directories provide a search box to save users from having to browse. If the directory is large, this can be quite useful.
- Origin – Who (or what organization) produced the site is sometimes a good indication of the quality you can expect from the site. Unfortunately, many sites do not give a clear indication of who produced them, and you may have to rely on the URL for a clue.
- Portal features – If, in addition to the collection of links, other features are included, the site can be especially powerful. Look for such features as news headlines, lists of events (conferences, etc.), professional directories (e.g., a list of members if it is a site produced by an association), directories of companies in that area, and so on.

SOME PROMINENT EXAMPLES
OF SPECIALIZED DIRECTORIES

The examples of specialized directories included here are mentioned for a variety of reasons: Some were chosen simply because they are sites that most serious searchers should be aware of; some demonstrate particularly good or unique characteristics of a specialized directory; some are very wide-ranging (as well as having other values as a specialized directory). In some categories, such as Government, more than one example is listed to show contrasts between sites. (Sometimes multiple directories are listed for an area because I just could not make up my mind which one to choose.)

Don't forget that effective use of a directory approach for identifying relevant sites can mean using a combination of the general web directories covered in the previous chapter and the specialized directories covered here. In one sense, each section of a general directory such as Yahoo! Directory or Open Directory is itself a specialized directory.

General, Academic, and Reference Tools

The first site that follows provides an extensive collection of links to reference tools such as encyclopedias, dictionaries, and so forth. The next three focus on a broad range of subjects, but their coverage is limited primarily to sites of interest in the academic/research setting. The last two included in this section—Project Gutenberg and the Library of Congress Gateway—provide links to books and library catalogs available online.

Refdesk

refdesk.com

This fairly extensive collection is actually arranged more as a portal, with news headlines and other features, as well as links to valuable reference resources. (It had achieved a well-deserved status on its own but got a boost when then-U.S. Secretary of State Colin Powell said something to the effect that it should be on the screen of every State Department employee.) Most of the reference tools are found toward the bottom of the page.

INFOMINE

infomine.ucr.edu

A well-organized, categorized, and searchable collection of more than 100,000 links (some chosen by librarians and some identified by robots/crawlers), this directory is specialized in that it focuses on "scholarly" internet resources. Look here for sources that will be useful at the university level. The advanced search page has quite extensive searching capabilities for a specialized directory. INFOMINE comes from the University of California, with contributions from librarians at a number of other universities.

BUBL LINK

bubl.ac.uk/link

This site, from Strathclyde University, includes more than 12,000 resources, covering all academic areas. Part of its uniqueness is that the main categories used are based on the Dewey Decimal Classification, and it has a particularly strong focus on library and information science. It is very easily browsable, with indexes by subject, country, and type, and BUBL LINK also has good search capabilities on its search page.

Intute

www.intute.ac.uk

Intute (formerly the Resource Discovery Network) contains more than 125,000 sites and is provided by a consortium of seven U.K. universities and a number of other partners. The collection is arranged in 19 main categories, covering the broad range of academic disciplines. The entire collection can be searched using the search box on the main page or by using its advanced search page, or it can be browsed by using the categories (Figure 2.4).

Library of Congress Gateway to Library Catalogs

lcweb.loc.gov/z3950/gateway.html

Going beyond just a "collection of links," this site uses a consistent interface to bring together the capability of searching (one at a time) the contents of the online catalogs for nearly 500 libraries in the U.S. and elsewhere. All of these are catalogs that use the Z39.50 standard for online library catalogs.

Figure 2.4

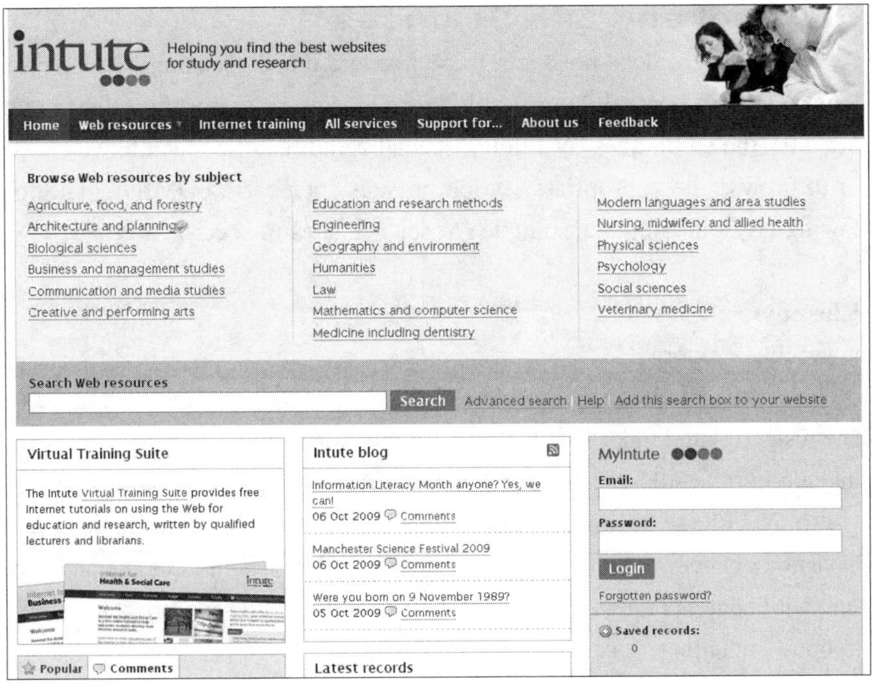

Intute

Social Sciences and Humanities

In addition to the more specific sites that follow, for a broader range of social sciences and humanities, use Intute (www.intute.ac.uk).

Best of History Web Sites

www.besthistorysites.net

Best of History Web Sites furnishes annotated and rated links to more than 1,200 history-related websites in categories such as Prehistory, Ancient/Biblical, Medieval, U.S. History, Early Modern European, 20th Century, World War II, Art History, General Resources, and Maps. There are also categories for Lesson Plans/Activities, Maps, and Research.

Virtual Religion Index

virtualreligion.net/vri

With a focus on scholarly sites, this directory site contains extensive links on the world's major (and minor) religions and on the academic study of religion and religious issues.

Physical and Life Sciences

At present, there does not seem to be a single broad-reaching directory for the sciences in general. Your best bet for focusing on a specific science may be to try the techniques for finding specialized directories mentioned earlier or to browse the appropriate section on sites such as INFOMINE. The following are some notable examples of science sites in specific areas.

Chemdex

www.chemdex.org

This site, from the University of Sheffield, contains more than 7,000 chemistry-related links. The links are arranged by 13 top-level categories and include both scholarly sites and links to chemical companies and suppliers. Go to WebElements for an outstanding online periodic table. Even if you have no connection with chemistry, you will find the site interesting and even fun, with contents ranging from the usual periodic table data for each element to bond enthalpies to cartoons about the elements.

healthfinder

www.healthfinder.gov

From the U.S. Department of Health and Human Services, this site provides reliable health information aimed at consumers. It includes links that range from a medical encyclopedia to background on diseases to directories of physicians, hospitals, and nursing homes, and a variety of other easily understandable resources.

MedlinePlus

www.nlm.nih.gov/medlineplus

MedlinePlus, from the U.S. National Library of Medicine and National Institutes of Health, is a portal that offers a combination of information provided directly on the site and an extensive collection of links. The Health Topics section contains more than 800 topics related to medical conditions, diseases, and wellness. Other parts of the MedlinePlus site include Drug Information, Medical Encyclopedia, Dictionaries, News (health news from the past 90 days), Directories (doctors, dentists, and hospitals), Go Local (for local resources), and Other Resources.

Business and Economics

In addition to the specialized directories listed here for business-related information, be sure to look at the sites listed in Chapter 6 for company information. Some of the sites listed there, such as CorporateInformation, can also be considered specialized directories.

Rutgers University Libraries—Subject Research Guides: Business

www.libraries.rutgers.edu/rul/rr_gateway/research_guides/busi/business.shtml

Though designed primarily for the Rutgers University community, this frequently updated site provides links to more than 3,000 business and management resources publicly available on the internet. This is an excellent example of a library pathfinder. As such, even though many of the links point to resources that are restricted to local users, the information provided by those links should itself be useful to others in that it identifies non-free-internet content with which business researchers in general should be familiar.

New York Times > Business > A Web Guide: Business Navigator

www.nytimes.com/ref/business/business-navigator.html

This bare-bones collection of business-related links includes categories for Markets (exchanges, etc.), Investing, Company Information (directories, news, etc.), Banking & Finance, Government (Federal Reserve, IRS, BLS, etc.), Business and Financial News, Business Directories, and Miscellany. Only about half of the 150 or so sites listed are annotated (and just briefly), but the clarity, selectivity, and categories into which they are divided make it an easy and quick guide to critical business resources.

CEOExpress

ceoexpress.com

CEOExpress is a cluttered-looking but rich site with a strong emphasis on business news sites (Figure 2.5). For a good understanding of what it can provide, spend three or four minutes browsing the unique arrangement of category links. The main site is free, but a paid subscription provides customization of the home page, email, and other tools and benefits.

Figure 2.5

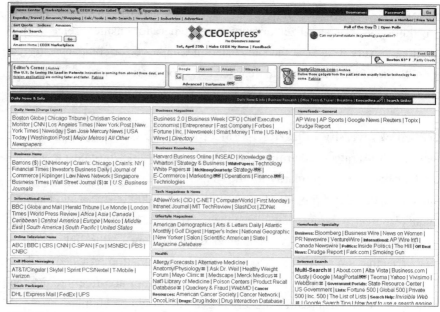

CEOExpress main page

globalEDGE

globaledge.msu.edu

From Michigan State University, globalEDGE includes well-organized, annotated links to thousands of sites on global business activities.

Resources for Economists on the Internet

rfe.org

Edited by Bill Goff and sponsored by the American Economic Association, this site lists more than 2,000 resources categorized into 97 sections. These sections range from the obvious things of interest to economists, such as data, to less obvious but very useful categories, such as software and mailing lists. (If you need a break, check out the Neat Stuff section.)

Government and Governments

Although some countries have a single site that provide links to sites for individual government departments or ministries, many do not, and it is not always easy to identify the particular agency site you need. The first two sites that follow are directories that make this task much easier by bringing together large collections of government sites, organized by country or other category. The next three sites are examples of portals for specific countries, and the final site in this section is a resource guide for political parties worldwide.

Governments on the WWW

www.gksoft.com/govt

Although rather tardy in updating, this site contains links to more than 17,000 websites from governments and multinational organizations around the world, including parliaments, law courts, embassies, cities, public broadcasting corporations, central banks, political parties, and the like. There are no annotations, but the names of the sites are translated into English.

Explore GovDocs

www.lib.umich.edu/government-documents-center/explore

This collection from the University of Michigan Library contains links to thousands of government-related resources. Note particularly the sets of links for Federal Government (U.S.), Foreign Governments (non-U.S.), and International Organizations. Click on any of the main categories for a further breakdown by region, topic, etc.

USA.gov

www.usa.gov

This site, which is the official portal to U.S. government sites, also contains links to state sites (Figure 2.6). The main tabs shown on the home page (For Citizens, For Businesses and Nonprofits, For Government Employees, and For Visitors to the U.S.) allow browsing by who is seeking the information or who the information is for. The Government Information by Topic section provides a subject approach, and the Government Agencies menu will take you to links arranged by branch of government and also provides an alphabetic index to agencies.

Directgov (U.K. Online)

www.direct.gov.uk

As the official U.K. government portal site, this site provides links to U.K. public sector information. The main portions on the site are arranged

Figure 2.6

USA.gov main page

by subject (Education and Learning, Home and Community, etc.) and by resources for specific groups of people (Parents, Disabled People, Over 50s, Britons Living Abroad, Caring for Someone, Young People). The A–Z of Central Government link leads to an alphabetic list of government departments, agencies, and other public bodies.

Government of Canada Official Website
canada.gc.ca

The home page of the Government of Canada Official Website offers sections on Governance and Services, a Resource Centre (with contact information and links to departments and agencies), and links to specific services for citizens, plus a variety of news and special features.

Political Resources on the Net
www.politicalresources.net

This site is an excellent resource for quickly identifying the sites of political parties for any country. On the map on the home page, click on a continent and then the country. Links for international parties and other related resources are also provided.

Legal

FindLaw

www.findlaw.com

This very rich portal contains links to a broad range of legal subjects, from lawyers and law firms to cases and codes. Don't expect it to turn you into an expert legal researcher, but if you are one, you are probably already making good use of this site. If you aren't one, it will point you in the right direction for many of the best legal resources on the internet. FindLaw's main page is aimed at consumers, but on that page, you will find a link that takes you to the legal professionals' site (lp.findlaw.com). Most of the legal resources are primarily focused on the U.S., but under the FindLaw for Legal Professionals portion of the site, you will find substantial non-U.S. content, including links to legal information organized by country.

GlobaLex

www.nyulawglobal.org/globalex

GlobaLex is much more than a specialized directory—it is also a "research guide" that includes articles about the legal systems of more than 100 countries and international jurisdictions. Within these articles, you will find thousands of related links (including links to individual departments, agencies, etc., for countries) and extensive bibliographies of print resources.

Education

Kathy Schrock's Guide for Educators

school.discoveryeducation.com/schrockguide

This well-known directory for K–12 teachers and parents contains links to hundreds of sites, each with a brief annotation. You can browse by subject or use the alphabetic index. It is a good source for links to lesson plans, among other things.

Education World

www.education-world.com

Education World contains a browsable and searchable database of more than 500,000 education-related sites. The site itself is more a portal, not merely a directory, and contains much original content by the producers of the site (such as articles and lesson plans) as well as the links to other sites.

Education Atlas
www.educationatlas.com

Education Atlas is a clearly organized resource guide containing 45,000 education websites arranged in six major sections (Early Childhood, K–12 Education, Higher Education, Distance Learning, Special Education, Teacher's Corner). It also has categories for a variety of topics such as Home Schooling, Instructional Technology, and Regional (international).

News
Kidon Media-Link
www.kidon.com/media-link

Although a number of sites serve as directories of newspapers and other news sources on the internet, Kidon Media-Link is one of the most extensive and seems to have relatively few dead links (a common problem with some of the other news directories). The site is arranged by continent and then country, and provides more than 19,000 links to newspapers, news agencies, magazines, radio, and TV sites (Figure 2.7). (Additional news resource guides can be found in Chapter 8.)

Genealogy
Cyndi's List of Genealogy Sites on the Internet
www.cyndislist.com

This is perhaps the best known of the numerous genealogy directories and has links to more than 260,000 sites. You can browse through the 180 categories or take advantage of the search box. Both beginners and experienced genealogists should find it useful.

Travel
Traveler's Web
extremesearcher.com/travel

The site for *The Traveler's Web* contains links to more than 500 internet travel resources covered in the book by the same name (and written by the author of the book you are currently reading).

Figure 2.7

Kidon Media-Link main page

GENERAL WEB PORTALS

Portals, or gateway sites, are sites that are designed to serve as starting places for getting to the most relevant material on the web. They typically have a variety of tools (such as a search engine, directory, news, etc.) all on a single page, so that a user can use that page as the "start page" for his or her browser. Portals can often be personalized with regard to content and layout. Many serious searchers choose a portal, make it their start page, and personalize it. Thereafter, when the searchers open their browsers, they have in front of them such things as news headlines in their areas of interest, the weather for where they are or where they are headed, stock performance, and so on.

The portal concept goes considerably beyond the idea of web directories as we have been discussing them. However, this chapter seems the appropriate place to discuss them since general web portals, like directories, embody the concept of getting the user quickly and easily to the most relevant web resources. In addition, the natures of directories and portals are melded so tightly that it is not feasible to try to totally separate them.

Well-known general portals include Yahoo!, iGoogle (google.com/ig), AOL (aol.com), and Excite (excite.com). Most countries have their own popular general portals, for example, the French portal Voila! (www.voila.fr).

General portals usually exhibit three main characteristics: a variety of generally *useful tools*, positioning as a *start page*, and *personalizability*.

General Web Portals as Collections of Useful Tools

In line with the idea of a "gateway to internet resources," general portals provide a collection of tools and information that allows users to easily put their hands on information they frequently need.

Instead of having to go to different sites to get the news headlines and weather, or to find a phone directory, general web directory, search engine, and so forth, a portal can put this information—or links to this information—right on your start page. General portals usually include some variety of the following on their main pages:

- News
- Weather
- Stock information
- White pages

- Yellow pages
- Sports scores
- Free email
- Maps and directions

- Shopping
- Horoscope
- Calendar
- Address book

General Web Portals as Start Pages

Most general portals are designed to induce you to choose the site as your browser's start page. Because at least part of their support comes from ads, you may find some ads on the page, but portal producers know that the useful information must not be overpowered by ads or no one will come to the page. The overall thrust is to provide a collection of information so useful that it makes it worthwhile to go to that page first.

General Web Portals—Personalizability

Most successful general portals make their pages personalizable, allowing the user to choose which city's weather appears on the page, which stocks are shown, what categories of headlines are displayed, and so on. If you look around on the main pages of these sites, you will usually see either a Personalize link or a link to a My... option, such as My Yahoo!, which will allow you to sign up and personalize the page or will direct you to your personalized page if you have already done so. A sign-in link will do likewise.

Yahoo!'s Portal Features

A look at Yahoo!'s main page offers a good idea of the types of things general portals can do. Yahoo! is undoubtedly one of the best of the general portals, particularly with regard to personalization features. As a matter of fact, a case could be made that for the serious searcher, Yahoo!'s personalized portal (My Yahoo!) is more important than the Yahoo! Directory (and with the disappearance of the directory from Yahoo!'s home page, Yahoo!'s designers seem to agree).

Yahoo! has a number of portal features on its main, nonpersonalized page (yahoo.com). Some of them, such as news headlines, are displayed directly on the page, along with links to more than 30 other portal features, such as Autos, Real Estate, and Finance. Many of these links lead to more specialized portal pages provided by the site with, again, a collection of tools and links specific to the topic of the channel. Other links on Yahoo!'s main page take you to a phone directory, maps, groups, and more. The best way to understand a portal such as Yahoo! is to lock yourself in your office and not leave until you have clicked on every link on the page. (Skip the ads, though.)

Internet Explorer: From the main menu bar, select Tools > Internet Options. Then under the "General" tab, enter the URL (including the http://) in the Address box.

Firefox: From the main menu bar, select Tools > Options > General > Home Page. Then enter the URL (including the http://) in the Location box.

Safari: Click the "gear" icon on the toolbar. Select Preferences. Then under the "General" section, enter the URL (including the http://) in the Home Page box.

TIP:

Follow these steps to make a chosen page your browser's start page.

My Yahoo!

An example of a personalized general portal page (My Yahoo! at my.yahoo.com) is shown in Figure 2.8. Yahoo! provides one of the most personalizable general portals, with possibly the widest variety of choices, including many other Yahoo! "personal" products such as Yahoo! Mail, a calendar, etc. It also provides personalized versions for many of its 42 country or language-specific versions.

Figure 2.8

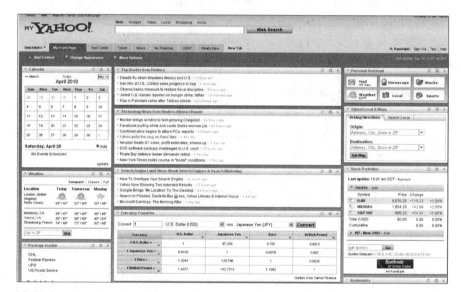

My Yahoo! personalized portal page

iGoogle

Google tends to know a good thing when it sees it. Though it made its reputation on the simplicity of its home page, Google also recognized a few years later the benefits of having a personalizable portal similar to My Yahoo! The result is iGoogle, a personalizable page similar (not surprisingly) in many ways to My Yahoo! and including Google's calendar, Gmail, newsfeeds, weather, gadgets, etc.

Some Other Popular General Portals

The following sites also all exhibit the three characteristics of general portals to varying degrees and with varying content. Determining which is the best for any individual probably depends on what content is available on the portal and how it is presented. Try more than one before deciding. Most of the better-known general portals have dozens of options to choose from (many, many more if the portal allows you to add any RSS feed you wish). Such items as Word of the Day and Pregnancy Watch may or may not be of interest to you. Your personal stock portfolio is handled very differently by various portals, and what data the portal displays and how it displays that data may make the difference in your choice. A portal may allow very detailed specification of what categories of headlines are displayed, or it may allow for only very general categories, and so on. The following portals, along with My Yahoo! and iGoogle, are among the best known in the U.S. For non-U.S. portals, take a look at the World section of Open Directory (dmoz.org/world), choose your country, and then search for the term *portal* in the relevant language.

Other Selected Examples of General Portals

Excite (excite.com) – Once the best and still used by many people

AOL (aol.com) – The first popular general portal

MSN (msn.com) – Relatively few customizable content options compared to My Yahoo! and iGoogle

Other Resources Relating to General Directories and Portals

Traffick: Frequently Asked Questions about Portals

www.traffick.com/article.asp?aID=9#what

This site provides a concise but quite informative overview and history of the web portal concept.

SUMMARY

Remember that web directories provide sites that are evaluated and selected by human beings. With general web directories, the fact that sites are placed in categories to allow browsing makes these tools a good starting place when you want selected sites, when you want only a few sites, and when your question is general rather than specific. Specialized directories provide the searcher with at least *some* immediate "expertise" in knowing the most important internet resources for a specific subject area. Take advantage of one of the general, personalizable portals as a starting place, so you can easily go to your own selection of frequently needed information.

CHAPTER 3

SEARCH ENGINES: THE BASICS

General web search engines, such as Google, Yahoo! Search, and Bing, stand in contrast to web directories in three primary ways: (1) They are much larger, containing billions instead of a few million (or fewer) records; (2) there is virtually no human selectivity involved in determining what webpages are included in the search engine's database; and (3) they are designed for searching (responding to a user's specific query) rather than for browsing, so they provide more substantial searching capabilities than directories.

For someone using internet resources, a workable definition of a web search engine is a service on the web that allows searching of a large database of webpages by word, phrase, and other criteria. There is actually some ambiguity involved when one speaks of "search engines." From a slightly more technical perspective, when we use a site such as Google, we are utilizing a service that facilitates the searching of a database. In the narrower sense, the "search engine" is the program utilized by the service to query the database. Almost any site that provides a search box could be considered to have a search "engine." Here, when we speak of "search engines," we will really be referring to a service, such as the three just mentioned, that provides searching of a very large database of webpages and may provide other services as well, such as translations, shopping, and others.

HOW SEARCH ENGINES ARE PUT TOGETHER

To take full advantage of search engines, it is useful to understand the basics of how they are put together. Four major steps are involved in making webpages searchable by a search engine service. These steps also correspond to the "parts" of a search engine: the spiders, the indexing program and index, the search engine program, and the HTML user interface.

1. Spiders (aka crawlers) – These are programs used by the search engine services to scan the internet to identify new sites or sites that have changed, gather information from those sites, and feed that information to the search engine's indexing mechanism. For some engines, popular sites (likely to have many links to them) are crawled more thoroughly and more frequently than less popular sites. Tied into this crawling function is a second way for webpages to get identified—by the process of submitted URLs. A link found on most search engines' sites will let anyone submit a URL, and with the exception of those pages that are identifiable as "spam" (pages that are designed to mislead the search engine and search engine users and/or illegitimately lead to high rankings) or pages that are unacceptable for other reasons, the pages will be indexed and added to the database.

2. The indexing program and the index – Once a new page is identified by the search engine's crawler, the page will typically be indexed under virtually every word on the page. Other parts of the page may also be indexed, such as the URL, metatags (see Glossary), the URLs of links on the page, and image file names.

3. The search "engine" itself – This is the program that identifies (retrieves) those pages in the database that match the criteria indicated by a user's query. Another important and more challenging process is also involved, that of determining the order in which the retrieved records should be displayed. This "relevance-ranking" algorithm usually takes many factors into account, such as the popularity of the page (as measured by how many other pages link to it), the number of times the search terms occur in the page, the relative proximity of search terms in the page, the location of search terms (for example, pages where the search terms occur in the title of the page may get a higher ranking), and other factors.

4. The HTML-based (HyperText Markup Language) interface that gathers query data from the user (the "search page") – The home page and advanced search pages of the search service are the parts we usually envision when we think of a particular search engine. These pages contain the search box(es), links to the various databases that are searchable (images, news, etc.), and perhaps a number of other features.

HOW SEARCH OPTIONS ARE PRESENTED

Exactly what search options are available varies from search engine to search engine. With any particular search engine, some available options are presented on the home page, but on the advanced search page, usually several more options are clearly displayed. Options are typically made available in one of two ways: (1) by means of a menu or (2) by the searcher directly qualifying the term when it is entered in the main search box.

An example of the menu approach is shown in Figure 3.1, where (in Yahoo!) a pull-down menu allows the term entered in the box to be qualified. In this example, the search is requesting that only those pages be retrieved that have the term *antioxidants* in the *title* of the page.

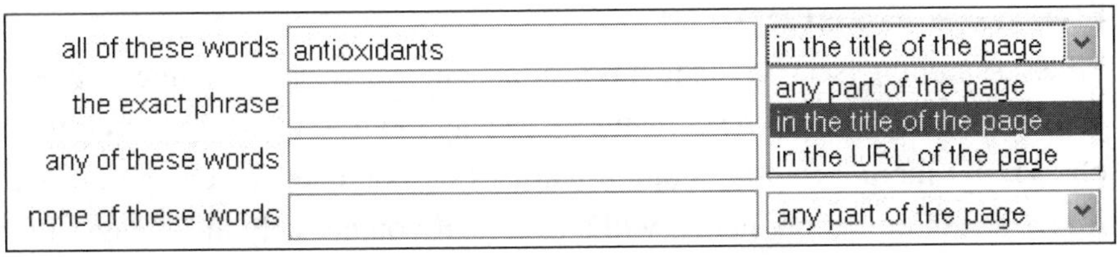

Figure 3.1

Example of the menu approach to qualifying a search term

Figure 3.2 shows an example of qualifying a term directly. Here (in Google) the *intitle:* prefix is inserted to do the same thing as shown in the menu example in Figure 3.1. (Whenever using prefixes such as this to qualify a search term, be sure not to put a space on either side of the colon.)

Figure 3.2

Example of using a prefix to qualify a search term

Usually you have a choice as to which approach to use. The menu approach is easier in that you do not need to know the somewhat cryptic prefixes. If you do know the prefixes, you may accomplish your search more quickly and easily.

TYPICAL SEARCH OPTIONS

A number of search options are fairly typical. These include phrase searching, language specification, and specifying that you retrieve only pages where your term appears in a particular part (field) of the record, such as the title, URL, or links. Now that major engines include more than just HTML pages, for some engines you can also specify file type (webpages, PDF files, Excel files, etc.). Every engine also offers some form of Boolean operations.

The following gives a quick look at why you might want to use (or not use) those options. Table 4.1 near the end of Chapter 4 identifies which options are available in which engines, and the search engine profiles in Chapter 4 provide some details for using the search options in the major engines. Expect occasional changes in exactly which options are offered by which engines.

Phrase Searching

Phrase searching is an option that is available in every search engine, and perhaps surprisingly, it can be done the same way in all of them. To search for a phrase, put the phrase in quotation marks. For example, searching on *"Red River"* (with quotation marks) will ensure that you get only those pages that contain the word *red* immediately in front of the term *river*. You will avoid records such as one about the red wolves of Alligator River. Whenever your concept is best expressed as a phrase, be sure to use quotation marks. You are not limited to two words; you can use several. For example, to find out who said "When I'm good I'm very good, but when I'm bad I'm better," search for a few of the words together, such as *"when I'm bad I'm better."* (Search engines have limits on the number of words you can enter.)

Some engines automatically identify common phrases, and most engines give a higher ranking to pages in which your terms appear next to each other. To be sure, though, that you are only getting records with your terms adjacent to each other and in the order you wish, use quotation marks.

Title Searching

This is often the most powerful technique for getting to some highly relevant pages quickly. It may also cause you to miss some good ones, but what you do get has an excellent chance of being relevant. All the major engines have this option, and most of them let you search titles by means of either menu options or prefixes (see Figures 3.1 and 3.2).

URL, Site, and Domain Searching

Doing a search in which you limit your results to a specific site allows you, in effect, to perform a search of that site. Even for sites that have a "site search" box on their home page, you may find that you get better results by doing a site search in a large search engine. If you want to find where on the FBI site the term *internship* is mentioned, use a search engine's advanced search page and specify the term *internship* in the search box and *fbi.gov* in the box that lets you specify the site (or domain or URL). Most engines will let you accomplish the same thing using a prefix. For example, in Google, Yahoo!, Bing, and Ask.com, you could search for

> *internship site:fbi.gov*

Most engines allow you to be more specific and search a portion of a site, for example (in each of the four engines just mentioned):

> *internship site:baltimore.fbi.gov*

As well as specifying an exact site, you can, in some engines, specify that you want a term to be somewhere in the URL by using the *inurl:* prefix, for example:

> *members inurl:aiip*

In many search engines, domain searching is identical to URL searching. The use of the term, though, points out that you can use this approach to limit your retrieval to sites having a particular top-level domain, such as .gov, .edu, .uk, .ca, or .fr. This strategy could be used to identify only Canadian sites that mention tariffs or to get only educational sites that mention biodiversity.

Link Searching

There are two varieties of link searching. In one variety, you can search for all pages that have a hypertext link to a particular URL; and in the other, you can search for words contained in the linked text on the page. In the former, for example, you can check which webpages have linked to your organization's URL. In the latter, you can see which webpages have the name of your organization as linked text. Either variety can be very informative in terms of finding out who is interested in either your organization or your website. It can be very useful for marketing purposes, and it can also be used by nonprofits for development and fundraising leads. Also, if you are looking for information on an organization, it can sometimes be useful to know who is linking to that organization's site.

This searching option is available in some search engines on their advanced page and/or on the main page with the use of prefixes. Engines may let you look for links to an overall site or to a specific page within a site. If you want to search exhaustively for who is linking to a particular site, definitely use more than one search engine. In link searching, the difference in retrieval is even more pronounced than in keyword searching.

Language Searching

Although all of the major engines allow you to limit your retrieval to pages written in a given language, they differ in terms of which languages can be specified. The 40 or so most common languages are specifiable in most of those engines, but if you want to find a page written in Esperanto, not all engines will give you that option. If you find yourself searching by language, be sure to look at the various language options and preferences provided by the different engines, particularly if a non-Western character set is involved.

Searching by Date

Searching by date is one of the most obviously desirable options, and most major engines provide such an option. Unfortunately, it may not have much meaning. Through no fault of the search engines, it is often impossible to determine a definitive "date created" or the "date of publication" of the content of the page. To get around this, engines may use the date when the page was last modified or the date on which the page was last crawled by the engine. When searching webpages, keep this approximation in mind and do not expect much precision. (In other databases an engine may provide, such as news or groups, the date searching may be very precise.)

Searching by File Type

Now that search engines are indexing non-HTML pages, including Adobe Acrobat (PDF) files, Word documents, Excel files, and so on, there are times when you may want to limit your retrieval to one of those file types. For example, if you wanted to print out a tutorial for Dreamweaver, you might prefer the more attractive PDF format over the format of an HTML page. If you want a nice summary of a topic, try finding a document in PowerPoint format. Collections of statistics on a specific topic can sometimes be easily identified by limiting your retrieval to Excel files. Specifying file type may not be required very often, but at times it will be very useful.

Boolean Search Options

In the context of online searching, Boolean searching basically refers to a process of identifying those items (such as webpages) that contain a particular combination of search terms. It is used to indicate that a particular group of terms must all be present (the Boolean AND), that any one of a particular group of terms is acceptable (the Boolean OR), or that if a particular term is present, the item is rejected (the Boolean NOT). These relationships are represented by the dark areas in the Venn diagrams shown in Figure 3.3.

Figure 3.3

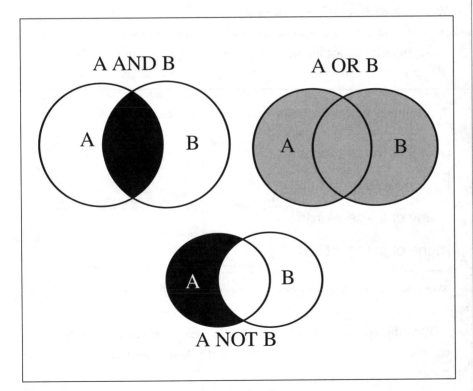

Boolean operators (connectors)

Very precise search requirements can be expressed using combinations of these operators along with parentheses to indicate the order of operations. For example:

(grain OR corn OR wheat) AND (production OR harvest) AND oklahoma AND 1997

The use of the actual words AND, OR, and NOT to represent Boolean operations has been downplayed in web search engines and has been replaced in many cases by the use of menus or other syntax. Even if you have never typed the AND, OR, or NOT, you have probably still used Boolean. (One point here being that Boolean is "painless.") If you choose the "all the words" option from a pull-down menu, you are requesting the Boolean AND. If you choose the "any of the words" option from a menu, you are specifying an OR. Because all major search engines automatically AND your query terms (if you do not specify otherwise), any time you just enter two or more terms in a search box, you are implicitly requesting an AND (even if you do not realize it).

Varieties of Boolean Formats

As with title, site, and other search qualifications, Boolean usually provides two options for indicating what you want: (1) a menu option, or (2) the option of applying the syntax directly to what you enter in the search box. Using the menu option can be thought of as "simplified Boolean" or "simple Boolean." An example of a Boolean menu option is shown in Figure 3.4.

Figure 3.4

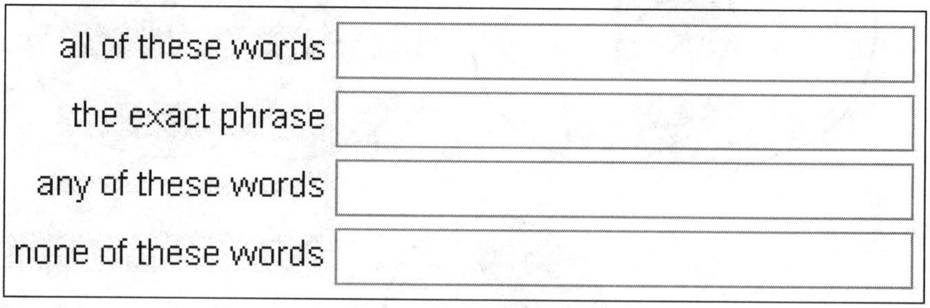

all of these words	
the exact phrase	
any of these words	
none of these words	

Menu form of Boolean options (and phrase option)

With the syntax approach, the exact syntax used varies with the search engine. All major engines now automatically AND your terms, so when you enter:

prague economics tourism

what you will get is more traditionally described as:

prague AND economics AND tourism

Figure 3.5 shows an example of Boolean syntax (from Yahoo!'s main search page).

| roma population (hungary OR hungarian) | **Web Search** |

Example of Boolean syntax

Full Boolean

Even though most engines provide syntax to allow near-maximum Boolean capabilities, engines assert their independence by varying the particular syntax used for entering a Boolean expression. For example, Google and Yahoo! do not require parentheses when using an OR, but Bing does require parentheses around ORed terms.

Table 3.1 shows how a typical Boolean-oriented search would be structured in the major search engines. For all practical purposes, a search engine can be considered to have full Boolean capabilities if it provides for all three Boolean operations (AND, OR, and NOT).

Boolean Syntax at Major Search Engines

Search Engine	Boolean Pattern	Full Boolean?	Expression
Ask.com	A –D C OR B –D C	No	"endangered species" –rockfish maryland OR "endangered species" –rockfish virginia *(Very convoluted syntax. Use Ask.com's advanced search page or another engine.)*
Google	A B OR C –D	Yes	"endangered species" maryland OR virginia –rockfish
Bing	A (B OR C) –D	Yes	"endangered species" (maryland OR virginia) –rockfish
Yahoo!	A B OR C –D	Yes	"endangered species" maryland OR virginia –rockfish

NOTE: Since Google and Yahoo! ignore parentheses anyway, the following will work in Google, Bing, and Yahoo!: "endangered species" (maryland OR virginia) –rockfish

SEARCH ENGINE OVERLAP

It is important to recognize that no single search engine covers everything. Due to differences in crawling, indexing, and other factors, each engine's database includes and delivers webpages that the others do not. In a typical search, if you search a second engine, it may significantly increase the number of unique records you find. Searching a third and fourth engine can also yield records not found by the first engines. Therefore, if you need to be exhaustive—if it is crucial that you find everything on the topic—do your search in a second and third engine. (At the end of this chapter, you will see why metasearch engines are *not* the solution to this problem.)

RESULTS PAGES

One of the most useful things a searcher can do is to take a few extra seconds to look not just at the titles of the retrieved webpages, but also at the other things included on results pages and at the details provided in each record. Most engines provide some potentially useful additional information besides just the webpage results. At the same time they search their web database, they may search the other databases they have, such as news, images, video, and directories. You may find some news headlines that match your topic; a link to images, audio, or video on your topic; background information; and more.

One thing offered on search results pages by all of the major engines is a spell-checker. If you misspelled a word, or the search engine thinks you might have, it graciously asks something like "Did you mean?" and gives you a likely alternative. If it was indeed a mistake, just click on the alternate suggestion to correct the problem.

Be aware of Sponsor Results or Sponsored Links on results pages. These are ads for websites and are there because the site has paid to appear on the search engine's results pages. Most major engines keep these sponsor sites easily identifiable, for example, by putting them on a blue background or off to the side of the page. When placed at the top of the results pages, though, they may send less experienced users to an ad while thinking they have gone to a regular search result.

Also look closely at the individual web results records. In most search engines, results from individual websites are "clustered," that is, only the first one or two highly ranked records from any site will be shown, and there will be a link in the record leading you to "more from … " or "Show more results from …". If you are not aware of these links, you may miss relevant records from that site.

One other option you will notice on search results for some engines is a "Translate this page" link. If a page is in French, German, Italian, Portuguese, Spanish, or another language, in some cases, you may see such a link attached to the record. Click on it to receive a machine translation of the page. As with other machine translations, what you get may not be a "good" translation, but it will probably be an "adequate" translation, in that it will give you a good idea of what the page is talking about. Also keep in mind that only "words" are translated. The translation program cannot translate words displayed on a page that are actually images rather than text. (Many purists flagrantly reject the use of these translation tools. That attitude, it can be argued, is analogous to saying I should never attempt to read a German newspaper article because my own translation will have a lot of mistakes, that being totally ignorant of the content of the page is better than having just a general idea of what is being said.)

SEARCH ENGINE ACCOUNTS

For many features provided by the major search engines, you must have an account, particularly for using features that involve personalized services such as personalized portals, email, search histories, etc. In most cases, signing up for these free accounts requires your divulging only a bare minimum of personal information (sometimes just an email address). (For any readers who may be intensely spamophobic, you may find it worthwhile to know that the author has accounts with all the major search engines and some minor search sites as well, and has yet to identify having gotten anything he regards as "spam" as a result of having signed up with them.) Considering the benefits these account provide, it is worth the few seconds it takes to sign up.

SPECIALTY SEARCH ENGINES

Numerous specialty search engines are available. Some are geographic (focusing on sites from one country), and some are topical (focusing on a particular subject area). To locate examples of these, check out the following category in Open Directory (dmoz.org): Computers > Internet > Searching > Search Engines > Specialized.

METASEARCH ENGINES

Metasearch engines are services that let you search several search engines at the same time. With one search, you get results from several engines. (They should not be confused with "metasites," another term for specialized directories, which were discussed in Chapter 2.) Considering the usefulness of using more than one engine, the metasearch idea seems compelling—and it is indeed a great idea. However, the reality is often something else. You may find that you like a particular metasearch engine and have legitimate reasons for using it, but it is important to note some particularly important shortcomings.

First, though, it should be noted that this section addresses the free sites on the web that allow the searching of multiple engines. There are also metasearch programs (software) that can be purchased and loaded on your computer to help you search multiple engines. These client-side programs may do a more complete job, but they involve downloading (and eventually purchasing) a program and sometimes involve several more steps to get to your results.

Free metasearch engines on the web are numerous. New ones frequently appear, and older ones disappear just as quickly. Among the better known are Dogpile, Ixquick, Clusty, MetaCrawler, and Search.com. They can cover portions of a large number of search engines and directories in a single search, and they can sometimes be useful in finding something very obscure.

However, each metasearch engine usually presents one or more (and sometimes all) of the following drawbacks:

1. They may not cover most of the larger search engines. If you have a favorite metasearch engine, see if it covers Google, Yahoo!, Bing, and Ask.com.

2. Most only return the first 10 to 20 records from each source. If record No. 11 in one of the search engines was a great one, you may not see it.

3. Most search syntax does not work. Some metasearch engines let you search by title, URL, and so on, but most do not. Some do not even recognize even the simplest syntax: the use of quotation marks to indicate a phrase.

4. Some present paid listings first.

Also, by now you know that on search engine results pages, the additional content presented (besides just the listing of websites) can often be very valuable. You usually lose this with metasearch engines.

Where metasearch engines can provide definite value is when they truly offer something above and beyond what you get in a single regular search engine. An example of this kind of feature is the subject clustering of results provided by Clusty (clusty.com).

If you find that a metasearch engine meets your needs, use it. However, they are not the solution for an exhaustive—or even a moderately extensive—search.

SEARCH ENGINE SHORTCUTS

Several search engines, particularly Yahoo!, Google, and Ask.com, provide shortcuts for quick answers, including phone numbers, stock prices, calculations, conversions, etc. With these, you can just enter a brief statement in the main search box and click on search, and an answer will appear at the top of the results page. Some of these will be mentioned in Chapter 4, but for a fuller list, take a look at www.extremesearcher.com/shortcuts.

DESKTOP SEARCH PROGRAMS

Some major web search engines (and other companies as well) provide a desktop search program that you can download for free. Once downloaded, it will index the contents of your computer, which you can then use to "instantly" search almost all of your files for any particular term or combination of terms.

All of the desktop search programs provided by major engines have fast search speed (virtually instantaneous), and all index hundreds of basic file types (documents, images, text, PDFs, etc.). None search every word of every file on a computer. Desktop search programs differ as to how many and exactly which file types are indexed, which email clients are indexed, how much control you have over what gets indexed, what searching options are provided, whether they provide quick previews of the files in your desktop search results, how they are integrated into your web searches, whether your network drives are indexed, and whether they provide an enterprise version (for your entire organization to use). For a typical user, any of these desktop search products will probably do a good job and may do a better and faster job than the file search that comes with some Windows operating systems. If there is any consensus among reviewers regarding desktop programs from the major engines, the favorites are either Yahoo! or Google. The biggest strength of Google's desktop search program is that it integrates desktop search results automatically into every search (unless you don't want it to), while Yahoo!'s program provides more searchability and sortability of results and a full preview for most files. Give one or both a try. It can save you hours when searching for lost files.

KEEPING UP-TO-DATE ON WEB SEARCH ENGINES

To keep up-to-date with what is happening in the realm of web search engines, take advantage of the sites listed in the section "Keeping Up-to-Date on Internet Resources and Tools" in Chapter 1.

CHAPTER 4

SEARCH ENGINES: THE SPECIFICS

Chapter 3 provided an overview of search engines, how they work, and their common features. This chapter, however, provides detailed profiles of each of the top search engines. The descriptions give an overview of the service, take a look at the features on the home page and advanced search page, and call attention to any notable additional features.

For some features, such as news and image databases, only a brief mention is given in the profile because the subject is covered in detail in a relevant chapter elsewhere in the book. As you use these engines, expect to occasionally find new features, new arrangements of home pages, and other changes.

The engines presented here are the four most popular among serious searchers. (If you look at many published lists of "most popular" search engines, you will often see AOL Search listed among the top five. It is not discussed here because AOL is still the "internet on training wheels," and its search interface and results are "enhanced by Google," as its search page says. It provides no significant search features or content beyond what Google itself provides.)

See Table 4.1 at the end of the discussion on the major search engines for an outline of which options are available in which search engines.

GOOGLE (GOOGLE.COM)

In about four years, Google went from being the new kid on the block to being the favorite search engine for the majority of users. For the most part, its popularity stems from using the popularity of a website as a major ranking factor, its simplicity for the casual user, and its vigorous efforts to increase both the size of its database and the provision of additional features and types of content. In ranking records, Google puts the emphasis on the popularity of a webpage, measured by how many other pages link to that page and the popularity of those linking pages. (Webpages are known by the

Figure 4.1

Google home page

friends they keep.) Google was the first major engine to provide a "cache" feature to let you go to a cached copy of the page as it looked when last indexed by the engine. Besides webpage searching, Google also provides excellent image, video, news, newsgroup, and shopping databases, plus more specialized searches such as for journal articles and books, as well as an increasing number of non-search services including email, satellite images, and maps. The last time Google officially reported the size of its database, way back in 2005, it contained more than 8 billion records.

Google's Home Page

One of the reasons Google is so popular is its insistence on a simple, uncluttered home page (Figure 4.1). Even though the home page is simple, exploring the few links on the page will uncover several features. The home page includes the following:

- Search box – Enter one or more words. Use a minus sign in front of a term to exclude that term (Boolean NOT). You can also use OR, as well as several prefixes such as *intitle:*. Google will ignore small, common words unless you insert a plus sign immediately in front of them (e.g., +*the*), or if they are part of a phrase within quotation marks.
- Links to Google's databases and other services
  - Web database (the default)
  - Images – Leads to one of the largest image search databases on the web

- Video – A search of video that appears in Google's own YouTube plus video from other sites
- Maps – Maps, directions, and "yellow pages," and a search for much of the world, plus driving directions (and where appropriate, walking directions and directions for public transit) and satellite images
- News – Covers 25,000 English-language news sources going back 30 days (plus a news archives search going back much further, and searches for news from other languages and countries)
- Shopping – Google's shopping database
- Gmail – Google's free webmail service

(The following may be under the "more" link at the top of the page, as Google occasionally switches which databases and services have direct links on the main page and which are found under "more.")

- Groups – Searching of Usenet postings back to 1981, plus other groups that are created by Google users
- Books – A search of the full text of millions of books, plus the ability to view actual pages from many
- Scholar – A search of scholarly literature from peer-reviewed journals, preprints, theses, books, etc.
- Finance – A portal for financial news and information
- Blogs – Google's blog search
- YouTube – Google's video sharing site
- Calendar – A sharable online calendar
- Photos – Online photo albums using Google's Picasa
- Documents – Online collaborative software applications: word processor, spreadsheet, presentations, etc.
- Reader – An RSS reader
- Sites – Create your own website
- "Even more" – This link takes you to the page that lists virtually all of the major services provided by Google
- Advanced search link
- Language tools:

- Translate both your search terms and your search results into any of 42 languages
- Translate text or a webpage from one language to another for 42 languages
- Display the Google interface in any one of 129 languages
- Link to the Google country-specific versions for 174 countries

- I'm Feeling Lucky – Takes you to the page that Google would have listed first in your results (mostly a gimmick)
- Various special options – Includes links for information on advertising, the company, and sometimes a featured service; the About Google link is Google's Help link and leads to help screens and the range of special Google offerings and tools
- Personalized Home/Sign In – If you have signed up for any of Google's services, such as the iGoogle personalized portal page, Documents, Search History, or Subscribed Links, etc., use the link at the top of the page to sign in or sign out, go to your account, etc.
- Search Settings:
  - Language search and interface preferences
  - SafeSearch option (adult content filter)
  - Number of results per page
  - Option to have results opened in new window
  - Turn "query suggestions" (that appear as you enter a search) on or off
  - Subscribed links (a library of special content that can automatically be added to your searches)

If you are not using Google's English-language page but are using one of the country-specific versions of Google, you will probably also see, beneath the search box on the home page, options to search only pages from that country and options to search just for pages in the language(s) of that country.

Google's Advanced Search

As with other engines, many Google searches can be accomplished by putting one or two terms in the home page search box. If you need enhanced capabilities, Google's advanced search page provides all the common field

Figure 4.2

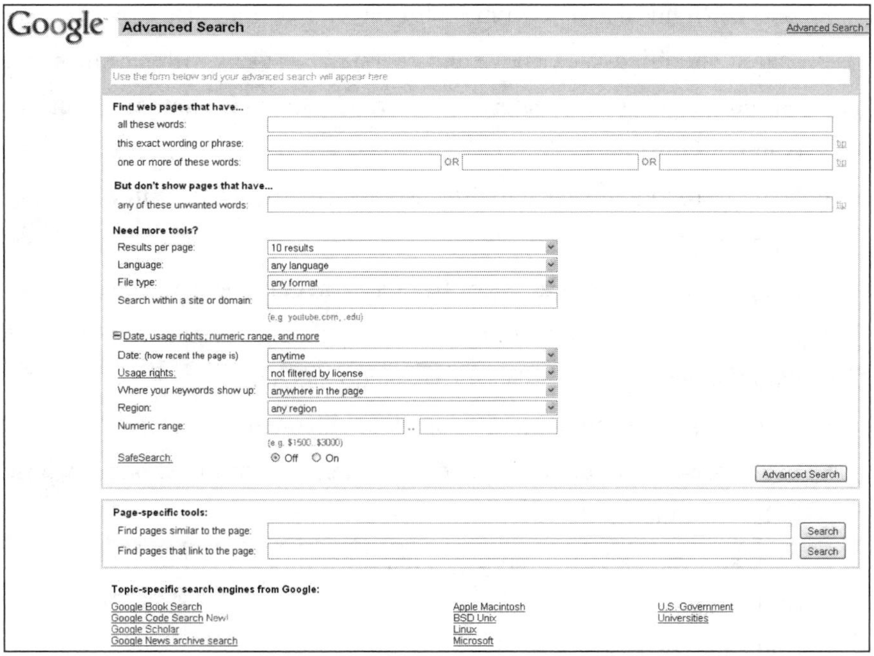

Google advanced search page

search options (title, domain, link, language, and date) as well as some less common ones (Figure 4.2).

You will find the following on Google's advanced search page (in roughly this order):

- Boxes to perform simple Boolean combinations ("all these words," etc.)
- Choice of 10, 20, 30, 50, or 100 results per page
- Choice of searching for documents in all languages or any one of 46 languages
- Option to retrieve only a specific file format (.pdf, .ps, .dwf., kml., .kmz, .xls, .doc, .ppt, .rtf, .swf)
- Box for limiting to a particular site or domain

To get to the next six options, you may need to click on the "Date, usage rights, numeric range, and more" link on the advanced search page:

- Date restriction (anytime, past 24 hours, past week, past month, past year)

- Usage Rights menu to limit retrieval to material that can be used, shared, modified, etc., above and beyond "fair use," without infringing on copyright (this material has a Creative Commons [creativecommons.org] license)
- Window to limit retrieval to title, text, or URL fields, or within the links on the page
- Region menu to limit to pages from a particular country
- Numeric range option to limit retrieval to pages containing numbers with the range you specify (for years, dollars, etc.)
- A filter option (SafeSearch) to block adult content
- Page specific tool to "Find pages [that are] similar to the page" whose URL you enter in the box
- Page specific tool to "Find pages that link to the page" (enter the URL of the page of interest)
- Links to topic-specific searches:
  - Google Book Search – Searches full-text books
  - Google Code Search – Searches within programmers' code
  - Google Scholar – Searches scholarly publications
  - Google News Archive – Searches news from historical archives
  - Apple Macintosh – Searches for Mac-related pages
  - BSD Unix – Searches webpages about the BSD operating system
  - Linux – Searches Linux-related pages
  - Microsoft – Searches Microsoft-related pages
  - U.S. Government – Searches all .gov and .mil sites
  - Universities – Searches pages from selected universities

Search Features Provided by Google

Using the menus on the advanced page and prefixes on the main page, Google provides field searching for all of the commonly searchable webpage fields (title, URL, link, language, date), plus searching by file format, date range, country, usage rights, and for "similar" pages.

Boolean

On the home page, Google automatically ANDs all of your words. You can also use a minus sign to NOT a term, and you can use one or more ORs (the OR must be capitalized).

Example: *warfare chemical OR biological -anthrax*

This search expression would find all records that contain the word *warfare* and also contain either *chemical* or *biological* but would eliminate all records containing the word *anthrax*.

On Google's advanced search page, simple Boolean is done by use of the "all these words," "one or more of these words," and "any of these unwanted words" boxes.

Title Searching

Searches can be limited to words appearing in the page title in one of two ways. First, on the advanced search page, you can enter your terms in the search boxes, then choose "in the title of the page" from the "where your keywords show up" pull-down menu.

Second, on the home page, you can use the prefixes *intitle:* or *allintitle:*. The *intitle:* prefix specifies that a certain word or phrase is included in the title.

Examples: *intitle:online   intitle:"online strategies"*

Use *allintitle:* to specify that all words after the colon be in the title but not necessarily in that order. For example, the following would retrieve titles with both words somewhere in the title, not necessarily in the specific order:

allintitle:nato preparedness

These prefixes can be combined with a search for a word anywhere on the page.

Example: *summit intitle:nato*

You cannot achieve this kind of combination using the menus on the advanced search page because your single menu choice (for where your terms show up) will apply to all terms you enter in the search boxes.

URL, Site, and Domain Searching

If you want to limit retrieval to pages from a particular URL, it can be done in a way parallel to title searching. You can do it either using menus on the advanced search page or using prefixes on the home page. On the advanced search page, enter a URL (or a top-level domain such as .edu or .ac) in the "Search within a site or domain" box.

On the home page, you can use the prefixes *site:* or *inurl:* or *allinurl:*

> Examples: *site:yale.edu*
> *inurl:bbc*
> *inurl:"bbc.co.uk"*
> *allinurl:bbc co uk*

To do a site search for a specific topic, on the advanced search page, enter terms for your topic in the search boxes and the URL in the "Search within a site or domain" box. A site search can be done on Google's home page using the *site:* prefix, as follows:

> *hybrid site:ford.com*

Link Searching

To find pages that link to a particular site, enter the URL in the box labeled "Find pages that link to the page" in the page-specific tools section of the advanced search page. Alternatively, you can perform the search on Google's home page by using the *link:* prefix. For example, to find pages that link to the Modern Language Association site, search for:

> *link:mla.org*

Language Searching

To limit retrieval to sites in a particular language, use the Language menu on the advanced search page. The default is "any language," but you can choose any one of 46 languages. If you want to set a particular language or languages as your default choice, use Google's Search Settings page. On that same page, you can also request that the Google search pages appear in any one of 124 languages (including Bork! Bork! Bork!, Elmer Fudd, and Klingon, as well as "real" languages).

Searching by Date

The Date window on the advanced search page allows you to limit results to pages that are new in the past 24 hours, past week, past month, or past year.

Keep in mind that date searching is only an approximation because the origination date or last updated date is often not clearly identified on most webpages.

Searching by File Type

Using the File Format menu on the advanced search page, results can be limited to any of the following formats: Adobe Acrobat (.pdf), Adobe Postscript (.ps), Autodesk DWF (.dwf), Google Earth (.kml, .kmz), Microsoft Excel (.xls), Microsoft Word (.doc), Microsoft PowerPoint (.pdf), rich text format (.rtf), and Shockwave Flash (.swf).

On Google's home page, you can accomplish the same thing (or exclude files of a particular type) by using the *filetype:* prefix. For example, if you want a 1040EZ IRS tax form to print out, search for:

1040EZ IRS form filetype:pdf

Searching for Related (Similar) Pages

You can search for pages that are similar to a particular page by using the "Find pages similar to the page" box in the page-specific tools section of Google's advanced search page. Enter the URL of the page in the box or use the *related:* prefix on Google's home page.

Example: *related:searchengineland.com*

Searching by Other Prefixes

The following prefixes can be used on Google's home page to search for other specific information.

cache: Enter a URL after the colon to get Google's cached version of the page.

Example: *cache:www.aps.org*

info: Enter a URL after the colon and you will be shown the record for that specific site and also given links that take you to (a) "similar" sites, (b) sites that link to the site, (c) all webpages indexed from the site, and (d) pages that contain the URL as a term on the page.

Example: *info:cyndislist.com*

stocks: Enter a stock symbol after the colon to get stock quotes.

Example: *stocks:csco*

define: Search the collection of glossaries that Google has found on websites. This is particularly useful for word definitions that will not be found in standard dictionaries, such as slang, neologisms, and technical terms.

Example: *define:mashup*

safesearch: Use to filter out adult content.

Example: *safesearch:underwear*

inanchor: Use to find pages that have a specific word in a link on the page (i.e., the clickable text contains that word)

allinanchor: Use (followed by one or more words) to find pages that have links containing your search terms.

Example: *allinanchor:extreme searcher*

numrange: Use to find any pages that contain a number that is within the range you specify.

Example: *american pottery numrange:1900..1920*

Actually just using the range, with the two periods but without the prefix, also works just as well.

Example: *american pottery 1900..1920*

You can do a less-than or more-than search by leaving out the first or last number.

Example: *skyscraper height numrange:1000.. ft*

"Wildcard" Words

Google allows the use of one or more asterisks for "wildcard" *words* (not to be confused with "truncation," which is a technique for searching wildcard *characters* within or at the end of a word). You can use the asterisk for unknown words in a phrase search. The use of *each asterisk insists on the presence of one word.*

Example: *"erasmus * rotterdam"*

That search will retrieve "Erasmus Universiteit Rotterdam" and "Erasmus von Rotterdam." It will not necessarily retrieve any "Erasmus Rotterdam" records.

Example: *"erasmus * * rotterdam"*

That search will retrieve "Erasmus University of Rotterdam" but not necessarily the "Erasmus Universiteit Rotterdam" records.

If you want "Franklin Roosevelt" and "Franklin D Roosevelt" as well as "Franklin Delano Roosevelt," search for:

*"Franklin Roosevelt" OR "Franklin * Roosevelt"*

Synonym Searches

As with other search engines to varying degrees, Google really tries to be "helpful." To do so, in some cases at least, it automatically recognizes and retrieves words that it considers "synonyms," a term that Google defines rather broadly to include word variants and closely related words. For example, a search on *diet* may also retrieve pages with the word *diets*, without you specifically asking it to do so. This does make it easier for searchers in that it means that it is not necessary to "OR" a lot of similar words. This in general is probably good, but Google's implementation of the idea is also a bit unpredictable.

You can force Google to more emphatically search for synonyms by adding a tilde in front of a search term:

Example: *apples children ~nutrition*

In some cases at least, searching *~nutrition* causes items to be retrieved because terms such as *nutritional, eating, food*, or *health* are on the page.

However, there are times when you don't want it to be so helpful, and you only want one specific word. You can insist that a term be searched exactly as you entered it by placing a plus sign in front of the term, for example, if you want the family name, "Price" but find you are getting things about "pricing" you may want to try*: +price.*

Search Suggestions

Unless you have turned the feature off (using the Search Settings page), Google will offer you search suggestions as you type your query (see Figure 4.3).

Subscribed Links

On Google's Preferences page, you will see an option for Subscribed Links. These are "reference" sites, and when you subscribe, information from the sites will appear in your search list when you do a related search.

Figure 4.3

Google search suggestions

For example, one of the options is Drugs.com. When one or more of your search terms seems related to drugs, drug data from the Drugs.com site will appear (as approximately the fourth item) in your search results list.

Calculator

For a quick arithmetic calculation, you can use the Google search box. Enter *46*(98-3+32)*, and Google provides the answer. For addition, subtraction, multiplication, division, and exponents use +, -, *, /, and ^ respectively. You can also nest using parentheses, for example, *15* (14+43)*. Google seems to want to hide the neat details on using this feature, but if you do a search on *calculator site:google.com* it should lead you to wherever Google is currently hiding the instructions.

Metric-Imperial Conversions

From the main search box, you can easily convert measurements between metric and imperial systems for all common units of length, volume, mass, and temperature. (See Google's "calculator" help page for details on this.)

Examples:

32 feet to meters

30 km to miles

8 liters to quarts

68 f to c

Some Miscellaneous Points About Search Statements on Google

Remember these points about search statements on Google:

- The order of words in your query may matter in terms of how Google ranks the results. Try placing your more important search terms at the beginning of your query.
- Punctuation is usually ignored, with some exceptions, particularly in situations where the punctuation is known to have meaning, such as C++ or a dollar sign in front of a number.
- As with all major search engines, capitalization is ignored.

Google Results Pages

On Google results pages, it pays to look closely at the entire page and also at the content of the individual records (Figure 4.4).

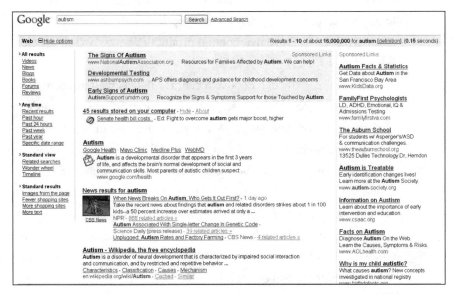

Figure 4.4

Google search results page

Start with the line where Google reports your results, for example,

Results **1 – 10** of about **18,500,000** for autism

Look for underlined terms. Depending upon the nature of the terms, clicking on them may lead to dictionary definitions, encyclopedia articles, maps, local time, a currency converter, statistics, etc., from 180 reference tools included in Answers.com.

Google also searches its other databases whenever you do a web search. If your topic has been in the news recently, above, below, or among your results you will see a section on "News Results for ..." with up to three headlines and a link to more. Click on the headlines to go to the news stories, or click on the title of the section to go to the full search in Google News.

Most importantly, Google results pages now contain a "Show options" link. Click on it and you will see, on the left side of your results page, four lists displaying several options for further refining your results:

- Type of results – This list narrows results to those that include videos, news, blogs, books, forums, and reviews. Make a choice and your results are not just narrowed to that kind of content, but you are also given further narrowing possibilities specific to the kind of content. (For example, for reviews, new options will be shown for narrowing results to those that contain product reviews, review articles, book reviews, etc.)

- Age of results – You can choose recent results, as well as those from the past hour, past 24 hours, past week, or past year, or you can choose a specific date range. When you make one of these choices, you are additionally given a sort option (by relevance or by date).

- View of results – Here you can choose from Related Searches, Wonder Wheel, or Timeline. The first choice puts a list of related searches at the top of the results page. The Wonder Wheel option shows a circle with related topics/subtopics attached as spokes. Click on one of the related topics and that spoke gets its own wheel. (Keep in mind, however, that the new results list then shown on the right side of the page is *not* necessarily a subset of the first set.) The Timeline option provides a clickable timeline based on dates mentioned on webpages.

- Standard results – This set of options allows you to narrow your results to pages that have images (giving you thumbnails next to each result) or to limit or expand the number of shopping pages in your results. You can also choose "more text," which results in a longer excerpt for each search result; instead of the standard website excerpt of less than 30 words, you may see descriptions of more than 70 words.

If you are using Google's Desktop Search, and you have your preferences set to do so, Google will automatically search your computer and list the results of that search above the web search results.

If Google "thinks" you may have misspelled a search term, you will see a "Did you mean" message, with a suggested alternative spelling.

A few additional parts of individual records are also worthwhile examining (Figure 4.5).

Figure 4.5

> **Spontaneous Human Combustion**: SHC: Living People Mysteriously and ...
> Mysterious fires and lights are considered anomalies, falling in the scope of **Fortean** phenomena. SHC is probably the most feared because it nearly always ...
> paranormal.suite101.com/.../**spontaneous_human_combustion**_shc - Cached - Similar

Example of an individual record in a Google search result

By clicking the Cached link in the record, you will be directed to a cached copy that Google stored when it retrieved the page. This feature is especially useful if you click on a search result and the page is not found, or it is found, but the terms you searched for do not seem to be present. If this happens, go back to the Google results page and click on the Cached link.

Clicking on the Similar link will lead to pages with similar content ("More like this"). Take advantage of this capability to find related pages that may be difficult to find otherwise.

If you encounter a record for a page that is in one of three dozen languages, you will see a link to "Translate this page." Click on that link for an English translation of that page.

If your search results include any Adobe Acrobat, Adobe Postscript, Excel, PowerPoint, Word, or Rich Text Format files, a link will be available to view those records as HTML. Click on "View as HTML" to see an HTML version of the page as "translated" by Google.

On search results pages, you can simply click on any of the links above the search box to have the same search done in those additional databases (Images, News, etc.).

Other Searchable Google Databases

In addition to its main database of webpages, Google provides searchable databases of images, groups, news, videos, blogs, products, maps and satellite images, books, and journal articles. Using Google's main search box, you can also search databases of phone numbers, businesses, and stock prices. The images, maps, groups, news, and video databases are accessible by clicking the appropriate link at the top of Google's main page (and on many other Google pages). Others can be accessed by the "more" link at the top of the page. Because the Google images, groups, news, and product databases are discussed in some detail in the chapters that follow, they are only mentioned briefly here.

Images

Google has one of the largest searchable image collections on the web, with billions of images. Details on image searching are covered in Chapter 7.

Google Groups (Newsgroups)

Google provides access to the Usenet collection of newsgroups, going back to 1981 and containing hundreds of millions of messages. In 2005, Google added its own user-created groups. More details on Google groups are available in Chapter 5.

News

Google's news search is reachable through the link on Google's home page or directly at news.google.com. It covers about 25,000 news sources and is updated continually. Records are retained for 30 days, but the site also provides a search of a large archival collection of news. Read more about news searching in Chapter 8. Also in the news category, Google provides a search of blogs (weblogs) at blogsearch.google.com.

Google Product Search

Formerly known as Froogle, Google's shopping database contains pages of products for sale that Google has identified by crawling the web and also contains product pages submitted by merchants. For more details on Google Product Search, see Chapter 9.

Google Maps

The map searches provided by various search engines all allow you to locate businesses in or near a particular city or other location, plus get road maps

Figure 4.6

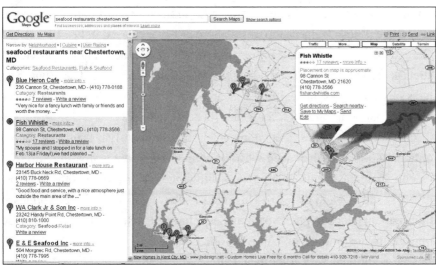

Google Maps search result

and driving directions. In the case of Google, its map search combines a search of a yellow pages database, information it has found from crawling the web, and its maps and satellite images databases, to provide not just names, phone numbers, and addresses of businesses but also an accompanying (draggable) road map with the locations of the businesses shown, with options to get driving directions, a satellite view of the location, and for some areas, even a view of the terrain and photos associated with the location (Figure 4.6). Google Maps, which originally covered just the U.S. and Canada, now covers much of the "drivable" world, with satellite photos at least of virtually the entire planet. Google Maps is very closely integrated with Google Earth, which will be discussed shortly.

To find businesses, enter the topic (e.g., restaurants, hotels, pet massage) and the location. For location, you can enter a city or ZIP code (or post code or postal code) and/or city, state, country, etc. (e.g., *pizza Doha Qatar*). You can also be more specific as to the location, for example, *london hotel near westminster*. Results show both a list and the map. Above the results listing, you are usually also shown categories (e.g., Hotels & Inns, Hotel Booking Agents) and options to narrow your search by such things as neighborhood, cuisine, and user rating.

For a rapidly increasing number of cities, towns, and even some rural areas, and in an increasing number of countries, Google Maps (and Google

Earth) now provide a "Street View," with draggable and tiltable horizontal and vertical 360-degree panoramic photos of real streets. Taken by special Google vehicles systematically roaming the streets, these photos provide a street-level view of what someone who is actually there would see (but, perhaps obviously, not in real time). Search for a location, click on the place-marker "balloon," and look for a link for "Street View."

One way Google has integrated content that previously was only available only on Google Earth is seen when you click the "more" tab at the top of a Google map. A menu will pop up allowing you to add photos, videos, reviews, and so on to the map. This feature allows you to easily see and learn things about a location that you may never have expected and to get to a wide range of related information quickly and easily.

One additional very important feature of Google Maps is the My Maps section, which enables anyone who has a Google account to easily create a "mashup." Wikipedia describes a mashup as "a website or web application that seamlessly combines content from more than one source into an integrated experience." Though mashups can refer to the mixing of lots of different kinds of data on the web, the most common mashups involve integrating information into a Google Map. (Those maps you've probably seen in numerous places that have a "balloon" you can click on are mashups.) Many other sites such as Yahoo! and Amazon provide opportunities to incorporate their data with other data, but Google Maps is the most popular source, and Google makes the process unbelievably easy. If you want a map that shows points of interest to you, a map that you can point people to on Google Maps, email to people, or put on your website, you can easily do so using Google's My Maps. Plus, you can add text, images, and videos to the balloons. If you want to get an idea of the possibilities that mashups offer, a great collection of them can be found at Google Maps Mania (googlemaps mania.blogspot.com).

Phone Book and Address Lookup

A phone book lookup for U.S. phone numbers and addresses can be done on Google directly from the home page search box. For a business, type the business name and either city and state or ZIP code. For individuals, give the first name, the last name, and either state, area code, or ZIP code. As with all phone directory sites on the web, do not expect perfect results all the time.

You can also do a reverse lookup just by entering the phone number in the search box, with or without punctuation. Include the area code.

Google Book Search

Through arrangements with publishers and several major libraries, Google Book Search provides bibliographic information on and, in some cases, full text access to, a large collection of both new and old books. Google Book Search is discussed in some detail in Chapter 6.

Google Scholar

Google Scholar covers peer-reviewed papers, theses, books, preprints, abstracts, articles, and technical reports. The availability of this scholarly material on Google is a result of agreements with publishers, associations, universities, and others, allowing Google to index databases that search engine crawlers usually cannot penetrate ("Deep Web" material). For more on Google Scholar, see Chapter 6.

Google Blog Search

Google's Blog Search has the intention of covering any blog that provides a site feed (either RSS or Atom). The main page of Google Blog Search shows the current top stories, and category links on the left of the page enable you to browse the top blogs in any of 11 categories. Blogs can be searched using the same operators as a regular Google search and the following fields prefixes can be used: *link:, site:, intitle:, inblogtitle:, inposttitle:, inpostauthor:, blogurl:*. The first three of those are the same as in a regular web search, and the remaining ones are unique to blog searching (but hopefully self-explanatory).

The Google Advanced Blog Search page provides simple Boolean and searching by blog title, URL, author, dates, and language. A SafeSearch option is also provided.

Patent Search

The 7 million patents in Google Patent Search come from the U.S. Patent and Trademark Office (USPTO) and are all full-text searchable. As of this printing, Google includes patents back to 1790 but does not include the most recently issued U.S. patents. Researchers should also be aware that the Google Patent Search does not provide the level of searchability of some other patents databases. In perspective, the USPTO's own site (www.uspto.gov) is completely up-to-date (updated every Tuesday when patents are issued), but full-text searchability on the USPTO site is available only from the beginning of 1976. Both the Google site and the USPTO site contain full images of all patents in the database.

While Google's interface is simpler and/or more intuitive than the interface for USPTO's own site and for commercial patent search services, Google offers fewer search options. Google provides searching by eight fields—in contrast to the 31 fields searchable on the USPTO site and more than 80 fields searchable on some commercial patent search services. Google Advanced Patent Search page allows use of the usual combination of text search boxes (all the words, phrase, at least one of the words, without the words) plus search options for the following fields: Patent Number, Title, Inventor, Assignee, Current U.S. Classification, International Classification, Issue Date, and Filing Date. Alternatively, most of these search options are available on the main page by means of Google's Boolean connectors and the following prefixes: *patent:, intitle:, allintitle:, ininventor:, inassignee:, uspclass:,* and *intlclass:.*

Google Earth

In addition to being a tool for serious research, one of the most "fun" tools offered by Google is Google Earth (Figure 4.7), a searchable database that provides aerial/satellite views of places throughout the entire planet. Google

Figure 4.7

Google Earth

Earth is also notable because it represents effective integration of a variety of trends and technologies, including nontextual content search and retrieval (in this case maps and images), streaming data, local search, and sharing.

Google Earth is a combination of a downloadable program and online data that provides satellite and aircraft imagery and allows users to integrate and superimpose their selection of related data.

Once the program has been downloaded, Google Earth's main page presents a control console and an image of the Earth. Click on an area of your choice, and then zoom in on exactly what you want to see—your own backyard, Maui, or Timbuktu. You can also zoom directly to your destination by typing in an address. At an "altitude" of your choice, you can have Google Earth superimpose roads, railways, schools, parks, hotels, restaurants, and other landmarks as well as political boundaries, statistics, driving directions, and more. You can tilt and rotate your image and "fly" over an area, and for some metropolitan areas, you can see 3D images of buildings and terrain. You can add your own placemarks and annotations and even share these with others.

Images are available for the entire world, with higher resolution versions for many locations, especially major cities. Google Maps search features and road maps are provided for most major metropolitan areas as well as non-urban areas. For the lower resolution sites, such as remoter parts of the world, the resolution will enable you to at least see major geographic features and towns. The higher resolution sites allow you to identify something the size of a car or smaller. A more powerful version, Google Earth Pro (with higher resolution and more sophisticated tools), is available for an annual subscription fee.

Google Earth includes rapidly increasing amounts of subject content associated with locations. Spend some time browsing the Layers and Places panels on Google Earth to get a feel for the possibilities. Content is provided by Google partner organizations, by the Google Earth Community (the major online forum for Google Earth users), and by the public at large. Searching for content on Google Earth can be done by using its search panel, searching on regular Google, or searching the Google Earth Community site (at bbs.keyhole.com). To find Google Earth subject content (text, videos, images, etc.) through a regular Google search you can use the "file type" search option and specify .kml and .kmz files (the two file types for Google Earth content). Along with your subject terms, either use the *filetype*: prefix in the main search box (e.g., *filetype:kml*) or use the corresponding menu on the advanced search page. Alternatively, in Google's main search box, simply try your topic and the phrase *Google Earth*.

Stock Search

Enter a ticker symbol for a U.S. company in Google's main search box, and you'll get current stock quotes, prices, volume, and links to more information about the stock and the company from multiple finance and market-related sources (MSN Money, CNN Money, etc.). This information, which will appear above the regular Google search results, is an example of search engine "shortcuts" discussed in Chapter 3.

SearchWiki

SearchWiki is a feature that allows you to change the order of results for a specific search. If you do that search again, your results will reflect your own preferences. SearchWiki is active while you are logged in to Google. For any particular search, using the icons displayed next to a result, you can *Promote* a site to the top of your ranking, *Remove* it, or *Comment* about the site. You can also add a site to your results. Comments from others who have used SearchWiki for a similar search are available through a link at the bottom of the search results page.

Google Toolbar

The Google Toolbar is a free downloadable feature that allows you to add the Google search box and additional features as a toolbar on Internet Explorer or Firefox browsers. You can add buttons to your toolbar to take you immediately to feeds, Google tools such as Gmail and Google Docs, and other features and "gadgets." Go to the "more" link on Google's home page (then to the "even more" link) to find out about what the Google Toolbar provides, including:

- Google Search – With the toolbar showing, the search box always appears on your browser screen.
- Search Site – Allows you to search only the pages of the site currently displayed.
- PageRank – Allows you to see Google's ranking of the current page.

- Page Info – Use this to get more information about a page, similar pages, and pages that link to a page; you also get a cached snapshot.
- Highlight – Highlights your search terms (each word in a different color).
- Word Find – Allows you to find search terms wherever they appear on the page.
- Spell Check
- AutoFill – Automatically fills out forms on a webpage.
- Translate – Hold the cursor over a word for an instant translation to or from English and Chinese, Japanese, Korean, French, Italian, German, Russian, or Spanish.
- Your choice of buttons for a variety of other Google services.

The Google Toolbar can be customized to include most of the features (image search, etc.) on the regular Google home page.

Other Google Features and Content

The folks at Googleplex, Google's headquarters, let no grass grow beneath their thousands of computers. While on the one hand some Google announcements receive inordinate attention, others receive relatively little press and even less attention from the majority of Google users. Informal polling indicates that many Google users have not even clicked on more than one or two of the links on Google's home page to see what is there, and even many very experienced searchers have not taken time to fully explore everything Google offers. The following Google offerings include some of the more significant features and content that may be easy to miss. These can be found through either the "more" link above the search box on Google's homepage or the "About Google" link at the bottom of Google's home page (some of these are still in beta mode):

- Alerts – This feature enables you to be automatically notified of news stories on topics of your choice or new or changed webpages. These are discussed in Chapter 8.
- Gmail – Google's free email service provides standard email functions and virtually unlimited storage, and comes with an integrated chat, instant messenger, and voice message function (Talk).

- Talk – Google's own instant messaging service includes a voice call option, voicemail, and file transfers.
- iGoogle – Google's version of a personal portal offers a choice of sections, including weather, Gmail, Google Calendar, movies, word-of-the-day, quotes-of-the-day, bookmarks, and a selection of news sources. You can also have, as one of your sections, Google's Search History, which records (when you wish) your searches and the sites you have visited. (Compare iGoogle to My Yahoo!.)
- Finance – This finance portal page provides stock information, news, and a personal stock portfolio. (Compare this to Yahoo!'s Finance section.)
- Calendar – This personal online calendar can be viewed by day, week, month, or next few days. You can also share with others, have multiple calendars, get email reminders, import events from other calendars, send invitations for events, and more.
- Blogger – Blogger lets you create a blog of your own.
- Picasa – This free downloadable program allows you to edit, organize, and share photos stored on your computer.
- Code – From Google's Code page, web developers can download Google APIs (Application Program Interfaces) and take advantage of other developer resources provided by Google. APIs are interfaces that allow an application program to communicate and interact with another program. Google provides such interfaces so that a developer can integrate its own data with a Google program.
- Mobile – Google provides a number of its services, such as Search, Maps, Gmail, SMS, Blogger, Calendar, and YouTube, in a format compatible with your mobile device. Go to www.google.com/mobile to get started.
- Video – Google's video search is discussed in Chapter 7.
- YouTube – Google's famous video sharing site is discussed in Chapter 7.
- Custom Search – With this tool, users can construct a custom search form that searches only websites or webpages that the user specifies (one site or page or many), with further capabilities to tag sites with keywords enabling further narrowing by those categories. Sites can be shared with others or with the general public, and the search form can be housed on your own website or on a page provided by Google.

- Google Health – Google Health, available for U.S. use only, provides a place for people to store personal health and medical information both for their own use and for sharing that information with family, doctors, and others. Access is limited to those for whom the user has given permission.

- Desktop Search – This feature indexes the contents of your own computer and provides an almost instantaneous search of your files. If you wish, results of the desktop search are shown along with your regular Google web search results.

- Google Docs – This is a suite of web-based, collaborative productivity tools, including a word processor, spreadsheet, slides presentation program, and forms generator. Documents are stored on Google's servers but can be uploaded from, or downloaded to, your own computer and are compatible with a number of formats such as Microsoft Word, PowerPoint, and Excel. A very strong point is the collaborative nature of this feature, making it very easy for those you choose to share in creating, editing, and using documents.

- Google Sites (sites.google.com) – This free website service allows users to easily create a website and allows others to share in editing and managing it and to embed other Google services such as Google Docs, Google Calendar, etc.

- Google Chrome – Google's own version of a web browser is intended to compete with Internet Explorer, Firefox, and other browsers.

- Goog-411 – This is a free voice-activated yellow-pages-type service. On your phone, you call 1-800-GOOG-411, say what you want to find and the city and state (or ZIP code), for example, *"Chinese restaurants Vienna Virginia."* The service will reply with matching business listings and connect you to the one you choose. This service is available only in the U.S. and Canada and only for U.S. and Canadian business listings.

- Checkout – This is a "shopping cart" service for online shoppers. You can use it whenever you do a search on Google and see the Google Shopping Cart icon in a sponsored link (ad) or are on the site of a participating merchant and see the icon. Google stores your shipping address(es), credit card information, and other information so that you don't have to deal with logins, passwords and other information for each merchant.

- Reader – This is a feed (automatic website and news updates) reader that allows you to easily subscribe to, organize, and read RSS and Atom feeds that you choose.
- SketchUp – This is a free, downloadable, computer-aided-design (CAD) program with which you can create 3D models of buildings, places, inventions, spaceships—anything you want. If you haven't used such a program before, it may take an hour or so to begin to get comfortable with it, but you will be amazed at what it can do and even more amazed that it is free.
- Google Labs – This is where Google provides demonstrations of a variety of projects on which it is currently working, which may or may not be destined for "prime time."

YAHOO! (YAHOO.COM)

Yahoo! made dramatic changes over the last decade, moving away from the directory function to the search function. In 2004, Yahoo! created its own new webpage database to challenge Google's database. Yahoo! also developed extensive databases for images, video, local, news, and shopping, as well as providing a search of the Yahoo! Directory. The My Yahoo! feature has provided the best general portal on the web, and Yahoo! has a broad collection of additional content accessible from its main page. In addition to the search box and search-related links on Yahoo!'s main page (yahoo.com), Yahoo! also provides a minimalist Yahoo! Search page (search.yahoo.com; see Figure 4.8). Comparing the sizes of web databases has become increasingly more difficult.

Figure 4.8

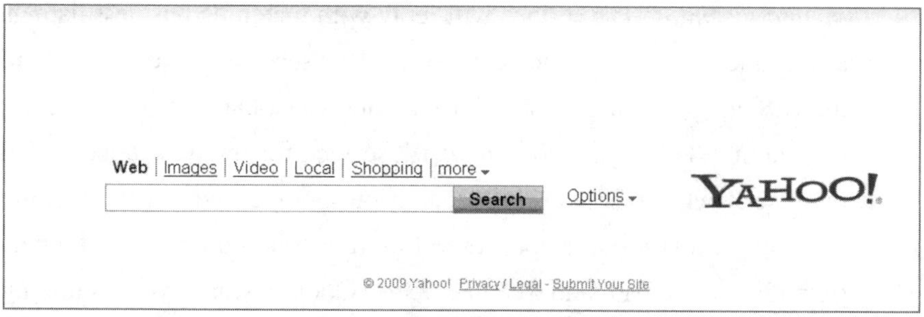

Yahoo! search page

Some quick comparative searches indicate that Yahoo! may stand up well against Google for the number of regular webpages indexed, but it may fall behind in total numbers because of the amount of "hidden web" content now covered by Google, particularly with regard to books and scholarly journal content the latter covers. The significance of the numbers is largely overshadowed by the search functions that can be applied to the databases.

Yahoo!'s Home Page

The Yahoo! home page is in the format of a general portal, with sections for search, news, and weather, Yahoo! Mail, and links to more than 40 Yahoo! services and sections. The search section at the top of the main page is virtually the same as on the streamlined Yahoo! Search page and on personalized My Yahoo! pages. From Yahoo's home page you can search the web database, or you can choose an alternate database and search Images, Video, Local (yellow pages), or Shopping. The "more" link above the search box provides links to other searchable databases (Answers, Directory, Jobs, News) and to All Search Services, a page that lists all of Yahoo!'s search-related services. As you enter your search terms in the box, you will see a list of suggested searches appear beneath the search box. (You may notice that neither on the home page nor under the "more" link has Yahoo! provided a link to the advanced search page.) If you would like to go to Yahoo!'s stream-lined search page (one that looks more like Google's home page, except that it doesn't show a link to the advanced search page), click on the Search button without entering anything in the search box.

The streamlined Yahoo! Search page includes the following:

- Search box – AND is implied between terms; and you can use OR, a minus sign for NOT, parentheses for nesting, and any of several prefix qualifiers.
- Options link – For some unfathomable reason, Yahoo! decided to not put the Advanced Search link directly on the Search page, but under this link, which also contains a link to the Preferences page.
- Links above the search box provide access to searches of alternate databases:
  - Images – A search of billions of images that Yahoo! has found by crawling the web

- Video – A search of millions of videos found by crawling the web or from submission by video producers
- Local – A yellow pages search by type of business and location that provides a listing of matching businesses, maps, driving directions, and more
- Shopping – Yahoo!'s product search with descriptions, photos, prices, ratings, and comparisons
- More – The link to other searchable databases and other Yahoo! services

Yahoo!'s Advanced Search

Users who miraculously manage to find their way to Yahoo!'s advanced search page will find extensive and easy search functionality (Figure 4.9), including the following:

- Boxes to perform simple Boolean combinations ("all of these words," "any of these words," or "none of these words"), plus a box for phrase searching
- Date restriction (anytime, past three months, past six months, last year); as with date searching in other search engines, this is not really reliable
- Options to limit to a particular top-level domain or a specific domain or site
- Creative Commons option for identifying copyright-free or shareable materials
- File Format option to retrieve only a specific file format (HTML, PDF, Excel, PowerPoint, Word, RSS/XML, and text)
- SafeSearch filter for blocking adult content
- Country origin option to limit to any of 100 countries
- Language option to limit to one or more of 41 languages
- Choice to specify the number of results per page (10, 15, 20, 30, 40, and 100)

Yahoo!'s Preferences Page

With Yahoo!'s Preferences Page (found under the Options link on Yahoo!'s search page), you can edit a number of options that govern what happens

Figure 4.9

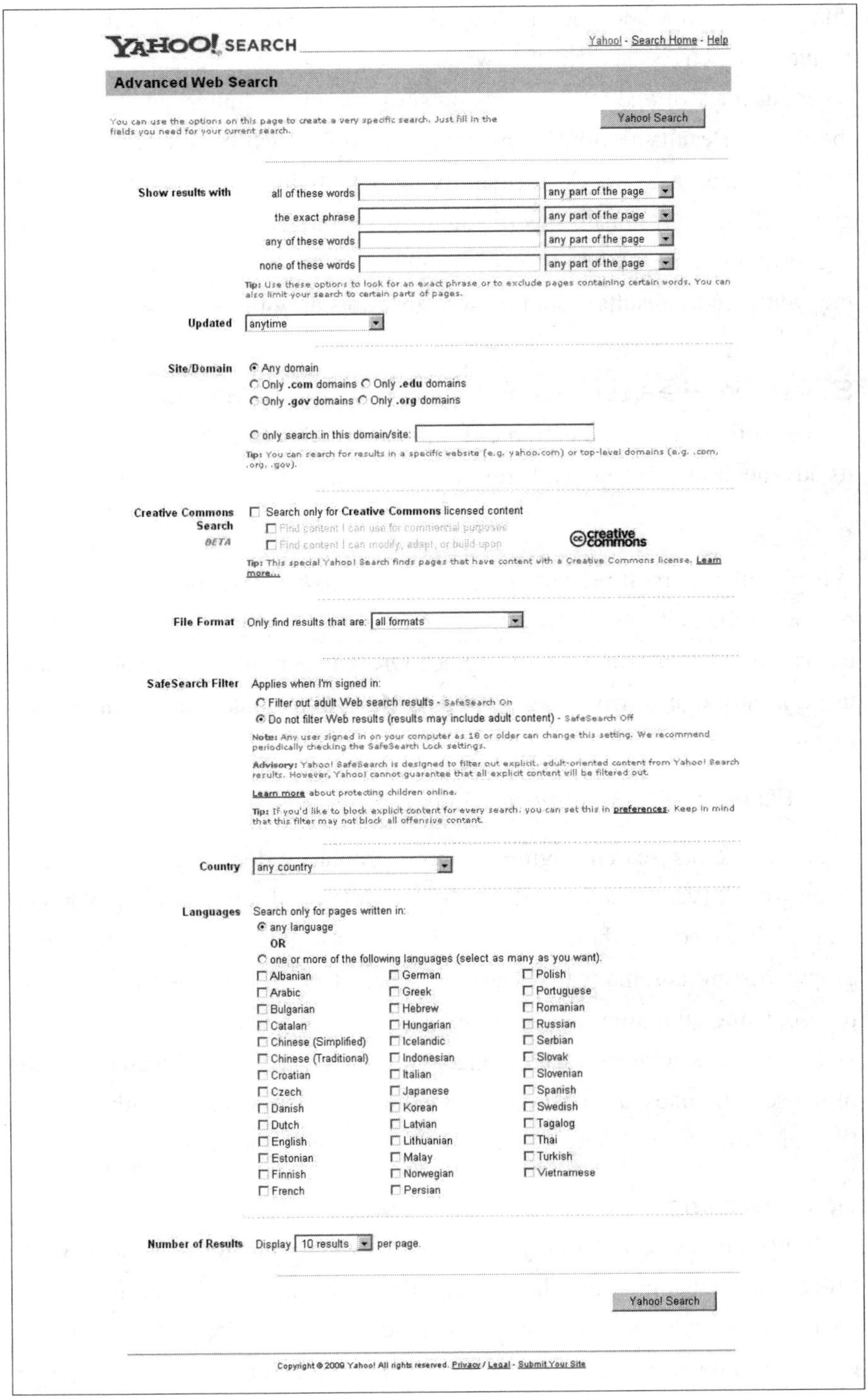

Yahoo! advanced search page

during a search when you are logged in under your Yahoo! account. These include: Search Assist (selecting when search suggestions appear); Search Pad (keeping track of and taking notes on sites you visit); Enhanced Results (see the Search Results section on this topic which follows); SafeSearch (limiting "adult content"); SearchScan (identifying potentially harmful websites); languages (limiting results to specific languages); and Display and Layout (opening results in a new window, setting number of results per page, and having the "Show more results from this site" link appear with records).

Search Features Provided by Yahoo!

Yahoo! offers a good collection of limiting and other search features, both on its advanced search page and from its main search box.

Boolean

When you enter multiple terms (e.g., *national debt*) in Yahoo!'s main search box, an AND is implied and you will only get back pages that use all of the terms. To OR two or more terms, place OR between the terms. You can also use a minus sign in front of a term as a NOT to exclude pages that contain that term.

> Example: *oil OR petroleum reserves iraq –war*

As with other search engines, Yahoo! ordinarily does not always search "stopwords" (very small words such as articles and prepositions). You can "force" it to do so, though, by putting a plus sign in front of the term. Stopwords are automatically searched when they are searched as part of a phrase, using quotation marks, for example, "in the limelight."

On Yahoo!'s advanced search page, you can use simple Boolean by means of the search boxes at the top of the page in the "Show results with" section ("all of these words," "any of these words," or "none of these words").

Title Searching

To limit your retrieval to only those pages where your terms appear in the title of the page, either use the "in the title of the page" option in menus that appear on the right side in the "Show results with" section of the advanced page or use the *intitle:* prefix in Yahoo!'s main search box.

> Examples: *intitle:"gross national product"   intitle:Obama*

URL, Site, and Domain Searching

With Yahoo!, you can limit your retrieval to pages from a particular site or kind of site by using the advanced search page or by using the *site:*, *url:*, *inurl:*, and *hostname:* prefixes.

On the advanced search page, use the Site/Domain radio buttons to limit your search to *.com, .edu, .gov,* or *.org* top-level domains. For other domains, enter the top-level domain extension (*.uk, .fr, .mil,* etc.) or combinations of these (e.g., *.co.uk*) in the text box there. In that box, you can also specify a particular site (e.g., *cruisemates.com*).

On Yahoo!'s main search page, you can use the *site:, url:, inurl:,* and *hostname:* prefixes. All of these can be combined with subject terms or other prefixes such as *intitle:*.

The *site:* prefix finds all pages from a domain and its subdomains; you can also use it to limit to a top-level domain (.edu, .com, .org, .mil, .fr, .ca, etc.).

When you use *site:* with a specific domain name, your results will appear on a Yahoo! Site Explorer page, which tells you how many pages Yahoo! has in its database for that site, provides a link to see pages linking to that site, allows you to either see pages linking to that specific domain or pages for all its subdomains, and provides a link to export the first 1,000 listings in a spreadsheet/database compatible format.

> Examples:
> *site:chrysler.com*
> *site:chile.chrysler.com*
> *human cloning intitle:ethics site:edu*

Use the *inurl:* prefix for searching a part of a URL:

> *inurl:worldbank*

The difference between the *hostname:* and *site:* prefixes is a bit esoteric and relates to subdomains (you may want to put this on your list of things to forget about). The *hostname:* prefix is used to get pages from a very specific domain or subdomain and exclude others. For both prefixes, results appear on a Site Explorer page.

> Examples:
> *site:chrysler.com* would get both *chrysler.com* and *chile.chrysler.com*
> *hostname:chrysler.com* gets precisely and only *chrysler.com* (not the records from subdomains such as *chile.chrysler.com*)

hostname:chile.chrysler.com would not get just plain *chrysler.com*

The *url:* prefix is used to find the Yahoo! record for a specific site and requires that you enter the *http://* part of the address:

url:http://onstrat.com

Link Searching

To do a link search in Yahoo!, use the *link:* prefix. This also leads to results on a Site Explorer page.

Example: *link:www.fas.org*

You may want to try variations on the address, for example:

link:fas.org OR link:www.fas.org

Language Searching

Use the Language checkboxes on the advanced search page to search any of 41 languages. Toward the bottom of Yahoo!'s main page, you will find a Y! International link to the Yahoo! sites for more than 40 countries or continents, with each country site in the language or languages of that country.

Searching by Date

Keep in mind that date searching for webpages is usually unreliable. But if you want to try it, use the Update window on the advanced search page to limit search results to the pages that Yahoo! identifies as updated in the past three months, past six months, or past year.

Searching by File Type

The File Format pull-down menu on the advanced search page lets you narrow your search to any one of the following document types: Word (.doc), Excel (.xls), PowerPoint (.ppt), Adobe PDF (.pdf), XML (.xml), and text (.txt).

Searching by Country

Yahoo!'s advanced search page lets you limit your search results to pages that are identified as coming from any one of 100 countries. The results are approximate and will both miss some pages and misidentify others.

Creative Commons

Creative Commons licensing provides a means by which copyright owners can easily grant some of their rights to the public, yet at the same time retain some of their rights. (For details, see the Creative Commons website at creativecommons.org.) Using the Creative Commons section of Yahoo!'s advanced search page, you can search specifically for materials that have a Creative Commons license and that you can therefore more freely and easily use in your own publications, etc. You can more specifically narrow your search to content that you can use for commercial purposes or content that you can "modify, adapt, and build upon."

Conversions

To find measurement conversions easily, use Yahoo!'s main search box and enter the conversion you want.

> Examples:
> *238.5 miles to kilometers*
> *19 celsius to fahrenheit*

The conversion feature works for most common units of length, weight, temperature, area, and volume. Abbreviations will usually work (m, in, ft., etc.); sometimes they won't.

Calculator

For a quick calculation, enter your problem in Yahoo!'s search box instead of pulling up a calculator.

> Example: *46*56.98*

For addition, subtraction, multiplication, division, and exponents use +, -, /, and ^ respectively. You can also nest using parentheses, e.g., 15*(14+43).

Stock Search

Stock quotes, charts, and news are available by entering the ticker symbol in the Yahoo! search box. The stock information will be shown at the top of the results page. The main Yahoo! site (yahoo.com) provides quotes for U.S. markets. Use other country sites (e.g., uk.yahoo.com) for markets in those countries.

Yahoo! Results Pages

Records on Yahoo! search results pages are listed (ranked) according to their relevance to the search terms (Figure 4.10).

In addition to the expected parts of a results listing—a title that links to the page, a snippet of text showing search terms that matched, and the URL

Figure 4.10

Yahoo! search results page

of the page—you may also find the following, depending on the record (Figure 4.11):

- Cached – Clicking on this link will take you to an archived version of the page. Use this when you encounter a Page Not Found message or when the word for which you searched is no longer on the current page.

- More from this Site – Yahoo! only shows one or two (highest ranked) pages from any site. If you have so chosen on the Yahoo! preferences page, this link will appear if there are other matching pages from a site.

- Translate – If a page is in Chinese (Simplified or Traditional), Dutch, French, German, Greek, Italian, Japanese, Korean, Portuguese, Russian, or Spanish, clicking this link will result in a machine translation of the page.

- View as HTML – When you retrieve a page that is in Adobe PDF, PowerPoint, or Word format, there will be a "View as HTML" link, from which you can view an HTML equivalent of the page (which may be quicker but probably not as pretty).

Figure 4.11

U.S. Food and Drug Administration - Bioterrorism
This site offers a menu of links to pertinent Web pages related to **counterterrorism**, including sites
from the Food and Drug Administration, Centers for Disease ...
www.**fda.gov**/oc/opacom/hottopics/bio**terrorism**.html - Cached - More from this site

---

Example of an individual record in a Yahoo! search result

- RSS: View as XML – If a site listed in your results is one that offers an RSS (Really Simple Syndication) newsfeed, you will see this link. Clicking on it will show you a page with the XML code for the news-feed page. The URL of that page is what you need if you want to sub-scribe to that feed. (For more on RSS, see Chapter 8.)

- Feed Discovery – If you have turned this feature on (using the Enhanced Results section of the Preferences page), you will see an indication of whether there are any recent RSS feeds from that webpage.

Additional Content Displayed on Search Results Pages

Above the regular search results list and beneath the search box, you will see the suggested search topics that Yahoo! will have displayed while you were typing your query, and, to the right of that, a list of related concepts. On the left of the page, you will see the following:

- Search Pad – This link brings up a notepad where you can keep track of sites you have visited during a Yahoo! search, add your own notes, copy and paste, rearrange your notes, print them, email them, share them via an HTML link, or save them on social networking sites such as Delicious, Facebook, and Twitter. The notes are stored on Yahoo!'s computers, so they are available wherever you go.

- Search Scan – This link turns on (or off) the feature (provided by McAfee) that is designed to protect you from harmful sites appearing among your results.

- Enhanced Results – These links may also appear on the left of the page. Depending upon which sources you have chosen, these may include sources such as Yahoo! Video, Flickr, Drugs.com, AllRecipes.com, etc.

- Phrases – On the left of the results pages, you may also see links for commonly occurring phrases that contain your term.

Remember, you can also click on any of the links directly above the search box on search results pages and have your same search done in those additional databases (Images, Video, etc.).

Just above your webpage results listings, you may also find other related items, depending upon the topic you searched. These may include:

- Did You Mean – If Yahoo! feels you misspelled one of your search terms, this feature suggests an alternate spelling. For some misspellings, you will see a message such as "We have included *parliament london* results - Show only <u>parlaiment london</u>". The last part is a link to click if you really do want to use your initial spelling.

- News – At the same time Yahoo! does your web search, it also automatically checks its news database; if there are matches for your search terms, you may receive up to three headlines, plus links to additional stories.

- Inside Yahoo! – Though Yahoo! is no longer calling this "Inside Yahoo!," the term still describes some links that may appear near the top of results pages. These lead to other places in Yahoo! that may be relevant to your search. For example, when you search for a city or country, you may see links to a visitor guide. A search on a disease may lead to a link to a page on that disease from Yahoo!'s Health section. Other topics will lead to other Yahoo! places.

Other Searchable Yahoo! Databases

Yahoo! also provides access to several major additional databases via the links above the search box on its main page: Images, Video, Local, and Shopping. (The choice of databases changes fairly frequently.) A "more" link there leads to links to Answers, Directory, Jobs, News, and other Yahoo! databases. There are at least a score of databases that can be found here or within the various Yahoo! sections on Yahoo!'s main page: The Autos section has databases of new and used car prices; the Health section has databases of health-related articles and other health information; HotJobs is an employment database; the Movies section has databases of old and new films; and Yahoo! Travel contains Yahoo!'s implementation of the Travelocity database as well as a database of destinations, and so on. The major offerings are described in the following section very briefly since they are covered in more detail in later chapters. The best way to get to know what searchable databases Yahoo! offers is to start with Yahoo!'s main page and spend time browsing the links you find there.

Images

Yahoo!'s image database, available through the link above the main search box, though once at least as large, may now be substantially smaller than Google's image database. See the section on searching images in Chapter 7.

Video

Here you can search the millions of videos that Yahoo! has identified by crawling webpages, plus video gathered directly from video publishers. Use the Video link above Yahoo!'s main search box to begin your search. For more details on Yahoo!'s video search, see Chapter 7.

Shopping

Yahoo! Shopping is one of the web's largest and easily searchable online shopping sites, with millions of products and tens of thousands of merchants (see Chapter 9).

Local

Yahoo!'s Local search, available from a link above the main Yahoo! search box, features a directory of U.S. businesses. (If you access Yahoo! from one of its international sites, check the main page to see if Yahoo! has a similar service for your country.)

To search for a business, enter a name or type of business (*Saks, Blockbuster, plumber, pizza, interpreter*, etc.) and either a ZIP code or the name of a city and the two letter postal code for a state. Yahoo! will retrieve a list of matching businesses with the name, phone number, and address of the business, a rating (by Yahoo! users), and the distance from your own default location (which you set by checking "Make this the default location for Yahoo!" in the pull-down menu on the right side of the location search box). A map is shown with the matching hits, and links are also provided for driving directions, reviews, and a link to further details on the business. You will also find, above the list of matching businesses, links to narrow your search by such things as category, location, distance, etc. The Category link lists related business categories for either narrowing or expanding the topic of your search. Click on one of the names in the results listings to get more detailed information, including the business web address (if there is one) and a map with a "Find nearby" link to locate nearby ATMs, hotels, parking, nightclubs, and movie theaters.

If you go directly to the Yahoo! Local site at local.yahoo.com, you will find a "City Guide" for your default location, with browsable business directory categories, a map, a list of upcoming local events, and user-recommended restaurants and other businesses.

Yahoo! Directory

You can search Yahoo!'s traditional web directory by clicking on the Directory link (found under the "more" above the search box) and entering your search terms in the search box. A search will yield a list of any matching categories and matching sites.

News

The Yahoo! news search (news.yahoo.com) covers 7,000 news sources in 35 languages. This is discussed in detail in Chapter 8.

Yahoo! Groups

Yahoo! Groups, which are all created by Yahoo! users, provides a very powerful communication tool. The content of "public" groups (those that the group creator decides can be public) is searchable and is an excellent place to gather advice and opinions. To get to Yahoo! Groups, go to groups.yahoo.com. Yahoo! Groups are discussed in more detail in Chapter 5.

People Search

Yahoo!'s People Search (found at people.yahoo.com) is a directory of U.S. and Canadian phone numbers, mailing addresses, and email addresses. The main People Search page indicates that it provides information for "U.S. Phone and Address," but if you put the two-letter code for a Canadian province in the *State* box, you can also find listings in Canada. (Apologies are probably due from the Yahoo! folks.) For other countries, check the country-specific Yahoo! site for a People section. Although you can search by first name, last name, city, and state, you may be able to get by with as little as the last name, which means you may not have to know the state in which a person lives.

Yahoo! Toolbar

The free downloadable Yahoo! Toolbar, available for Internet Explorer and Firefox, provides very easy access to most Yahoo! services regardless of what webpage is showing in your browser window, plus added features such as antispy software. Among the things the toolbar provides are:

- Search box – Available at all times with a pull-down menu for searching the alternate Yahoo! databases (Images, Video, etc.)
- A choice of buttons for more than 70 Yahoo! services and sections such as Mail, News, My Yahoo!, Calendar, etc.
- Antispy software
- Translate Page – Translate the current page into English
- Pop-up blocker (Internet Explorer version only)
- "Smart Tools" – Highlight any text on the webpage in your browser window and a Yahoo! Icon appears (for Internet Explorer 6.1 and higher); click it and search your highlighted text, email it, IM it, copy it, or translate it

Other Yahoo! Features and Content

Here are just a few of the additional services that can be accessed either directly from Yahoo!'s main page (yahoo.com) or through the More Yahoo! Services link on that page:

- Address Book – Store addresses and related information for use with Yahoo! Mail, Yahoo! Groups, or the calendar, or just use it as a convenient place for storing phone numbers and addresses. For the latter, it can be your "traveling" address book.
- Answers – Ask questions of other Yahoo! users and answer their questions.
- Autos – Research new or used cars and prices, as well as buy and sell cars.
- Calendar – Enter events and tasks, have email reminders sent to you, list and print events, tasks, and calendar pages in a variety of ways, and even share your calendar.
- Finance – Access a broad range of statistics, advice, news, background, tools, and services related to finance and investing, along with a personal portfolio option.

- Health – Find a range of information on diseases, conditions, and health-related issues, including a drug guide, health news, and expert advice.
- Mail – Sign up for Yahoo!'s robust web-accessible email service, one of the most-used free email services in the world.
- Messenger – Send and receive instant messages.
- Mobile – Access a variety of Yahoo! services on your cell phone or other mobile device.
- Movies – Find reviews, showtimes, trailers and clips, news, and more—about new movies and old, about what's in the theaters and what's out on DVD.
- Y! Music – Purchase and download music online, and locate information, interviews, and videos about musicians, groups, and recordings.
- Travel – Make reservations for airlines, trains, autos, vacation packages, and cruises, and find country and city guides.

BING (BING.COM)

After a long period of promises, MSN delivered its "new" MSN Search in 2004, with a new interface and a crawler of its own (rather than, as previously, using someone else's). Analogous in more ways than one to Microsoft's Millennium Edition operating system, the delivery of MSN Search was fairly quickly followed, in late 2005, by the release (in beta mode) of Windows Live (live.com), Microsoft's "new" new web search engine. By late 2006, MSN Search was no longer available, having been replaced by Live or "Live Search," which in 2009 was enhanced and renamed as Bing. Bing has a different look and feel than the old MSN Search, with a main page that has the now-usual minimalist search engine interface but with a large, attractive photographic background image. In line with Bing's "decision engine" marketing theme, Bing enhances its search results with useful "facts," gathered from selected websites, particularly in the areas of travel, health, shopping, and local information.

Bing's Search Page

The attractive but simple Bing home page (Figure 4.12) provides the following search-related features:

Figure 4.12

Bing home page

- Search box – In the search box, terms you enter are automatically ANDed, and you can use OR, NOT, and several prefixes.
- Links to other databases – Images, Video, Shopping, News, Maps, and Travel databases can be searched by using the links above the search box.
- Link to the MSN portal page
- Sign-in link – This link enables participation in Bing's cashback program news alerts, etc.
- Regional link – This link allows you to choose from about 60 country versions of Bing.
- Preferences (SafeSearch adult content filter on or off; default location for local search and other geographically significant searches; language in which you would like the search interface to appear; number of results per page; whether to open links in a new browser window; whether to turn "search suggestions" on or off; default language of search results)
- Cashback – Information on your Cashback account (cashback credit for purchases you make through Bing)
- A changing variety of additional features, promotional "beta," and others.

Move your cursor around on the background image to discover some hidden "hotspots" that provide information about the subject of the photo. (See the example of this in Figure 4.12.)

Bing's Advanced Search

If you click on the Advanced Search link found on Bing results pages, you are provided with a menu of advanced options (Figure 4.13). You can use this to easily, one step at a time, build additional qualifications into your search. The options include:

- Boolean – A menu provides simple Boolean options for the terms you enter, including "All of these terms," "Any of these terms," "None of these terms," as well as "This exact phrase."
- Site/Domain – Limits your search to, or to exclude, a specific site or top-level domain (.com, .edu, .uk, .fr, etc.).
- Country/Region – Limits your search to pages from any one of more than 90 countries.
- Language – Limits your search to any one of more than 40 languages.

Figure 4.13

Advanced search   x

Search terms │ Site/Domain │ Country/Region │ Language

Look for results that meet the following criteria:

[   ] [All of these terms ▾]

[Add to search]

You can add words or phrases one at a time. Get more search tips.

Bing advanced search page

Search Features Provided by Bing

Boolean

All terms you enter are automatically ANDed. You can use the OR (or |) connector, but you should be sure to enclose your ORed terms in parentheses. To exclude words, you can use either NOT or a minus sign in front of the word. (To facilitate copying and pasting your query into another engine, you may prefer to use the minus for the NOT.)

Example: *muskrats (recipe OR cooking) -baked*

Bing automatically searches for some variant word forms such as plurals (*recipes* when you search for *recipe*). You can insist on just one form by placing a plus sign before the term, for example, *+tarp*.

Title Searching

To limit to pages that have your term in the title, you must use the *intitle:* prefix. You can use this with quotation marks for a phrase. To specify multiple words without insisting on a specific phrase, re-use the prefix.

Examples:
intitle:handel
intitle:"Georg Frideric Handel"
intitle:handel intitle:biography

Site, Domain, and URL Searching

To find all pages that Bing has indexed for a particular site (up to two levels deep), or for a subdomain of a site, use the *site:* prefix.

Examples:
site:fujifilm.com
site:phototips.fujifilm.com
shadows site:fujifilm.com

This prefix can also be used to limit your retrieval to a specific top-level domain.

Example: *esters saponification site:edu*

The advanced search also provides a Site/Domain search option. Bing accepts a *url:* prefix, but it only retrieves the one record for that specific URL.

Language Searching

The easiest way to search for items in a particular language is to use the Language portion of the advanced search menu. You can use the *language:* prefix if you know the two-letter code for the language.

Example: *biographie clemenceau language:fr*

Searching by File Type

You can search by file type by using the *filetype:* prefix.

Example: *photoshop tutorial filetype:pdf*

This prefix works for .html, .txt, .pdf, .doc, .xls, .dwf, and .ppt files.

Searching by Other Prefixes

In addition to the prefixes just covered, the following can be used in Bing:

country/region – Enter *loc:* or *location:* followed by two-letter country code.

Example: *Fledermaus location:de*

contains – Use to find pages containing a link to a particular media filetype, such as mp3 or wma.

Example: *Janice Joplin contains:mp3*

in the Anchor (link) – Use to find pages that have a particular word in the text of a link.

Example: *Texas restaurants inanchor:dallas*

in the Body – Use if for some obscure reason you want to identify pages that have a term in the body of the pages (as opposed to the title, etc.).

Example: *inbody:frog*

ip address – Use to identify sites that are hosted on a particular ip address.

Example: *ip:207.57.95.6*

Bing's documentation also talks about a *prefer:* prefix for adding emphasis to a term for ranking purposes. It does not seem to work.

Bing Results Pages

Associated with its claim of being a "decision engine," Bing integrates some useful "facts" into search results lists, utilizing content from selected "Deep Web" websites, particularly in the areas of travel, health, shopping, and local information. Do a search for hotels in a particular city, and you will find that your results listing may contain suggested "deals" and links to book a room. Do a search on hypertension, and as well as regular results, you will get categorized, enhanced results for statistics, guides, drug information, etc., from "vetted" sites such as MayoClinic.com. Product searches may give summaries, links, or data for top brands, categories, prices, guides, ratings, and reviews.

Elsewhere on results pages you will find other enhancements for "navigating" through a search. Easily missed are Bing's webpage previews. Instead of thumbnails of screens, as other services have provided, Bing gives excerpts from the page. (Place your cursor to the right of the result to see this pop-up). Depending upon the search, results pages may also show some categories related to your topic and a list of related searches, related news headlines, and selected images from Bing's images database or links to videos. Bing also displays a useful, clickable list of searches you have recently done.

As with results pages for other engines, Bing search results are ranked by relevance. Individual webpage results listings include the page title, a brief description or snippet of text, the URL, and a link to a cached version of the page (Figure 4.14). Some records will also show links to more specific topics/pages within that site, and non-English pages may show a "Translate this page" link. If more than one matching page from any site has been found, you will be shown a "Show More Results" link to see any additional pages.

Figure 4.14

Bing search results page

Other Searchable Bing Databases

Images

An image search in Bing produces significantly smaller numbers of results than does a similar search in Google, but the results may on the average have higher relevance, since Bing is apparently a bit more conservative in terms of the words it tends to associate with an image on a webpage. On image search results pages, you can narrow your results by size, layout (square, wide, tall), and color or black and white, and you can narrow to just images for people and even those images just showing faces or those showing head and shoulders.

Video

The Video search found on Bing covers a collection of commercial and non-commercial sources plus video sharing sites. Among other sources, you will find video here from CNN, USAToday, AP, Fox, MSNBC, ABC, CBS, Reuters, Comedy Central, MSN Video, AOL Video, YouTube, and MySpace. On video search results pages, just hold your mouse over the thumbnails for an immediate preview. See Chapter 7 for more on video search.

Shopping

Bing has an extensive easily browsable and searchable shopping site, with access to products from major and minor online stores, price comparisons, and user and product reviews. Bing's Cashback program provides cashback savings from partner sites.

News

Bing's news search covers thousands of news sources worldwide, including news services, newspapers, and blogs. You can also use it to easily set up free news alerts on specific topics for once-a-day, twice-a-day, or weekly delivery.

Maps

Bing's Maps Search provides searches for businesses, people, and locations, with road maps for much of the world and aerial views for the entire world, plus driving directions, and yellow pages-type information for many countries. It also incorporates imagery from what was formerly known as Virtual Earth (MSN's formidable competitor to Google Earth). For a number of cities, you will also find excellent "Birds' Eye" views, taken from planes and providing more detailed photos with more "perspective."

The businesses section of Bing Maps provides extensive yellow pages-type information with features such as 1-Click Directions, which with one click will give you directions to a business from several directions, and for many locations, you can get "traffic sensitive" directions, which utilize current traffic reports.

Travel

Bing's Travel section is what was previously known as FareChase and is a flight and hotel reservations site with booking capabilities and price comparisons, plus FareChase's predictions of when is the best time to purchase a reservation, based on pricing histories.

Other Bing Features and Content

Phone Book and Address Lookup

If you enter the name of a person and address (e.g., *Phineas Bluster Doodyville VA*) in the search box, you can search for phone numbers of individuals (as well as businesses).

Stock Search

Enter a ticker symbol in the search box and get current quotes, links to company news, etc.

Calculator

As with other engines, you can use Bing's main search box as a calculator. For addition, subtraction, multiplication, division, and exponents use, respectively, +, -, *, /, and ^. Parentheses can be used to nest operations, e.g., $(12+2.1-1)^2$. Unlike the calculator functions provided by other search engines, with the Bing calculator you can also solve some equations. For example, enter $8x + 5 = 244$, and it will tell you that the value of x here is 29.875.

Other Bing Instant Answers

As well as getting addresses, solving equations, and getting stock quotes, there are a variety of other facts that Bing will provide directly from the search box. Enter an area code to find its location or enter *area code* and a location to get the area code. Enter *define* and a word to get a definition. Enter *flights to* or *flights from* and a city to get flight deals. Enter a flight number to get its status. Enter a disease, condition, or drug name to get medical information.

Enter a shipper and a tracking number to track a package. Bing provides even more, so don't hesitate to try just about anything in the search box.

ASK.COM (ASK.COM)

Ask.com, formerly known as Ask Jeeves, has an interesting history going back to 1996. In its early days, it was not a search engine but rather a "question and answer" site, utilizing stored collections of answers and algorithms that made an attempt at understanding the question and then finding the probable answer. This approach changed significantly, and when it purchased the Teoma search engine technology in 2001, Ask Jeeves was very obviously moving into the more standard search engine arena. Its transition was complete when, in 2006, it changed its name to Ask.com, retired the butler, and completely redesigned its interface. It provides, in addition to its web search, a good collection of additional databases (images, etc.). As well as the U.S. site, Ask.com also has sites for France, Germany, Italy, Japan, The Netherlands, Spain, and the U.K. Each of those has a similar web search function and contains some, but not all, of the other features discussed here. In 2009, Ask.com decided to become part of the NASCAR scene, with a lot of attention to NASCAR on its pages and even a special NASCAR search engine. (An historical note: For the once-promising search engine, Northern Light, the emergence of a NASCAR fetish within its organization immediately preceded the doom of the search engine.) By mid-2009, the NASCAR period of Ask.com seemed to have run its course.

Ask.com's Home Page

Simplicity and focus on the search box is the theme of Ask.com's home page (Figure 4.15). Links to images, news, videos, and local databases are shown above the search box, with a link there to additional databases and features. Beneath the box is a link to the advanced search page and a link to change the "skin" (background image) of the page. The following items are found on the home page:

- Search box – The terms you enter are ANDed unless you specify otherwise. You can also use an OR, a minus sign for a NOT (though it works inconsistently), and prefixes to qualify a term. As you enter your

Figure 4.15

Ask.com home page

search terms, you may see a list of "search suggestions" appear beneath the search box.

- Links to change the "skin" (page background) of the advanced search page, to AskEraser (to delete your search history from the Ask.com servers), and to Settings (for changing results displays, content filtering, etc.).

Ask.com's Advanced Search

Ask.com's advanced search page (Figure 4.16) provides the following options:

- Menu and search boxes – To perform simple Boolean ("all of the words," "at least one of the words" and "none of the words"), with a box for exact phrases
- Location of words or phrases – To limit retrieval to occurrence of your words in the page title or in the URL
- Domain – To narrow your search to a top-level domain (.uk, .edu, .mil, etc.) or to a specific site (e.g., temple.edu)
- Language – To specify one of six languages (Dutch, English, French, German, Italian, or Spanish)
- Country – To limit retrieval to pages from one of 21 countries
- Page modified – To limit by time frame (last week, last month, etc.)

Figure 4.16

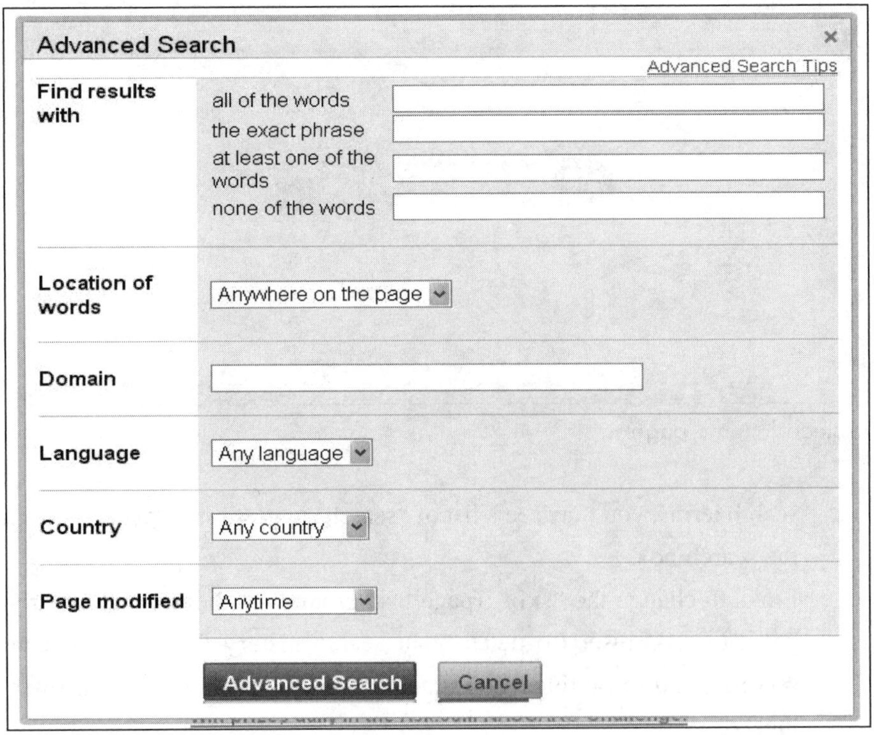

Ask.com advanced search page

Search Features Provided by Ask.com

By the use of the menu on its advanced search page or by the use of prefixes, Ask.com provides a number of ways to refine your search.

Boolean

As with other search engines, all terms you enter in the main search box are automatically ANDed unless you specify otherwise. Ask.com says you can also use an OR, but to make the OR work, you may have to use a very convoluted, non-intuitive syntax. Similarly, you can use a minus sign for NOT, but the feature often does not work. If you want to use those two Boolean operations with Ask.com, use its advanced search page. But just in case you are curious, to get articles on deterioration of concrete or cement, but excluding bridges, you would do the following:

Example: *deterioration -bridges concrete OR deterioration -bridges cement*

Title Searching

For higher precision, you can limit your retrieval to items where your term occurs in the title. Use the Location of Words menu on the advanced search page or use the *intitle:* prefix on the main page.

Example: *symbolism intitle:chrysanthemums*

URL, Site, and Domain Searching

To limit to sites with a particular term somewhere in the URL, you can use either the *inurl:* or *site:* prefix. To limit retrieval to a specific site or to pages that come from a particular top-level domain (.com, .fr, .org, etc.), use the *site:* prefix. The prefix cannot be used by itself; it must be used along with another term or terms.

Examples:
inurl:nato
NATO site:de
nonproliferation site:un.org

Language Searching

On the advanced search page, you can limit to pages that are in Dutch, English, French, German, Italian, Portuguese, or Spanish. Alternatively, in the main page search box, you can use the *lang:* prefix with the two-letter code for those languages (nl, en, fr, de, it, pt, es).

Example: *goethe lang:de*

Terms in Linked Text

The *inlink:* prefix enables you to find pages that have a specific term as linked text on that page.

Example: *inlink:stumbleupon*

Date-Related Prefixes

Ask.com offers four prefixes for narrowing by time frame corresponding to the Page Modified option on the advanced search page (*last:, afterdate:, beforedate:, betweendate:*).

Example: *putin beforedate:last year*

Keep in mind that with Ask.com, like other search engines, date searching for webpages is a very "iffy" proposition.

Calculator

You can perform calculations right from the main search box, as with other major engines. For addition, subtraction, multiplication, division, and exponents, use +, -, *, /, and ^ respectively. You can also nest using parentheses, for example, 15 * (14+43).

Ask.com Results Pages

Though at one point Ask.com's results pages also automatically (depending upon your search) provided a number of items of useful related information (related searches, news, selections from reference tools, etc.), it now provides a much more basic list of real search results and ads. Ask.com is not as rigorous as some other search engines in making a clear distinction between ranked webpages and "Sponsored Results," which it intermixes; in the same list you may find as many ads as regular pages, with only a light-colored background and an inconspicuous "Sponsored Results" label to distinguish the two (Figure 4.17).

Figure 4.17

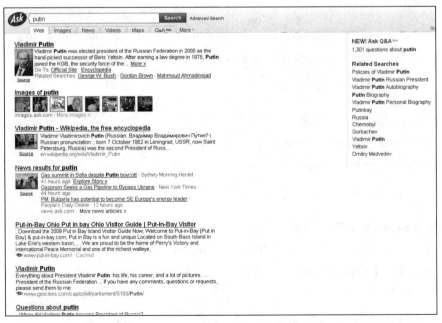

Ask.com search results page

Beside each webpage result, you will find a "binoculars" icon. Hovering your mouse over the icon will cause a small window to pop up showing a preview of the webpage.

Other Searchable Ask.com Databases

Images

Ask.com's image search is designed very similarly to that of Google and Yahoo!, but it is apparently (based on retrieval numbers and the relevance of images retrieved) substantially smaller.

News

The News search on Ask.com provides a browsable news home page and a search of a wide range of major news networks, newspapers, and magazines, as well as a wide variety of smaller news sources and blogs, plus, of course, a place for you to get all of the NASCAR news you hanker for.

Video

Ask.com's Video search gathers video from a number of news sites and video sharing sites across the web, including YouTube, Google Video, Revver, Viddler, Blip, Metacafe, etc.

Maps & Directions

Ask.com's Maps & Directions search offers maps and driving directions for the U.S. and Canada. In addition to draggable and zoomable maps showing streets, political boundaries, and physical features such as lakes and forests, Ask.com also provides aerial views, bird's-eye views, and for some areas, a view with current traffic conditions. For locating businesses, look for a local link, which will enable you to easily find businesses, nearby events, and movies.

Q&A

Ask.com's Q&A is a search of a database of "questions and answers" that Ask.com has found on a number of "question and answer" sites across the web, including Yahoo! Answers, Wikianswers, Internet FAQ Archives, Experts Exchange, and others.

Shopping

Ask.com's Shopping search offers browsing in 13 main categories and a search function (for either the entire catalog or specific product categories).

The Compare Prices link next to an item yields a price comparison chart for the stores selling that product.

Options

On most Ask.com pages, you will find an Options link with which you can set your preferences for a default location (used for maps, etc.), number of results per page, whether clicking a result will open it in a new window, whether you wish to see search suggestions, adult content filtering, a nickname, and your Ask.com password.

AskEraser

AskEraser is an optional setting that, when turned on, automatically erases your Ask.com search history from Ask.com's servers.

Table 4.1   Major Search Engines Features

	Ask.com	Bing	Google	Yahoo!
Boolean	*term term* (Defaults to an AND) *-term* (for NOT) Us advanced search for Boolean	*term term* (Defaults to an AND) *-term* (for NOT) *(term* OR *term)* Advanced search page	*term term* (Defaults to an AND) *-term* (for NOT) OR *term* OR *term* Advanced search page	*term term* (Defaults to an AND) *-term* (for NOT) *term* OR *term* Advanced search page
Stemming			Some automatic stemming	Some automatic stemming
Title field	intitle:term Advanced search page	intitle: *term*	intitle:*term* allintitle:*term1 term2* Advanced search page	intitle:*term* Advanced search page
URL field	site:*term* Advanced search page	site:*term* Advanced search page	inurl:*term* allinurl:*term1 term2* site:*term* Advanced search page	inurl:term site:*term* hostname:*term* url:term Advanced search page
"Links to" a site			link:*term* Advanced search page	link: *term*
File type		filetype:*extension*	filetype:*extension* Advanced search page	("File Format" window menu)
Language	lang:xx Choice of 6 languages on Advanced search page	Choice of 41 languages in Advanced search menu lang:xx	Choice of 46 languages on Advanced search page	Choice of 41 languages on Advanced search page
Media search	Images, Video	Images, Video	Images, Video	Images, Video
Also shown on results pages	Links to cached pages Encyclopedia News Headlines Related searches Save to My Stuff Ask Q&A	Links to cached pages News headlines Related searches	Links to cached pages Similar pages link Translation option Link to definitions, etc. News headlines Related searches	Links to cached pages Shortcuts, etc. Link to cached page Translation option Link to definitions, maps News headlines Related searches

MyStuff

When you are logged in under your Ask.com account, you can use your MyStuff page to save and record your selected searches and results (pages and/or pictures), arrange them in folders, tag them, sort them, annotate them, and email, print, or delete them.

Ask.com Toolbar

The downloadable Ask.com Toolbar has the Ask.com web search box, plus your choice of buttons for any of the Ask.com Search Tools, links to save webpages and images to MyStuff, translations, and quick stock quote lookups.

ADDITIONAL GENERAL WEB SEARCH ENGINES

The web search engines covered in this section are additional engines that the serious searcher should be aware of. For these, most searchers may not want to absorb the level of detail provided for the four engines just covered, but you should be aware of special features these provide or at least of their existence. The "special features" point applies particularly to the first one, Exalead. The others are listed here, to some degree at least, for "historical" purposes.

Exalead (www.exalead.com/search)

When a new web search engine appears, most searchers can probably ignore it unless it provides two things: (1) unique and useful features, and (2) a database of competitive size. Although the size of Exalead's web database is now in the billions, it is still small compared to the "big guys." But for some searches, the uniquely powerful features it provides will more than make up for the size of the database. Exalead still identifies its public search engine as a "demo," but searchers may want to take good advantage of it (see Figure 4.18).

Exalead provides all the basics expected of a search engine including an advanced search page with Boolean and limiting by title, language, file format, domain, date, and country. In the main search box, AND is implied, and you can use OR, a minus sign for NOT, and the *intitle:*, *site:*,

Figure 4.18

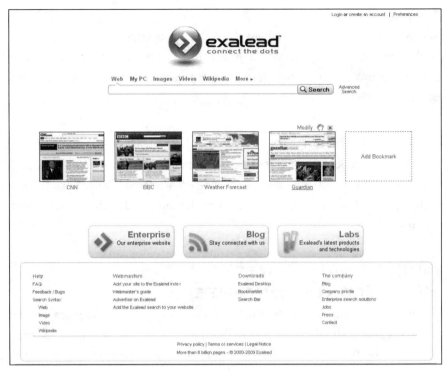

Exalead home page

lang:, and *before:* and *after:* date prefixes. It is, however, in Exalead's special options—truncation, proximity, and more—that its search really excels.

Perhaps the most important of these options is truncation (searching on the stem of a word to get all of the variant endings). From the main search box, add an asterisk to search on a word stem (e.g., *bank**). Enter NEAR between two terms to insist that the terms be within 16 words of each other. On the advanced search page, menus offer the truncation and NEAR options, and also the following types of matches: exact phrase, phonetic spelling ("sounds like"), and approximate spelling.

As well as these search features, Exalead has a good collection of features on its results pages including very effective "categorization" of search results. On the side of results pages are lists of Related Terms, File Type, Site Type (e.g., blog, forum, commercial, non-commercial), Multimedia (audio, video), Languages, and Directory categories (and subcategories). Click on any of the headings there to narrow your search by that criterion. To the left of each search result is a thumbnail image of the page.

At the top of each results page are links that will take your search to Exalead's fairly small images and video databases, to Wikipedia, and to the contents of your computer (if you have installed Exalead's desktop search software). The images database, though small, does offer a "face filter" for identifying portrait-type images. Exalead should definitely be in the toolbox of "power searchers."

Virtually Defunct But Still Out There

There are four web search engines that have been around for a long time but whose current lack of functionality, features, interest, and size means that they do not offer anything of real significance to the power searcher. However, their names do come up occasionally.

HotBot (hotbot.com) is one of the oldest web search engines and was once one of the most powerful, with some pioneering and unique features. After years of neglect and downgrading, there is virtually nothing left of its former glory, and the site is now merely a watered-down interface for Yahoo!, lyGo (beta-mode visual search engine), and Live web databases.

Lycos (lycos.com) was once a major contender on the search engine scene. The searches it provides are now "powered" by other search engines.

Once among the top three or four search engines, AltaVista (altavista.com) and AllTheWeb (alltheweb.com) are now Yahoo! properties. AltaVista's unique and powerful search technology (including truncation and the NEAR connector) has been discontinued, and the databases of both have been replaced with Yahoo!'s database and search technology.

VISUALIZATION SEARCH ENGINES

Visualization engines provide a very different "look"—literally—at search results.

Instead of the traditional linear, textual list of retrieved items, results are shown on a map that displays conceptual connections spatially. Visualization continues to be an area of extensive research, and several sites demonstrate various visualization approaches. The conceptual and visual mapping done by these sites can be especially useful for a quick exploration of the concept possibilities, directions, and terminology for a particular search. Consider this approach for competitive intelligence and other searches where you need to start by understanding relationships rather than just browsing lists of results. Among the leaders in this area are KartOO, TouchGraph, and Quintura. Each uses the content of one or more of the larger search engines' databases.

KartOO (kartoo.com)

KartOO provides multiple ways of viewing search results, all of which are significantly different than search result displays provided by more mainstream search engines. Though KartOO is technically a metasearch engine, since it relies on databases of other engines, its approach to the display of results can provide very useful and interesting perspectives. Though KartOO offers a variety of results display options, the most unique (and interesting) is the default, which provides a semantic map of results, showing linkage patterns and common terms found among the websites identified by the search. To search, enter one or more search terms in KartOO's search box (including, if you wish, OR, NEAR, *, and any of a variety of prefixes such as *intitle:*, *domain:*, etc.). You will see a map with each site represented by a "page" icon, plus a pattern of lines indicating terms that link the sites (commonly occurring "associated" terms that were identified when KartOO analyzed the retrieved records). Hold your cursor over a site icon to see a description of the site. If you click on a term on the map, lines will be displayed connecting that site to the most closely associated pages. The Options link provides a number of additional ways of modifying both the content and the display of results pages. The best way to understand the possibilities of KartOO is simply to simply play around with it.

TouchGraph (touchgraph.com)

TouchGraph offers a dynamic and interactive display of the relationships between entities such as (in the case of the free demo sites it provides) webpages from the databases of Amazon and Google, and images from Facebook. To try TouchGraph, go to the Demo section of its site. For the TouchGraph Google search, enter a term or a URL. For the Amazon search, enter a keyword (title, author, etc.). For Facebook, log into Facebook, and TouchGraph analyzes photos connected to your photos. The results are displayed by a network of lines connecting the various nodes, or websites (Figure 4.19). From each, site lines radiate to sites to which they link. Hold your cursor over a node to highlight the links from that node. When you do so, an Info button will display that you can click to get a pop-up window with more detail about the site. Other URLs can be added to see how relationships to them fit in with your first site. You can choose to label nodes by title, by URL, or as points, while taking advantage of several other controls that modify how results are displayed.

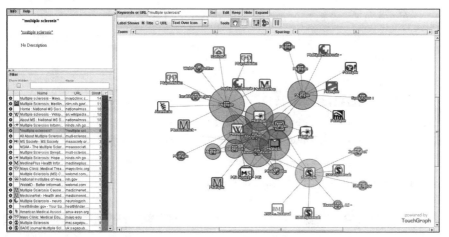

Figure 4.19

TouchGraph results page

Quintura (quintura.com)

Of the visualization engines discussed here, Quintura is the newest. When you search on a term using Quintura, the most obvious feature you see on the results page is a "cloud" of terms—similar to a "tag cloud" but showing the "concepts" that Quintura has identified as dominant among the concepts found in the search results set (which it gets from a Yahoo! search). Terms in the cloud have a size relative to their "importance," and the distance between terms is used to indicate the degree of connection. Details of hits are shown in a "regular" search results list to the right of your screen. If you hold your cursor over one of the terms in the cloud, that concept is automatically added to your search and the new list and cloud are shown. In addition to webpage searches, Quintura also offers an image search (using Yahoo! Images), a video search (with results from blinkx), and a search of Amazon. Quintura also provides a kids' version that utilizes content from Yahoo! for Kids (formerly Yahooligans).

SEARCH ENGINE COMPARISON SEARCHES

There are a number of sites that provide a comparison of results from various search engines. Unlike metasearch sites, which extract and amalgamate the top few results from multiple engines, these comparison sites give more of a side-by-side comparison, with a much truer look at what is actually available in each engine. Though each has a unique approach and may cover a different selection of search engines (and different types, such as web, images, blogs, video, etc.), a feel for what this type of tool can do can be determined from a quick look at Zuula and TurboScout.

Zuula (zuula.com)

Zuula allows you to view the actual results from nine web search engines, displayed in separate tabs, with a single click (Figure 4.20). Zuula also provides a similar comparison for images (10 engines), video (10 engines), news (four engines), blogs (nine engines), and job searches (four engines).

Figure 4.20

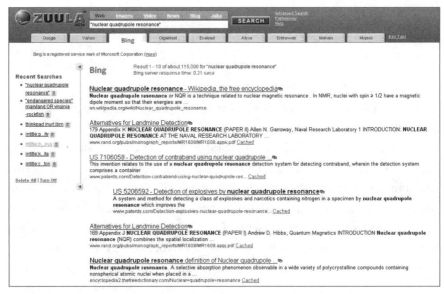

Zuula main page

TurboScout (turboscout.com)

TurboScout allows a quick look at the results from more than 90 engines, arranged under seven categories (Web, Images, Reference, News, Products, Blogs, Audio/Video). Enter your term or terms, click on a category, and then choose an engine.

CHAPTER 5

DISCUSSION GROUPS, FORUMS, NEWSGROUPS, AND THEIR RELATIVES

Groups, newsgroups, discussion groups, lists, message boards, and other online interactive forums are tools that are often under-used resources in the searcher's toolbox. Particularly for competitive intelligence (including researching and tracking products, companies, and industries), for other fields of intelligence (including security, military, and related areas), and for technical troubleshooting and advice, discussion groups and their relatives can be gold mines (and, analogously, the product is sometimes difficult to find and to mine). These resources can be essential when you need to see the subjective side of something—politics, travel, products, people, technology—anything where opinions can be useful.

You may find yourself making use of groups without even realizing it. When you enter a "how-to" or troubleshooting query into a search engine, many of the best answers that come up are likely to come from groups. Indeed, if for example, you run into a computer problem (you get an error message you don't understand and can't remedy, your software isn't behaving as it should, etc.), enter a few words describing the problem, or, in quotation marks, just enter a string of words from the error message. Chances are the most relevant answers returned may actually be on forums.

Groups, mailing lists, and a variety of their hybrids represent one aspect of the interactive side of the internet, allowing users to communicate with people who have like interests, concerns, problems, and issues. Unlike regular email, where you need the addresses of specific persons or organizations in order to communicate with them, these channels allow you to reach people you don't know and take advantage of their knowledge and expertise. This chapter outlines the resources available for finding and mining this information, and it suggests some techniques that can make it easier.

A major barrier to understanding these tools is the terminology. Though *discussion groups* is probably the most descriptive term applied to most of this genre, other terms are also used. *Newsgroups*, which was the first term used, usually have little to do with news, and *mailing lists* are definitely not to be confused with the junk mail you receive in either your email or traditional mailbox. Newsgroups, narrowly defined, usually refers to the Usenet collection of groups that actually originated prior to the internet as we now think of it. *Groups*, more broadly defined, includes newsgroups and a variety of other channels, variously referred to as discussion groups, bulletin boards, message boards, forums, and even (by dot.com marketers, primarily) communities. In this chapter, the terms *groups* and *forums* will be used interchangeably to refer to all of the incarnations just mentioned.

In terms of the type of communication channels they provide, it would not be unrealistic to include blogs in this chapter. However, the blog phenomenon is different enough to be addressed separately and is covered later in this book (see Chapter 10). Groups can be thought of as primarily a communal, participatory, democratic experience, whereas blogs are usually exclusively controlled, top-down, by an individual (with, however, some participatory possibilities). Though they existed prior to the creation of the term Web 2.0, the interactive, collaborative, sharing nature of groups makes the whole concept of groups very Web 2.0-ish.

Many groups provide both an online forum and a "mailing list" service. The biggest distinction between these two services lies in how the information gets to you. On the forum side, messages are posted on computer networks (e.g., the internet) for the world to read. Usually anyone can go to a group and read its content and, usually, anyone can post a message. With a mailing list, content goes, by email, only to individuals who subscribe to the list, and past messages usually are not accessible. Messages that appear in groups are usually more fully archived and, therefore, more retrospectively available than the content of something that is purely a mailing list.

Both groups and mailing lists can be moderated or unmoderated. With unmoderated groups (and lists), your posting appears immediately when you submit it. If the group or mailing list is moderated, your posting must pass the inspection of someone who decides whether to approve the posting, and, if it is approved, then posts it to the list. Among other things, this means that moderated groups and lists are more likely to have postings that really are directly related to the subject.

The messages within each individual group are usually arranged by "threads"—a series of messages on one specific topic, consisting of the original message, replies to that message, replies to those replies, and so on. Users can post messages to either the original message or to any of the replies, or they can start a new thread.

GROUPS OF GROUPS AND INDIVIDUAL GROUPS

Groups can be found on sites that offer a collection of many individual groups and on websites that host one or more groups relevant to the specific area of interest of that site. Collections of groups include the grandparent of all groups, Usenet, commercial portals such as Yahoo!, and sites such as Delphi Forums and Yuku that serve as hosts for discussion groups. Individual groups are found in such places as professional association sites and travel sites such as Lonely Planet. The next few pages will give an overview of the nature of these various collections and individual groups, and outline how you can most easily access them and participate.

Usenet

Before going into how and where to find groups of interest and how to search for specific messages of interest, a few words should be said, for background and historical purposes, about Usenet. Usenet is the original and probably still best-known collection of groups, created in 1979 at the University of North Carolina and Duke University by Jim Ellis, Tom Truscott, Steve Bellovin, and Steve Daniel. Usenet (a "users' network," originally spelled USENET) started as a collection of network-accessible electronic bulletin boards and grew quickly both in terms of use and in its geographic reach. Not only does Usenet predate the web, it predates the internet as most of us know it today. With the popularization of the internet and the web, however, Usenet access is now, for all practical purposes, through the internet (and in most cases through Google), and most users use a web-based interface rather than the older specialized software known as Usenet newsreaders.

Until probably the late 1990s, most Usenet access was through an Internet Service Provider (ISP), and messages were read and posted by means of special software called newsreaders or through such software built into browsers such as Netscape. ISPs received newsfeeds from the computers that hosted Usenet groups and then made that content available to the ISP's customers.

Web access to Usenet newsgroups first became widely available through a site called Deja News, which was created in 1996 and later became "deja.com." It was great—until the people responsible for its design and marketing began to miss the point and decided to make it into a shopping site, with the newsgroup access relegated to a minor position. Deja.com went out of business and can now best be remembered as an early pioneer of the dot.com bust.

To the rescue comes none other than almost-every-serious-searcher's favorite site, Google. In 2001, Google bought Deja's remains, began loading the archive, and quickly added the capability to not just search Usenet postings but to post messages as well. By the end of the year, it had made a 20-year archive of Usenet postings available and easy to access. Details of how to make use of Usenet through Google is coming up a few pages from now.

Other Groups

Although Usenet is the best-known collection of groups, it is not the only one. Collections of groups can be found on commercial sites and portals such as Yahoo!, and on group-hosting sites such as Delphi Forums (www.delphiforums.com) and Yuku (www.yuku.com). Google's own user-created and hosted groups are not only now available but may be overshadowing the Usenet groups on Google. You will also find a lot of specialized groups on association and club sites, such as the Utah Cycling Association, the Institute of Electrical and Electronics Engineers (IEEE), and the Australian Tarantula Association. These web-based groups vary considerably in terms of the appearance of the interface, but they all function in about the same way. For most sites, you can read what group members have posted without belonging to the group and without logging in. To post questions and other messages, you will probably have to join the group, although often your email address and a name (real or otherwise) is about all you need to do so. On sites such as Yahoo! Groups, you must sign up for a password, and on most association sites, you must be a member of the association to participate in the discussions.

Resources for Locating and Using Groups

The following resources (and others) can be used to locate either *groups* of interest or *messages on specific topics*:

- Groups search engines – Search engines devoted to searching large numbers of groups from sites across the web, among them Omgili, BoardReader, and BoardTracker

- Google Groups search – For searching Usenet groups, the newer Google Groups, and also other groups that Google has identified on the web

- Google's web search – For locating some non-Google, non-Usenet groups; search results will also include those things found by searching Google Groups

- Yahoo! Groups – Search covers only groups on the Yahoo! site (there are hundreds of thousands of them)

- Delphi Forums – More than 8,000 active forums on the Delphi Forums site

- Yuku (formerly ezboard) – Another provider of forum services

- Big Boards – A resource guide for locating very large message boards and forums (www.big-boards.com)

Also, don't hesitate to simply use a search engine search to find a group. Searching on your topic and the term *forum* usually works well, as in the first example below, but if you want a more inclusive search, follow the second example:

> Examples:
> *physics forum*
> *"multiple sclerosis" (forum OR "discussion group" OR "message board")*

Sites of Associations Related to Your Topic

Look on the site of an association related to your search topic for an indication of a *forum*, *discussion*, or similar term suggesting the presence of a group. This tip also applies to locating mailing lists.

GROUPS SEARCH ENGINES

There are search engines designed specifically to search the contents of groups from across the web, not just, as is the case with Google Groups and Yahoo! Groups, content stored on their own site. You can use these search engines either to locate individual messages that mention a topic or to locate forums that cover a broader area of interest you wish to follow.

Omgili (www.omgili.com)

Omgili searches more than 100,000 forums, newsgroups, and mailing lists. It differs from some of its competitors by providing significantly more "searchability," allowing the user to much more precisely refine a search.

To get a good feel for Omgili's searchability, take a look at the advanced search page, where you will find options for narrowing your search by phrases, by language, and by occurrence in the title, topic, or replies, and for searching within a specific forum. On the advanced search page, you can also specify the sort order (relevance or date) and date range, and limit to those messages with a minimum number of replies, unique users, or "engaged" users (those who have a reply containing at least 100 characters). For most of the options, there is a corresponding prefix (*intitle:*, *intopic:*, *inreply:*, *inforum:*, etc.) that you can use directly in the search box on the main page. As for language, you can search in any language you wish by using search terms in that language as your search query.

As with general web search engines, the search terms you enter in Omgili's main search box are automatically ANDed, you can use quotation marks for phrases and a minus to exclude terms, and you can use wildcards ("?" for a single character within or at the end of a search term, and "*" for multiple characters). Also, you can boost the relevance weighting of a term by adding a caret and a number (for example, *"medvedev^3"* will boost that term's relevance ranking by a factor of three); stemming is automatic but you can (theoretically) turn it off from the advanced search page.

On Omgili results pages, take advantage of the Preview and "More from [this forum]" options and the sort option. Also look at the "chatter" graph that shows the frequency of occurrence of your search terms over the last month. (Omgili provides a free widget with which you can place such a chatter graph on your own website.)

BoardTracker (www.boardtracker.com)

BoardTracker tracks 37,000 forums and contains more than 1.7 billion posts. It provides a number of search options, plus other features such as automatic alerts. In its main box, AND is implied between your search terms. You can search on the stem of a word by using an asterisk at the end of the term (e.g., *disarm**) and use quotation marks for phrase searching.

On the advanced search page, you can use simplified Boolean, narrow retrieval to words in the title, to a specific domain, by language, by author, and by date. You can also limit retrieval to original posts only (i.e., excluding replies to a post). You can apply the SafeSearch filter and have your results shown either by relevancy or by date. Of considerable usefulness for some searches is the ability to narrow by one of 19 subject categories. The categories are also found under the Browse tab, where you can browse easily through categories and subcategories to locate forums of interest. If you sign up (it's free), you can set up alerts that automatically notify you when a posting has been made that mentions your search terms.

BoardReader(www.boardreader.com)

With BoardReader, you can search more than 100,000 unique message board domains for words within individual posts (messages), in the topic (title) of the post, or within the name of the forum. You can also search for images that have appeared in messages, and there are options on the main page allowing you to search specifically for messages on IMDb (the Internet Movie Database) message boards, to search within groups hosted on the Yuku website (Yuku is a site that hosts groups, which are referred to by Yuku as "communities"), and to do a video search (provided by blinkx). Another search category, Microblogs, searches Twitter and Identi.ca, and BoardReader plans for its search to move considerably further into the social networking realm.

On BoardReader's advanced search page, you can search using simplified Boolean, and by language, by date, or by domain, and sort results by time, by relevance, or by a combination of time and relevance. An "advanced links search" page allows you to search for messages that have linked to a specific URL or part of a URL ("path"). Like Omgili, BoardReader shows, on results pages, a graph indicating the recent frequency of occurrence of terms.

Using Google to Find Groups and Messages

When Google first got into the realm of groups, the main and only focus was on the Usenet collection, with its archives going back to 1981. In 2004, Google launched its own user-created groups, mimicking to a significant degree the types of groups offered by Yahoo!. The focus has now moved away from Usenet to Google's own groups. More recently, Google has added threads and messages from many other sites on the web that have groups. Overall, Google lists more than 3 million groups. The following is a quick overview and some highlights.

Browsing Google Groups

From the main Google Groups page (click on the "more" link on Google's main page to get to the Groups link or go directly to groups.google.com), you can click the Browse Group Categories link to browse through the 12 main top-level hierarchies or browse by Region, Language, messages per month, number of members, or days since last post. A Browse All of Usenet link takes you to an alphabetic listing of Usenet-only groups. That list is far from "all" and contains just a portion of actual Usenet subcategories.

As you browse throughout the levels, you will see links to additional lower levels in the hierarchy or related categories and, beneath that, specific groups at that level. Clicking on the group name will take you to the messages threads for that group.

You will in some places see references to specific Usenet groups (which are arranged in a hierarchy that at first glance appears a bit arcane). The hierarchy consists of 10 main top-level categories—alt (alternative), biz (businesses), comp (computers), humanities, misc, news, rec (recreation), sci (science), soc (social sciences), and talk (politics, etc.)—and thousands of other next-level hierarchies, based mainly on subject, geography, and language.

Examples:
sci.bio.phytopathology
rec.crafts.textiles.needlework

Searching for Groups and Messages

When you use the search box on the main Google Groups page, Google will retrieve all groups that have your term(s) in the group name or description, plus any threads containing that term. Those groups with your term in the group name will be shown at the top of the results. On results pages, beneath the search box, you are given an option to search all of the groups or just Google groups. The advanced groups search page (Figure 5.1) allows you to specify the following attributes:

- Simple Boolean expressions:
  - Use the "all these words" box to specify a Boolean AND
  - Use the "one or more of these words" box to specify an OR
  - Use the "any of these unwanted words" box to eliminate records that contain a particular word (NOT)
- Number of results per page
- Messages from a specific newsgroup only
- Subject, author, language, domain, date or date range, message ID
- Safe Search Filter

Search results are ranked by relevance, but you can click the Sort by Date link on the results page to view the newest first.

Figure 5.1

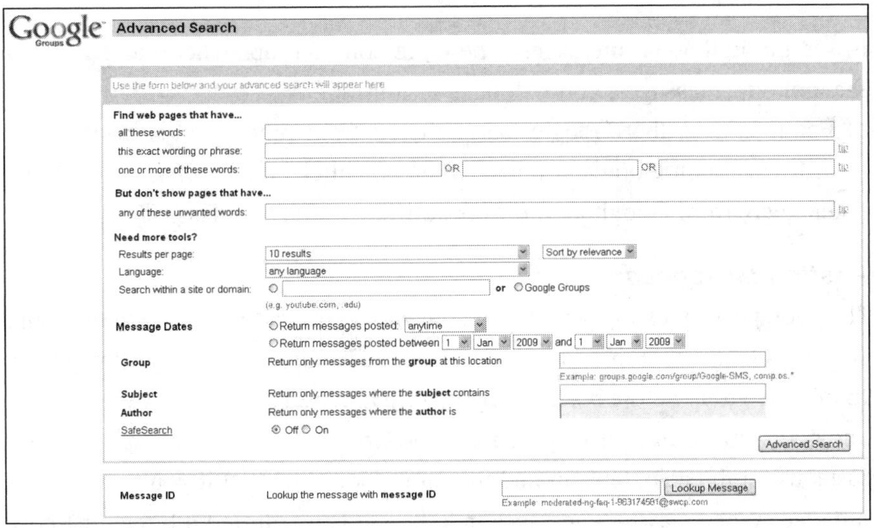

Google Groups advanced search page

Viewing Messages

Either browsing or searching will lead you to a list of threads, showing for each the thread title (linked to the entire thread), an excerpt of text around retrieving words, a link to the group in which it was found, a date, and the number of messages and authors in the thread (Figure 5.2). Click on the subject of the thread

Figure 5.2

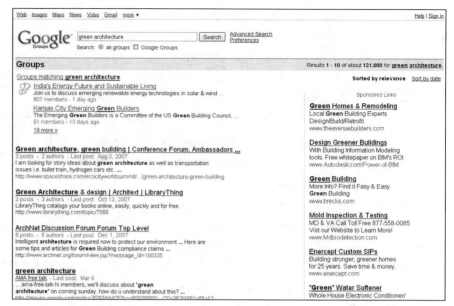

Google Groups search results page

to see the individual messages. There are some groups where, to even read the archived messages, you will have to join.

For messages that Google has gathered from other groups on the web (non-Usenet, non-Google Groups), when you click on the thread, you will be taken away from Google to the website from which the message came.

Posting Messages

How you post a message will depend on where you start and the kind of group. If it is a Google Group or a group from elsewhere on the web, you may have to join the group before posting. If you have browsed the directory or searched and gotten to the main listing for a Google Group or a Usenet group itself (not just a list of threads), look around for a link for a New Post if you want to start a thread. When viewing messages in a thread, you will find a Reply or Reply to Author link. To either start a new message (thread) or reply to a message, you will be required to be logged in to Google with your Google password.

Starting a Google Group

Participating in discussions on Usenet is easily done, but starting a new group on a topic of your own choice is a long, complicated, and usually not even feasible process. On the other hand, starting a group of your own on Yahoo!

and elsewhere can be quick and easy. It was therefore natural for Google to begin offering an easy-to-use groups feature to go along with the Usenet groups.

To create your own group in Google, first sign in with your Google user name and password. Then click on the Create a Group link on the main Google Groups page. Follow the next several steps, which include naming your group, providing a description, and selecting the level of public access. Options for access levels include Public, where anyone can read the archives and join the group; Announcement-only, where anyone can read and join but messages can only be posted by moderators; or Restricted, where only those you invite can participate and the archives are not searchable by others.

Though it is easy to set up a Google group, at the same time (using the group owner's "Management Tasks" options), you have a very broad range of options: how widely the contents are available, whether the group is moderated, how messages are distributed, categories under which the group is listed, and who can join, post messages, view the membership list, create pages, upload files, or invite members. For members, subscription options for getting messages include the following: no email (access only available on the web); email (email messages are automatically sent to members for each new posting); abridged email (daily email summaries sent); or digest email (all messages sent in a single email daily). This can all be done in as few as a couple minutes and is quite simple. The result is a group with varying levels of public access, archives, and searchability, and depending upon the subscription type you choose, something that can be more of a "mailing list" than a group.

Using Web Search to Identify Non-Usenet, Non-Google Groups

A Google Groups search will lead you to many groups found on the web that are neither Usenet nor Google Groups and would not be uncovered by a Google Groups search. It doesn't work perfectly, but you can locate some of these groups messages in Google by using this trick: As part of your search, use the phrase "*next thread*." Because that phrase is present in many messages from other groups, it will locate messages from a variety of sources that have been indexed by Google because of the existence of a group on a website. Also try your topic along with the word "*forum*."

Using Yahoo! to Find Groups and Messages

Along with the groups search engines already mentioned and a Google Groups or Google web search, another place to find groups is Yahoo! (groups.yahoo.com, or look for the Groups link on Yahoo!'s home page). If you want to create a group of your own, for free and with powerful options, perhaps the first place to look is Yahoo! Groups. Yahoo! Groups is actually a hybrid of groups and mailing lists, because for each group you can receive messages either at the Yahoo! website or by email. Yahoo! allows you to search or browse through the groups, post messages, and create groups of your own. There are hundreds of thousands of Yahoo! groups, some with thousands of members and many with only a single member. (Join one of the latter and brighten someone's day.) There are a dozen or so "duct tape" groups alone, including one for people who enjoy being taped up with duct tape.

Searching or Browsing for Yahoo! Groups

You can find Yahoo! groups of interest to you either by browsing through the 17 categories on the main Groups page or by using the search box there. Be aware that a search there only searches group names and their descriptions, not individual messages. Yahoo! does automatically truncate, though, so a search for *environment* will also retrieve groups that have *environmental* in their title or description. Terms you enter in the search box are automatically ANDed. You can also use "-" (minus sign) to exclude a word.

Whether you use the search box or browse the categories to find groups on Yahoo!, the listing of groups that results will contain the name of each group, the description, the number of members, whether the archive is public or not, and when it was created. If it is public, you can browse through the messages without joining the group. Clicking on the name of the group will show you more detail about the group, including the number of recent messages and so forth, plus a calendar showing numbers of messages posted each month (Figure 5.3). The number of members and volume of postings are usually important indicators of the potential usefulness of the group.

Joining a Yahoo! Group

After identifying a group of interest, if it accepts new members, click on Join This Group. If you are not signed in to Yahoo! you will be asked for your Yahoo! password, and if you do not have a Yahoo! password, you can

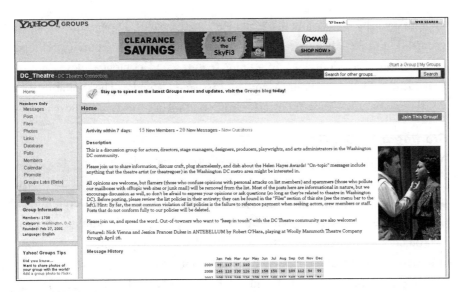

Figure 5.3

Yahoo! Groups

get one at this point. After joining a group, Yahoo! Groups will send you an email message containing a link for you to click that confirms that the email address you used is really your own. Once you have confirmed your address and selected a delivery method, you can go to the home page for the group and read and post messages. Delivery methods for messages include:

- Individual emails – To receive individual email messages
- Daily digest – To receive up to 25 of the posts for the day in one message
- Special notices – To receive update emails from the group's moderator
- Web only – The true groups approach, where you go get the messages, rather than receiving them by email

Once you have joined one or more groups, when you are signed on and go to the Yahoo! Groups main page, you will be presented with a page providing links to all of the groups to which you belong. The Manage link there takes you to a page where you can edit your memberships, with options to change delivery methods, your profile, and your email address for the group, and also to leave the group.

On both the pages that list messages and on the message pages themselves, you have a variety of options, such as viewing the message in brief (simple) form or expanded form, viewing the sender's profile, and viewing the messages by date (using the "calendar" on the page). Though most Yahoo! groups don't take advantage of all of the possibilities, each group is provided with options for adding the following features and content: Files, Photos, Polls, Links, Database, Polls, Members List, and Calendar. The availability of these features takes Yahoo! Groups far beyond most of its competitors.

Starting a Yahoo! Group

Yahoo! is definitely one of the easiest—perhaps actually *the* easiest—place on the web to set up a group. A group of your own can be a great tool for a course you are teaching, networking and support groups, family, community organizations, and so forth, and you can get one set up in 10 minutes or less.

You choose the category (although Yahoo!'s staff may change the category if they see it and feel the category is inappropriate), name the group, decide if it is to be public, moderated, and so on. Basically, all you have to do is fill in the blanks.

With Yahoo!'s large number of users and members, large number of groups, ease of use, range of options, and accessibility to both those who want to use and those who want to sponsor groups, Yahoo! Groups is a potent resource for those who wish to make use of the internet as a communications channel.

Other Sources of Groups

There are numerous other places where you will find groups, some large and some small, but most have considerably less reach and content than those available through Yahoo! or Google. Nevertheless, the group that may precisely meet your needs may be in one of the smaller collections. Two additional sources, not as large as Yahoo! but having both a large number of groups and members, are Delphi Forums and Yuku (formerly known as ezboard).

Delphi Forums

www.delphiforums.com

According to Delphi Forums itself, this site has more than 4 million registered users, 8,000 active forums, 100,000 messages a day, and more than 200 million total messages. As with Yahoo! Groups, with Delphi you can read most messages without registering, but to post messages, you must register. Registration is easy and free.

Delphi's lists are browsable using 22 categories (look for a "Browse Communities by Category" or similar link). A search box on the home page enables you to search for forums. Terms entered in that box will search both titles of groups and the content of the forum's home page. When browsing through categories, you are also given a search option to search just within that category. On the pages for individual forums, look for the advanced search link, which will give you the opportunity to search the messages themselves and by author, date, etc. "Basic" members can search three months back. Premium members can search the entire date range.

You can create a free forum on Delphi, but for fuller capabilities (chat room, blogs, polls, message and forum ratings, etc.), you would need the premium service, which is very inexpensive. If it is really important that you find as many groups out there on your topic as possible, don't ignore a search on Delphi Forums.

Yuku

www.yuku.com

Yuku, the forums site formerly known as ezboard, provides a place for people to create forums, but it also provides "profiles" (social networking), photo sharing, and blogs. A search box on the home page yields results from the Yuku forums, and you can narrow your search by category.

Big Boards

www.big-boards.com

Big Boards is a resource guide covering more than 2,300 of the largest message boards and forums (measured by the numbers of members and the numbers of posts). You can locate discussions of interest either by using the Big Boards search box or by browsing through the 12 main directory categories (and more than 130 subcategories).

MAILING LISTS

Most of what can be said about the usefulness and nature of groups also applies to mailing lists. As mentioned earlier, the biggest differences with mailing lists are: (1) the message arrives in your email rather than you having to request to see messages, with every message sent to the list coming to you; (2) you have to subscribe, often providing identifying information (and may need to be a member of the sponsoring organization); (3) the content of mailing lists is less likely to be archived and searchable than for groups; and (4) although the email delivery mode makes it easier to access and ensures that you don't miss anything important, mailing lists postings have been known to fill up mailboxes and be a nuisance to deal with. The comparison is analogous to a company bulletin board compared to the inbox on your desk: Some information is more appropriately accessed by your going to the bulletin board periodically, whereas for some information, you would prefer to get a copy on your own desk. If, on a particular topic, you want to make sure you don't miss anything, a mailing list may better serve you.

One change that has occurred in the last few years is that the concept of mailing lists has, for many users, been obscured somewhat by the "groups" that were just discussed. Many people read, join, and participate in groups and, as part of that process, somewhere along the line indicate that they would like to receive messages by email (instead of, or in addition to, seeing messages by going to the group's website).

In other cases, users can join many mailing lists from many other types of websites just by clicking a link there that says you would like to be put on that website's mailing list. This has made joining a mailing list a much easier process than it used to be. Whether a specific mailing list is just one function of a group, is provided by a website, or exists by itself in "pure mailing list" form (i.e., just email delivery) probably doesn't and shouldn't make much difference, as long as you get what you need. What is said in the following paragraphs about mailing lists will in some cases be more descriptive of mailing lists that exist mostly on their own, not as a part of a "group" function.

The receipt and distribution of messages on the older "purer" form of mailing lists (those that are not just one function of an online "group" or ones that are joined by just clicking a link on a website) are controlled automatically by "listserver" software. Lists are often referred to, inappropriately, as "listservs." LISTSERV is a registered trademark for listserver software produced by the L-Soft company, and the term (legally) should not be applied generically. The other most frequently encountered mailing list managers are Majordomo and Listproc.

For any kind of mailing list, you need to subscribe to participate. (How to find lists will be discussed shortly.) Some sites (for example, lots of association sites and commercial sites) provide a nice web interface where you just have to fill in the blanks. Other sites provide instructions for sending an email message to the mailing list administrative address and tell you what command you need to put in the header or message in order to join. For example, you might be instructed to send a message to majordomo@alektoro phobia.org with the message *subscribe fearofchickens* in the body of the message. The instructions will vary primarily depending upon the listserver software being used. You will usually receive a reply confirming your membership to the list and referencing an information file explaining how to use the list, ground rules, and so on.

The following are other important points about using mailing lists that are managed by listserver software:

- The email address to which you send administrative messages is different from the one you use for posting messages. It is a great annoyance to list members to see administrative messages in their mailboxes.
- Many lists offer delivery of a "digest" form in which a number of messages are bundled on a regular basis (e.g., daily or weekly). This is especially useful for lists that have a lot of traffic, and digests can avoid clogging up your email inbox. They may also have an option where you can suspend delivery while you are on vacation.
- Many (probably most) lists will provide an FAQ (Frequently Asked Questions) file or webpage, which is usually worth scanning.
- Some lists provide archives, many of which are searchable.
- Before you sign up, note (from descriptions you find of the list) the level of traffic. If you subscribe to several high-volume mailing lists, you will end up not being able to read them because of the hundreds of messages you receive. For high-volume lists, consider taking advantage of digest versions and "on vacation" options.

Tools and Techniques for Locating Mailing Lists

For many people, their first experience in using mailing lists is through organizations to which they belong. Numerous other lists of interest may be out there and, fortunately, there are some online sites that make them easy to find. Among these are Topica and L-Soft CataList. Yahoo! Groups and

Google Groups could also be included among these "finding tools" since, as pointed out earlier, their groups also have an email option.

Topica

lists.topica.com

Topica's thrust is providing mailing list services to companies, associations, and individuals. Many readers who use mailing lists may have noticed that instead of associations managing their own lists, many have taken advantage of this service. Topica (formerly liszt.com) hosts more than 100,000 email newsletters. In addition to association lists and lists created by individuals, many of Topica's lists are commercial, but keep in mind that these are opt-in lists—you only join if you want to. They can be valuable for competitive intelligence purposes, as well as for keeping up-to-date on products and special deals from your favorite suppliers.

You can search by list topic without signing up, but signing up will enable you to have a page that shows all the Topica lists to which you belong and allows you to manage them.

Lists of interest can be identified either by using the search box or browsing through the Topica categories. To browse, click on one of the categories at the bottom of Topica's home page, or better, click the More option there. The resulting page will give you a better idea of coverage of the categories.

You can search using the search box on the main page or on the categories pages. Once you are two levels down in the categories or on search results pages, the search box provides an option of searching either Lists (names and descriptions) or the content of messages themselves. Topica allows you to use AND, OR, and NOT (capitalization is not necessary). If you do not use any operator between words, Topica defaults to an OR. You can also use quotation marks to search for phrases. You may want use these techniques to get to a smaller, more relevant set of results because Topica searches return a maximum of 200 matches.

The list descriptions given usually make it easy to determine if this is a list for you (Figure 5.4). The description pages also make it easy to read and subscribe to (join) the list. On those and other pages you will find how to (very easily) start a list of your own. (First ask yourself, "Does the world really need my list?")

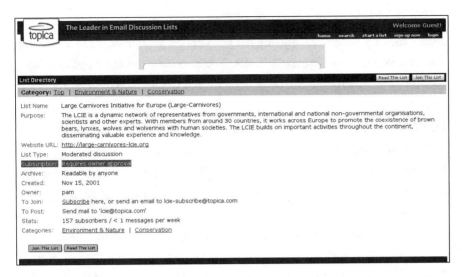

Figure 5.4

Topica list description

L-Soft CataList, the Official Catalog of LISTSERV Lists
www.lsoft.com/lists/listref.html

As the name says, L-Soft CataList is the official catalog for the 53,000 public lists that use LISTSERV software. In addition to searching list names and descriptions, you can view lists by host country or view only those with 10,000 subscribers or more, or those with 1,000 subscribers or more.

INSTANT MESSAGING

Instant messaging, pioneered by AOL Instant Messenger with variations by Yahoo! and others, is another incarnation of online interaction for people and is a hybrid of groups and email. Although it was first populated mainly by teenagers—an extension of the historic evolution of hanging out on the street corner or occupying the family phone—instant messaging spread beyond that. Though instant messaging is still going strong, its social role has been replaced at least somewhat by other technologies, particularly text messaging on cell phones, social networking sites such as MySpace and Facebook, and microblogging sites such as Twitter (see Chapter 10).

If you haven't used or seen it (unlikely at this point), the way instant messaging works is that participants create a buddy list of people they want to interact with online on an immediate basis. You send a message to someone on your list, and it will pop up on his or her screen. People who use the same instant messaging service who are not yet a buddy but who want to talk to you can send you a message asking to talk. You also have the option of creating a chat room in which multiple people are invited to join the conversation.

NETIQUETTE POINTS RELATING TO GROUPS AND MAILING LISTS

Readers of this book most likely already have a good sense of Netiquette (internet etiquette), but some may profit by these selected points relating to groups and mailing lists:

1. "Lurk before you leap." Lurking or hanging around just observing a discussion without participating is definitely a good idea. It may involve just reading a few messages or a few threads, and you may find yourself ready to leap in and join the conversation in a matter of minutes. Read enough messages (and preferably the FAQ or similar documentation) to be sure that the conversation is at the level appropriate to your needs and knowledge. If a group is very technical, the members get annoyed at beginners asking extremely simple questions. If there is a searchable archive, check it out. Don't get caught trying to start a discussion about a topic that has already been beaten to death.

2. Don't use newsgroups or email lists for advertising. Depending on the group or list, there might be times when it would be acceptable to respond to a posting that may have requested a service you provide, but be careful. You can easily irritate many people. In such a case, you can play it safe by responding directly to the poster by email, rather than responding to the group or list as a whole.

3. Don't get sucked into a flame war (an angry or unnecessarily strongly worded series of messages, aka flaming). Remember the sad truth that there are people out there who have nothing better to do than waste their time being nitpicky, rude, and generally obnoxious. The advent of groups and lists has become a wonderful channel for their frustrations and repressed feelings.

4. Only forward messages if allowed. Some associations, particularly, have rules regarding privacy of messages, often relating to such things

as client privilege and competitive intelligence. Follow those rules very carefully. This mistake can cause you to be banned from a group—and worse.

5. Use crossposting (posting the same message to multiple groups or lists) advisedly. It clutters up people's mail and time.

CHAPTER 6

AN INTERNET REFERENCE SHELF

All serious searchers have a collection of tools they use for quick answers—the web equivalent of a personal reference shelf. The challenge is to make sure that you have the right sites on your shelf. This chapter provides a selective collection of sites that should be on most researchers' shelves. Different researchers have different quick-reference needs requiring different tools. For many of us, we may have found out about most sites through a friend or by simply stumbling across them but may not have systematically assembled a complete collection. Here we highlight reference tools that provide quick answers to some of the most frequently asked questions, from the mundane to the esoteric.

This chapter goes hand-in-hand with Chapter 2. For subject areas of interest to you, many of the resource guides of the types covered in Chapter 2 should be in your reference collection, in the same way that the reference section of a library usually contains a good collection of resource guides. In addition to quick-answer sites, a number of resource guides for reference tools in particular areas, such as statistics, government information, and companies, are also included here.

Going from general to specific, we look first at some prime general tools, such as encyclopedias, and then move in the direction of tools that can provide specific bits of information. For many of the categories, as well as lists of specific sites, suggestions will be provided about using the resources effectively.

Remember that all of the links presented here, as well as links for all sites covered throughout this book, are available at www.extremesearcher.com.

THINKING OF THE INTERNET AS A REFERENCE COLLECTION

Especially with a greater and greater proportion of the population having broadband connections, going to the internet rather than to print resources for frequently sought information has become more and more common. With practice, web searching is clearly quicker and easier (and in some cases, such as telephone directory assistance, much cheaper). The biggest tricks are, first, simply understanding the range of quick-reference tools that are out there, and second, getting in the habit of using them—remembering to use them and bookmarking them. Another trick is to not fall into the trap of always going to the internet first. (I have a dictionary right behind me that I often grab rather than reaching for the keyboard.)

The tools listed in this chapter provide a start in making sure the reader has a sense of the breadth and variety of quick-answer sites. The next step in understanding the range of these tools is to spend some time browsing one of the several reference resource guides listed at the end of this chapter. Plan to spend at least 20 minutes poking around those sites. Almost anyone can find something new and interesting in them.

CRITERIA USED FOR SELECTING THE TOOLS COVERED

Selection of the tools covered here was based on several factors. The first factor is my own experience as a long-time internet user and former reference librarian as well as my experience observing and talking with thousands (literally) of internet users from a variety of organizations and countries. The second factor is the measure of a site's utility for a wide range of users. Some sites were chosen because they provide good examples of the range of these tools, and others were chosen because they provide examples of particular features to look for when examining and using reference sites. In several instances, multiple sites serve basically the same function (such as the travel reservation sites). In these cases, more than one site is included in order to point out the differences and the utility of using more than one, rather than choosing a favorite and always going there.

TRADITIONAL TOOLS ONLINE

A number of online tools are electronic versions of common print tools, including encyclopedias, dictionaries, almanacs, and the like. These are excellent sources for quick answers and for background relating to more specific research. In these (and many other) tools, a number of factors contribute to their usefulness. These factors are important to know in some circumstances, irrelevant in other circumstances, and often are the same ones to be considered when using print reference tools:

- Does the tool contain everything that the print version contains? Encyclopedia.com contains everything the print equivalent does (and more), whereas the free online version of *Encyclopedia Britannica* contains only a small portion of the printed content.
- Does it contain things the print version does not? Many online tools provide collections of links and often news headlines that the hard-copy version does not provide.
- How current is it? The version of Bartlett's *Familiar Quotations* available as part of Bartleby.com is the 1919 edition.
- Is the entire site free? Or is there a fee required to access part of the content? For many of the tools that require a subscription, the fee is not too high, and you may find the expenditure worthwhile.

The annotations for the sites discussed here, which are purposely brief and not intended to be reviews of the sites, include the major points that researchers should consider when determining whether to use the tool ("... too great brevity of discourse tends to obscurity; too much truth is paralyzing," according to Blaise Pascal in a quote located by using Bartleby.com).

ENCYCLOPEDIAS

Encyclopedia.com
www.encyclopedia.com

Encyclopedia.com not only includes 51,000 articles from the sixth edition of the *Columbia Encyclopedia* but also content from 48 other encyclopedias, 73 dictionaries and thesauruses, and other reference sources. Articles from the *Columbia Encyclopedia* and some of the other reference tools are free, but for many of the sources, particularly journal and magazine and news articles, you will only get a description and an excerpt. To see the full article, you will need a paid subscription. Articles can be located by browsing through categories or alphabetically, or by searching. On the search results page, Encyclopedia.com provides a very nice option for viewing multiple sources side-by-side (Figure 6.1). For students and researchers,

Figure 6.1

Results from Encyclopedia.com

Encyclopedia.com automatically shows a citation at the end of each article formatted in MLA, Chicago, and APA styles.

Encyclopedia Britannica Online
britannica.com

As the online version of the renowned *Encyclopedia Britannica*, this site provides *very* brief articles for free, but the vast majority of the content requires a subscription. Considering the quality of this encyclopedia, you may find that buying a subscription (with access to more than 120,000 articles) is well worth the price. You can either browse or search, and results include the encyclopedia articles and carefully selected websites. Take advantage of the free videos and images.

Wikipedia

wikipedia.org

Wikipedia, which is an internet-only encyclopedia, is by far the largest encyclopedia in existence. It is also an example of a *wiki* site, a collaborative project by internet users that allows easy input and online editing by any user. Because of this, intense debates have ensued about Wikipedia's quality, reliability, and accuracy. But remember that no other encyclopedia has ever had as many editorial eyes examining the content, and in contrast to print encyclopedias, Wikipedia provides an extremely high level of currentness.

Wikipedia contains over 3.7 million articles in its English version and also has versions in more than 80-plus other languages with more than 10,000 articles each (plus smaller versions for many other languages). It is both browsable and searchable.

HowStuffWorks

www.howstuffworks.com

HowStuffWorks is an example of a specialized but broad-reaching encyclopedia with articles on, indeed, how stuff works. Content is organized into categories for adventure, animals, autos, communication, computers, electronics, entertainment, food, geography, health, history, home & garden, money, people, and science, each with numerous subcategories. Find what you are looking for by browsing the categories or by using the search box, and explore subjects ranging from how solar cells work to how brainwashing works to how pop-up turkey timers work.

DICTIONARIES

yourDictionary.com

www.yourdictionary.com

yourDictionary.com is a resource guide that provides links to more than 2,500 dictionaries and grammars for more than 300 languages, as well as a variety of other language-related resources. The site features *Webster's New World Dictionary*, but perhaps more important are the links to multilingual dictionaries and specialized subject dictionaries, including technical and scientific dictionaries. The quality and extensiveness of the dictionaries varies, but for most languages, you will have a choice among a number of dictionaries. When you consider that relatively few libraries in the world have as many language dictionaries on their shelves as this site brings to your fingertips, you can better understand the potential of the web as a reference resource.

Dictionaries—Selected Examples

In addition to taking advantage of yourDictionary.com, you may find it worthwhile to bookmark one dictionary for each of the languages you are most likely to use. Following are some recommendations.

Merriam-Webster Online

www.merriam-webster.com

This is a full-featured English dictionary with pronunciation (with audio), parts of speech, etymology, inflected forms, and synonyms (Figure 6.2). It also provides a Spanish/English dictionary, medical dictionary, thesaurus, and visual dictionary. Give the word games a try as well. An unabridged version with an atlas and other tools is available for a subscription fee.

Diccionarios.com

www.diccionarios.com

This general Spanish dictionary includes translations between Spanish and eight languages: Catalan, Basque, English, French, Galician, German, Italian, and Portuguese. It contains 95,000 entries and provides audio for pronunciations. Without a subscription, you are limited to 25 lookups.

Figure 6.2

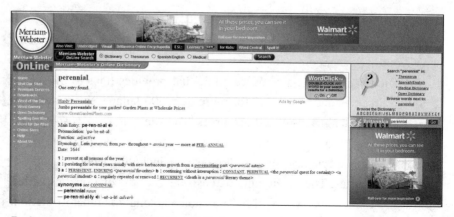

Definition from Merriam-Webster Online

LEO (Link Everything Online)

dict.leo.org

LEO contains more than 580,000 entries and provides a quick English/German and German/English lookup. You will also find audio pronunciations and a display of usage and idiomatic expression examples. Look under the information ("i") button for complete dictionary definitions, conjugations, and declensions.

COMBINED REFERENCE TOOLS AND ALMANACS

Answers.com

answers.com

Go to Answers.com to get multiple resources very quickly and simply on one page: dictionary definitions, encyclopedia articles, maps, local time, a currency converter, statistics, etc. These come from more than 250 reference tools, including multiple general encyclopedias, specialized encyclopedias, dictionaries, a thesaurus, glossaries, travel guides, a company directory, a recipe collection, and a collection of Answers.com proprietary information. The downloadable 1-Click Answers program (for Windows operating systems) lets you do an ALT-Click on any word on your screen and go directly to the Answers.com page for that word.

InfoPlease

www.infoplease.com

No brief description can substitute for spending time exploring this site, which is much more than just an almanac. Explore each of the main sections: World & News, United States, History & Government, Biography, Sports, Arts & Entertainment, Business, Calendar & Holidays, Health & Science, and Homework Center. The site contains the Information Please almanacs, an encyclopedia (*Columbia Encyclopedia*, sixth edition), InfoPlease Dictionary (125,000 entries), InfoPlease Atlas, biographies, and more. Lots of little gems can be found, such as timelines, statistics, slideshows, country profiles, and so on. For non-U.S. users, the World & News section will move you away from the U.S. orientation of the home page. One of the many interesting features is the Cite link, which shows you how to cite the item being viewed. When using the main search box, the search is performed automatically on all of the almanacs, the encyclopedia, biographies, and the dictionary. Terms you enter are ORed, but items with all of your terms (AND) will be listed first. Quotation marks can be used to search phrases. By using the pull-down window near the search box, you can limit your search to specific almanacs, biographies, the dictionary, or the encyclopedia.

ADDRESSES AND PHONE NUMBERS

There are many places to go on the web for phone numbers and addresses worldwide. For a specific country, start by identifying the available directories by using a resource guide such as Infobel or Wayp International White and Yellow Pages, but don't expect 100 percent success (or even 70 percent) in any of the directories. Some of the directories may be incomplete or a bit dated; depending on the country and the website, some of the yellow pages are internet-only (without an equivalent print version) and may be fairly limited. However, some are quite extensive. Searchability and extensiveness of the white pages listed here also vary considerably. But if you ordinarily use telephone directory assistance, these sites will allow you to find many people a lot more easily and a lot less expensively. For U.S. phone numbers, Yahoo! People search or Google (google.com) may be your best bet. When searching, remember that names may be listed in a variety of ways (for example, with first initial instead of the full first name).

Infobel

www.infobel.com

Infobel provides access to phone directories for more than 200 countries and contains links to white pages, yellow pages, business directories, and email directories. Which of these are available depends upon the country.

Wayp International White and Yellow Pages

www.wayp.com

Wayp is a resource guide for white and yellow pages directories, arranged by continent and country. Click on the name of a continent to see which directories are available for each country.

Yahoo! People Search

people.yahoo.com

For finding addresses, phone numbers, email addresses, and more, Yahoo! People Search covers U.S. numbers and addresses as well as provides a reverse phone number search and an email address search that works reasonably well. For non-U.S. numbers and addresses, use the relevant country-specific Yahoo! site and look on the main page there for links to phone directories.

AnyWho

www.anywho.com

AnyWho has U.S. yellow pages and white pages from AT&T, plus a few links to international directories (under the International link). Links are provided for maps and area codes. AnyWho also offers a reverse phone lookup. If you have a phone number and don't know the name of the person, click the Reverse Lookup link, enter the number, and you will probably get the owner's name.

Superpages.com

superpages.com

Though it covers just the U.S., Superpages.com provides not only a lookup of people and businesses but links to maps and driving directions. It also offers both a reverse phone lookup and a reverse address lookup, and a ZIP code and area code search.

QUOTATIONS

The Quotations Page

www.quotationspage.com

This is a resource guide with a searchable database of more than 26,000 quotations from more than 3,100 authors. You can either search or use the subject directory (Life, Love, Success, Change, Friendship, Dreams, Happiness, Attitude, Character, Education, etc.). The Quotations Page is a great source if you are preparing a talk, an article, or a paper. Quote something from Lucius Accius, and people may think you have actually read his works.

Bartleby.com

www.bartleby.com

Bartleby.com belongs in the category of "outstanding" sites (Figure 6.3). Chief among its quotation sources are Bartlett's *Familiar Quotations* (1919 edition), *Columbia World of Quotations*, and *Simpson's Contemporary Quotations*, but it also contains a wonderful collection of other quote sources, handbooks, anthologies, collected works of famous authors (including Shakespeare), and other reference tools. The content is primarily humanities, but Bartleby even throws in some science. The contents of all of these resources can be searched together, or you can use the pull-down windows from the main page or on the Reference, Verse, Fiction, or Nonfiction tabs to individually search more than 200 full-text works. The following list is just a selection of what is available at Bartleby.com:

> *Oxford Book of English Verse*, 1919
>
> *Yale Book of American Verse*, 1912
>
> *Columbia Encyclopedia*, sixth edition, 2001
>
> *Columbia Gazetteer of North America*, 2000
>
> *The World Factbook*, 2008
>
> *American Heritage Dictionary of the English Language*, fourth edition, 2000
>
> *Roget's II: The New Thesaurus*, third edition, 1995
>
> *Roget's International Thesaurus of English Words and Phrases*, 1922
>
> Bartlett, John, *Familiar Quotations*, 10th edition, 1919
>
> *The Columbia World of Quotations*, 1996
>
> *Simpson's Contemporary Quotations*, 1988 ("The most notable quotations since 1950")
>
> *American Heritage Book of English Usage*, 1996
>
> *The Columbia Guide to Standard American English*, 1993
>
> Fowler, H. W., *The King's English*, second edition, 1908
>
> Quiller-Couch, Sir Arthur, *On the Art of Writing*, 1916 and 1920
>
> Quiller-Couch, Sir Arthur, *On the Art of Reading*, 1920
>
> Sapir, Edward, *Language: An Introduction to the Study of Speech*, 1921
>
> Strunk, William, Jr., *The Elements of Style*, 1918
>
> The Bible, King James Version, 1999

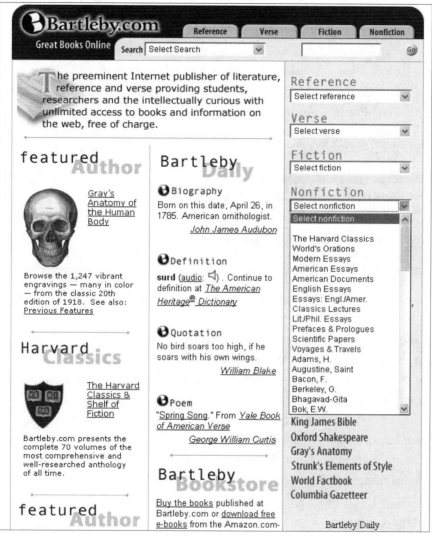

Bartleby.com home page

Figure 6.3

TIP:

If a quotation sounds like an old famous quotation, try identifying it in Bartleby.com first. If you don't find it here, try a search engine and search for the quote as a phrase. Bartleby.com has the advantage of greater authority, while the search engines have wider reach and cover more current material.

Brewer, E. Cobham, *Dictionary of Phrase and Fable*, 1898

Bulfinch, Thomas, *The Age of Fable*, 1913

Frazer, Sir James George, *The Golden Bough: A Study in Magic and Religion*, abridged edition, 1922

Cambridge History of English & American Literature (18 vols.), 1907–1921

Eliot, Charles W., ed., *The Harvard Classics and Harvard Classics Shelf of Fiction* (70 volumes), 1909–1917

Eliot, T. S., *The Sacred Wood*, 1920

Shakespeare, William, *The Oxford Shakespeare*, 1914

Van Doren, Carl, *The American Novel*, 1921

Gray, Henry, *Anatomy of the Human Body*, 20th edition, 1918

Farmer, Fannie Merritt, *The Boston Cooking-School Cook Book*, 1918

Post, Emily, *Etiquette*, 1922

Inaugural Addresses of the Presidents of the United States, 1989

Robert, Henry M., *Robert's Rules of Order Revised*, 1915

FOREIGN EXCHANGE RATES/ CURRENCY CONVERTERS

If you travel internationally, have family or friends living in other countries, or purchase items outside your own country, you may frequently need to know the equivalent of your money in a certain foreign currency. There are many sites on the web that do these calculations. Yahoo! has one of the best.

Yahoo! Finance—Currency Converter

finance.yahoo.com/currency-converter

You have to look fairly closely on Yahoo!'s Finance page to find the link to the currency converter, so you will want to bookmark this site. You will discover that it provides a conversion calculator that handles more than 150 currencies. Under the converter box is a link to View 5 Day Trend, which leads to a graph showing fluctuations. You can also view trends over other time periods, ranging from one day to five years.

WEATHER

Both for local weather and for travel planning, a good weather site is essential. A good option is a personalized portal, such as My Yahoo! or iGoogle, that automatically supplies the weather forecast for the cities you specify. If you use a news site as your start page, look there to see if you can select weather information for specific cities. If you want a weather-only site, try Weather Underground.

Weather Underground

wunderground.com

Click on the appropriate region of the U.S. map or the world map to get weather for a particular location. You can also choose to have temperatures appear in either Fahrenheit or Celsius (or both), and the site provides links for what seems like an endless collection of weather-related data and maps. You can personalize the home page by choosing favorite cities (worldwide) to be shown automatically.

MAPS

Perry-Castañeda Library Map Collection

www.lib.utexas.edu/maps

The Perry-Castañeda Library Map Collection is a tremendous collection of maps, plus links to gazetteers and so forth (Figure 6.4). Most of the more than 11,000 maps on this site are public domain, and no permission is required to copy or distribute them. The CIA actually produces a large portion of the maps. The site also has a fascinating collection of historical maps. Beyond the maps on the site, there are links that lead to thousands and thousands of maps found on other sites. Take time to read the FAQ, especially for the useful tips on printing the maps. The General Libraries at the University of Texas should be thanked profusely for providing this resource.

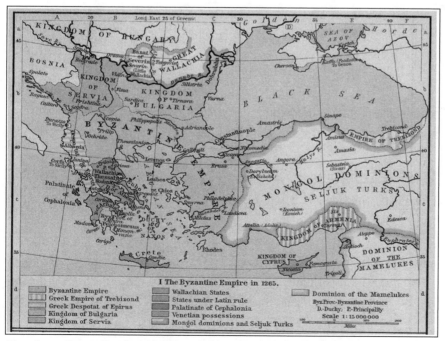

Figure 6.4

Map from Perry-Castañeda Library Map Collection

David Rumsey Historical Map Collection

www.davidrumsey.com

This collection contains more than 20,000 high-resolution maps and images online. It focuses on rare 18th- and 19th-century maps of North and South America, but it also includes historical maps of other continents. The various viewers provided on the site make it easy to navigate and examine the maps in detail.

GAZETTEERS

Global Gazetteer

www.fallingrain.com/world

This gazetteer provides a directory of more than 2.8 million cities and towns in more than 180 countries. Locate the place of interest by first browsing by country, then by region (state, provinces, etc.), and then alphabetically. Each place listed has a satellite or topographic image, latitude and longitude, elevation, population, weather data, nearby cities and towns, nearby airports, and more. Data comes from the U.S. government's National Geospatial-Intelligence Agency and other sources.

World Gazetteer

www.world-gazetteer.com

Latitude, longitude, current population, and other statistics are available at the World Gazetteer site for countries, administrative divisions, cities, and towns. The pronunciation table it provides for dozens of languages is useful not just here but also for other applications.

ZIP CODES

U.S. Postal Service ZIP Code Lookup

www.usps.com/zip4

If you have the street address, the U.S. Postal Service site can provide the nine-digit ZIP code, while the Search by City tab provides a list of ZIP codes associated with a particular city. You can also find the ZIP code for a company and all places in a particular ZIP code.

STOCK QUOTES

As with many other frequently asked reference questions, stock quotes can be found at numerous places on the web. For the searcher who needs stock quotes frequently, it will be worthwhile to investigate several sites and determine which one is the best for you by looking at ease of use, clarity of presentation, detail provided, personalized portfolio features, types of charts and graphs available, and presence of associated news stories. As with weather information, consider using a personalized portal, such as My Yahoo! that can integrate selected stock information and a personalized portfolio into your start page. Remember that these free quotes are typically delayed by 20 minutes. If you use a major brokerage house or an online trading service, also look at its site. You may qualify to sign in as a client and receive real-time data and order capabilities. CNN is one example of the many sites that offer free stock information online.

CNNMoney

money.cnn.com

CNN's financial site is very rich, packed with detailed stock quotes, financial news, company backgrounds, a currency converter, email newsletters, financial tools, and other kinds of market-related information. You can set up and track your own detailed portfolios for free.

STATISTICS

Although not every statistic you might want will be available on the internet, finding statistics via the web makes locating a needed statistic amazingly easier than just a few years ago. The expanse of statistical information is immense, as is the amount that could be said about finding statistics on the internet. A few very basic hints and resources are provided here. Because the topic of statistics is so broad, you are often best off starting with one of the numerous resource guides. Other than resource guides, only a handful of specific sources for the most commonly sought statistics are given here.

Keep the following hints in mind:

- There are three main ways of finding statistics on the internet:
    1. Go to a site you think may contain the statistic and search or browse. For example, try the relevant governmental department (e.g., the Department of Agriculture for U.S. agricultural statistics).

     Think about what agency or other organization would have an interest in collecting the data you are trying to find.

2. Go to a collection of links to statistics sites (such as those listed later).

3. Use a general web search engine such as Yahoo! or Google. Far more statistical material is indexed by search engines now than was the case a few years ago, especially because of the indexing of PDF files, Excel spreadsheets, and other document types. A search strategy can often be very straightforward. For collections of statistics in a particular area, try a search such as *health statistics*. For more specific statistics, try a combination of one or more subject terms plus the place and perhaps the year (for example, *avalanche fatalities norway 2008*).

- Good news: There is plenty of redundancy of identification and access; in other words, there are many routes online to the same statistic.

- When you find a statistics site you might use again, bookmark it. To make it easier to use bookmarks, create folders to organize similar types of sites.

- On statistics sites, take advantage of site search boxes and site maps.

- Watch for terminology. Unless you are familiar with the topic, the terminology may not be obvious. The term *housing starts* may not be what you think to look for immediately when searching for statistics on the number of new homes being built.

BEOnline—Statistics
www.loc.gov/rr/business/beonline/subjects.php? SubjectID=56

This collection of links from the Library of Congress is not extensive (just under 100 sites) but covers a wide range of carefully selected statistics sites, particularly for business, economics, and the social sciences.

Intute: SocialSciences—Statistics and Data
www.intute.ac.uk/socialsciences/statistics

Part of the broader Intute site, Intute's Statistics and Data section is maintained by subject specialists at U.K. universities. Sections include: General Statistics and Data; Educational Outcomes and Institutions; Elections and Public Opinion; Finance and Markets; Health and Nutrition; Housing and Migration; Land and the Environment; National and International

Indicators; Population and Area Statistics; Social Attitudes and Behaviour; Socio-economic Studies; and Statistical Theory.

U.S. Statistics

USA Statistics in Brief

www.census.gov/compendia/statab/brief.html

This site contains selected tables from the venerable *Statistical Abstract of the United States*, including summary tables for a broad range of subjects, plus basic state population data (Figure 6.5). The full *Statistical Abstract of the United States* is available at www.census.gov/compendia/statab.

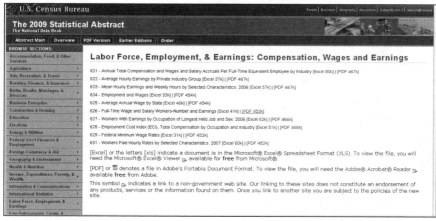

Figure 6.5

USA Statistics in Brief section listing

FedStats

www.fedstats.gov

FedStats contains links to statistics produced by more than 100 U.S. federal agencies. You can browse or use the search feature to search across agencies.

BOOKS

Most book searches on the internet fall into one of two categories: (1) finding information *about* books—in other words, what books are available on a particular topic or by a particular author—and verifying bibliographic information, or (2) trying to *locate the entire book online*. Unless the book was published close to a century ago, you shouldn't expect to get the complete book in full text online. Nevertheless, thousands of books are currently available in full text, and the number is growing rapidly. If the book is in English and is by a famous pre-20th-century author, you have a pretty good chance of finding the full text online.

Finding Information *About* Books— Bookstores

Keep in mind that the large online book vendors' sites are not just good for buying books, but also for identifying books currently in print on any topic or out of print but still available for sale by used- or rare-book dealers.

Amazon

amazon.com

Amazon lists millions of book titles (and lots of other products) for sale with good discounts. The site is searchable by keyword, author, title, subject, ISBN, or publication date, and it is browsable by subject. Click on Books, then on Advanced Search, for these search options. There you will also find additional options for narrowing and sorting your search results. As well as new books Amazon also includes millions of used, rare, and out-of-print books from hundreds of booksellers. Take advantage of the book categories on the left of the book search page. As you are browsing, look for books labeled with Amazon's Search Inside the Book feature, which provides images of selected parts of the book, including the covers, the table of contents, sample pages, the index, and more.

Barnes & Noble

barnesandnoble.com

Competing nose-to-nose with Amazon, Barnes & Noble also provides access to millions of books (and other merchandise). The search box on its home page lets you search by author, title, or subject. Click the Advanced Search link for a larger selection of searchable fields. The site also has a collection of millions of out-of-print, used, and rare books from dealers around the world (click on the Used & Out-of-Print tab).

Finding Information *About* Books—
Bibliographic Databases

To find what books have been published at any time on any topic, go to the online catalog of one or more of the major national libraries. For English-language materials (although, of course, they are not limited to English materials), you might start with either The British Library or the U.S. Library of Congress.

Library of Congress Online Catalog

catalog.loc.gov

The Library of Congress online catalog includes 14 million records for books, serials, computer files, manuscripts, maps and other cartographic material, music, and audio/visual materials (Figure 6.6). The Basic Search option searches by title, author, subject, call number, and keywords, and by LCCN (Library of Congress Control Number), ISSN (International Standard Serial Number), or ISBN (International Standard Book Number). Guided Search provides searches by a greater number of options, and the OR, AND, and NOT options can be used by means of the pull-down windows and radio buttons.

Figure 6.6

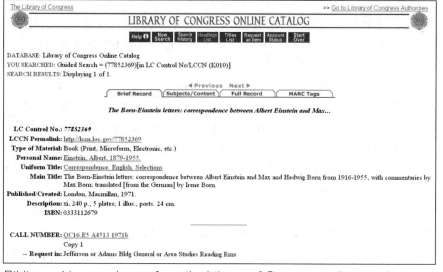

Bibliographic record page from the Library of Congress online catalog

The British Library

blpc.bl.uk

This site provides a search of 14 million books and more than 62 million other items, including patents, newspapers, sound recordings, and other materials. It covers items located in The British Library Public Catalogue, plus lots more. The main search covers the 10,000 pages of the library's website, 30,000 images from the library's Online Gallery, 14 million catalog records, and 9 million journal articles. These can be searched individually or in combination. Click on the Advanced Searching link to get to more detailed search options for each of these collections. The British Library site is far more than just a bibliographic search, and the site itself contains an impressive amount of multimedia content. Be sure to try the Turning the Pages section where you can view some books in a way you never have before.

Google Book Search

books.google.com

Google Book Search is a search of a collection of both new and old books (plus some magazines), made possible due to Google's arrangements with publishers and several major libraries. For books that are out of copyright, you can see the Full Book View with all pages of the book. For books under copyright, access will vary. You can see actual pages of the book (either the full book but more likely a "limited preview") if the publisher has given permission, although you will need to log in to your Google account in some cases. You can search using the same Boolean expressions as with regular Google (AND is implied, and you can use OR and a minus sign for NOT). You can also use the following prefixes: *inauthor:*, *intitle:*, *inpublisher:*, *date*: (e.g., *date:1960–2006*), and *isbn:*. On the advanced search page, you can elect to search All Books, or Limited Preview and Full View Books, or Full View only. Menus and boxes allow for searching by title, author, language, publisher, publication date, subject, and ISBN (or ISSN for magazines).

Your Local Library's Online Catalog

For something more local, check the online catalog of your local library. If it has a web-accessible catalog, you'll find the site for the catalog easily through a search engine, or you may find it by going to the Library of Congress Gateway to Library Catalogs (lcweb.loc.gov/z3950/gateway.html).

Full-Text Books Online

If you are trying to find a specific work online, a search engine usually works quite well. However, it may be easier to use a site that compiles a large number of such works and that will enable you to browse by title or author. Bartleby.com provides more than 200 full-text books including a number of useful reference works. But for a collection of more than 30,000 books, consult Project Gutenberg; and for locating more than 35,000 titles, look at The Online Books Page. The vast majority of the works in these collections are no longer under copyright; with a few exceptions, they are all from before the 1920s. (Unfortunately, the increased availability of 20th-century texts threatens to be slowed by attempts by both the EU and the U.S. Congress to extend copyright virtually into perpetuity.) The sites discussed here are definitely sites to which the word "amazing" must again be applied. Whether you want to find Cicero or the Bobbsey Twins, these are good places to start.

The Online Books Page

digital.library.upenn.edu/books

This resource guide contains links to more than 35,000 books in English. The creator and editor of the site, John Mark Ockerbloom, founded it in 1993, and he has been adding to it ever since. To be included, a book must be in English and in full text, and must qualify as significant by being listed in the online catalog of a major library or be otherwise recognized. The site, which is easily searchable by author and title, is also browsable by author, title, subject, and serial title.

Project Gutenberg

www.gutenberg.org

Want to read a good book? Come here. Project Gutenberg, established in 1971, was designed to place online, in easily accessible format, as many public domain electronic texts (etexts) as possible. So far, it has provided more than 30,000 texts, from Cicero to the Bobbsey twins. Although the majority of books are in English, Project Gutenberg contains (a few) books in about 60 other languages. The breadth of texts available makes this an excellent research site but also consider it a source of etexts to read on your laptop or other reader. Because most of the books are stored in ASCII text, they are small enough to be loaded on a flash drive. (You will also now find a number of books in audio format and a small collection of sheet music.) All the books are in the U.S. public domain, no longer under copyright (therefore, almost all are from before 1923). For many of the books, the entire text is available in a single file, allowing a researcher to quickly find all references to a particular word in a text (by using the Edit > Find in This Page function of a browser). Using this approach (not just here but elsewhere), you can go to the text of *The Odyssey*, for example, and quickly find each and every mention of Telemachus, if you are so inclined to do such things.

Bartleby.com
www.bartleby.com
For a partial list of the books covered by Bartleby.com, see the previous section on quotations.

HISTORICAL DOCUMENTS

EuroDocs: Online Sources for European History
eudocs.lib.byu.edu
A resource guide, the EuroDocs site provides links to Western European documents that are online in transcribed, facsimile, or translated form. They are arranged first by country and then chronologically. The site is now in a wiki format.

A Chronology of U.S. Historical Documents
www.law.ou.edu/hist
The Chronology of U.S. Historical Documents site contains links to more than 140 full-text documents from the pre-Colonial period to the present.

University of Virginia Hypertext Collection
xroads.virginia.edu/~HYPER/hypertex.html
The University of Virginia offers a collection on its site of classic and other texts (primarily books) in the area of American Studies.

Governments and Country Guides

In lots of situations, information about specific countries is needed—basics such as population, names of leaders, flags, or maps, or more detailed information on economics, geography, and politics. Numerous resources provide this information, and those resources differ primarily in terms of amount of detail and categories of data covered.

Governments on the WWW

www.gksoft.com/govt

Governments on the WWW is an excellent resource guide. Arranged by continent and country, the links on this site connect you to official government sites (including individual sites for parliaments, offices, courts, and embassies), banks, multinational organizations, and political parties. Though the site has gone for years without updating, it is a unique, useful collection, and most links are still valid.

CIA World Factbook

www.cia.gov/library/publications/the-world-factbook

This regularly updated work provides easily usable yet quite detailed country guides. Data for each country is arranged in the following sections: Geography, People, Government, Economy Communications, Transportation, Military, and Transnational Issues. This is an extremely rich site, and even if you do not think you will use it frequently, you will find the time spent exploring it worthwhile. As an indication of how widespread the respect for this site is, the Basic Facts on Iraq section of the official site of the former Permanent Mission of Iraq to the U.N. (under Saddam Hussein) was mostly taken word-for-word from the CIA World Factbook!

U.K. Foreign & Commonwealth Office—Country Profiles

www.fco.gov.uk/en/travel-and-living-abroad/travel-advice-by-country/country-profile

The profiles here, prepared by FCO desk officers, provide general facts and background about the country, history, geography, politics, economy, international relations, and trade and investment. The latter two sections typically focus on the relations between the country being profiled and the U.K.

U.S. Government

USA.gov

www.usa.gov

USA.gov (formerly FirstGov) is the official internet gateway (portal) to U.S. government resources and is a good starting place for locating information from or about government services and agencies. The site has four main divisions: For Citizens, For Businesses and Nonprofits, For Government Employees, and For Visitors to the U.S. Take advantage of the menu on the main page, which provides an alphabetic listing of federal government agencies and links to state, local, and tribal government information.

GPO Access

www.gpoaccess.gov

Use this site to search the Federal Register, Code of Federal Regulations, Commerce Business Daily, Congressional Record, Government Manual, and other U.S. government databases, either singly or together.

THOMAS: Legislative Information on the Internet

thomas.loc.gov

THOMAS has a variety of detailed and easily searchable databases with information related to federal legislation, including bills and resolutions, activities in Congress, the Congressional Record, schedules, calendars, committees, presidential nominations, treaties, and more. It also contains links to the Senate and House websites and to other government information. This is an excellent place to start a search on legislation currently in process or on a specific topic, or for tracking a particular current bill.

Open CRS

www.opencrs.com

On an ongoing basis, the Congressional Research Service (CRS) of the Library of Congress produces a collection of highly respected, nonpartisan reports on a wide variety of subjects relating to current political events and situations. Unfortunately, Congress (which, perhaps obviously from the name, controls the Library of Congress) pointedly prevents CRS from distributing the reports directly (though some members have fought hard to change this situation). To "democratize" the availability of non-confidential

CRS reports, the Center for Democracy & Technology has created this website, which collects reports that have been released. The reports included here represent only a portion of the reports produced by CRS, but this site is a good starting place to find out, as far as currently possible, what reports have been made publicly available and to access those reports online.

U.S. State Information

Library of Congress—State and Local Government Information

www.loc.gov/rr/news/stategov/stategov.html

The Library of Congress State and Local Government directory is a resource guide with a convenient collection of links to state, county, and local government information.

U.K. Government Information

Directgov—Web Site of the U.K. Government

www.direct.gov.uk

Directgov is a searchable and browsable collection of information, news, and links to U.K. public sector information, including both central and local government information. The content is arranged primarily by topic (Motoring, Education and Learning, Environment and Greener Living, etc.) and by audience (Parents, Young People, Disabled People, etc.). For a more detailed list of content, use the A–Z of Central Government link found on the main page.

COMPANY INFORMATION

Entire books have been written on finding company information on the internet. Anyone who searches for company information frequently will want to spend time with one of those books and may already be familiar with the quick-reference company sites included here. For those who have only occasional need for company information or who are just getting into the area, the following sites will provide a start.

First, we should cover a few basic pointers about tools for finding company information. For company information, it helps to start by thinking about what kinds of company information you might reasonably expect to find on the internet. You might think in terms of three categories:

1. Information that a company *wants* you to know, such as its stature, its products or services, and any good news about the company
2. Information that a company *must* let you know, such as information required by government laws and regulations (e.g., Securities and Exchange Commission [SEC] filings in the U.S. and Companies House filings in the U.K.)
3. *What others are saying* about the company

To find out what a company wants you to know, start with the company's home page. Depending on the company, you will probably find detailed background, products and services, company structure, press releases, and so on. To find a company's home page, you can just enter the name in any of the major search engines. The company home page will usually be among the first few items retrieved.

To find out what a company *must* let you know, first keep in mind that these regulations apply only to publicly held companies. Others typically do not have to divulge very much information publicly. For U.S. publicly held companies, SEC filings are available through several sites, including the SEC's own site. For public companies in other countries, the amount of mandated information is usually much less than that required of U.S. companies, but you can start by looking at the CorporateInformation website.

For the third category of company information—*what others are saying* about a company—some items to keep on your internet reference shelf are discussion groups (especially Google Groups and other groups sources discussed in Chapter 5) and news stories (through MSNBC, CNN, BBC, etc.). For some key news sites, see Chapter 8.

These resources, however, are basically most useful for finding information about a specific company you already have in mind. Many company questions focus on "What companies are out there that match a particular set of criteria?" For example, who are some of the largest seafood packers in Maryland? What is the name of a plumber who serves my neighborhood? These questions are often answered by using directories or online yellow pages of the types listed earlier in this chapter.

Company Directories

Company directories on the web differ in terms of:

- Number and type (public, private, U.S., non-U.S.) of companies included
- Free, paid subscription, or pay-per-view
- Searchability (by name, industry location, ticker symbol, size, etc.)
- Amount of information provided about each company (usually the more companies included, the less information about each)

CorporateInformation

www.corporateinformation.com

This site, from Wright Investors' Service, provides tens of thousands of company research reports, profiles, and analyses for companies in 55 countries. For many users, the most useful and unique part may be the links to company directories and other resources arranged by country. Use the Research Links link on the main page and choose the country. Full company reports from Wright Investors' Service require a fee, but free snapshot reports are provided for thousands of companies worldwide.

Hoover's

www.hoovers.com

Hoover's provides information on public and non-public companies worldwide (Figure 6.7), on company executives, and on more than 600 industries. For much of the information, a subscription is required, but especially for public companies, you will find very informative profiles with an overview of the company, basic financials, executives, etc. You will also find free overviews of hundreds of industries. The free portion is searchable by company name, ticker symbol, keyword, and executive name. Spend some time exploring this site to get a feel for how much information is there.

ThomasNet

www.thomasnet.com

If you need to buy a manufactured product and want to find out who makes it or who can get it for you, this website is the place to go. This online version of the well-known resource formerly published as *Thomas Register* allows you to browse or to search by company name, product/service, or

Figure 6.7

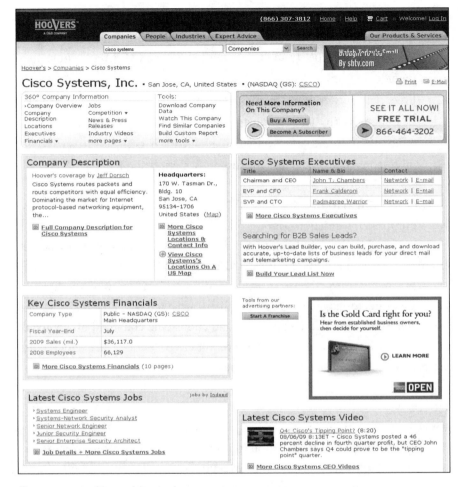

Company profile on Hoover's

brand name. It covers more than 600,000 North American suppliers, manufacturers, distributors, and service companies, arranged under 67,000 categories. You can browse by the categories or search, and searches can be
narrowed by location, company type, ownership, and certification. The information you find will contain company profiles, contact information, and links
to websites. A companion site, Thomas Global (www.thomasglobal.com), is a
directory of suppliers in 28 countries, available in nine languages.

Also see the following two product directories that are discussed in
Chapter 9:

Kompass
www.kompass.com

Kellysearch
www.kellysearch.com

Company Phone Numbers and Addresses

Don't forget that the company's home page will usually provide phone numbers. Also be sure to check the phone directories listed earlier in this chapter.

ASSOCIATIONS

If you know the name of an association and need further information, usually the best place to start is with the association's home page. From the other direction, if you need to find the names of associations that relate to a particular topic, there are a couple places to consider as starting points:

1. Use a search engine and search for the subject and terms such as association, society, organization:

   Example: *"solar energy" (association OR society OR organization)*
or,
   solar (energy OR power) (association OR society OR organization)
or just
   solar (association OR society OR organization)

2. Use the directory provided by the American Society of Association Executives.

American Society of Association Executives Gateway to Associations
www.asaecenter.org/Directories/AssociationSearch.cfm

This ASAE Gateway provides links to thousands of association sites, which you can search by name, location, geographic scope, and organization type.

PROFESSIONAL DIRECTORIES

To find directories for a specific profession, try a search on the name of the profession and the word *"directory."* It works sometimes; sometimes it doesn't. Two of the most widely useful directories, for physicians and lawyers, are listed here.

AMA DoctorFinder

webapps.ama-assn.org/doctorfinder

This AMA (American Medical Association) site offers "information on virtually every licensed physician in the United States" and includes more than 814,000 doctors. You can search by name, location, and specialty. Look on the main AMA site (www.ama-assn.org) under the Information for Patients tab for additional resources such as a Patient Medical Library, an Atlas of the Human Body, and to create an iHealthRecord of your own medical information (in conjunction with Google).

Lawyers.com

lawyers.com

Lawyers.com allows a search of 1 million attorneys and law firms in 160 countries by practice area, name, and location. Searches on Lawyers.com use the Martindale-Hubbell database, which will be familiar to any legal researcher.

OTHER INFORMATION ABOUT PEOPLE

Finding someone's phone number and address was discussed earlier. There is a lot more though that can easily (and legitimately and ethically) be found out. Sources include sites such as MySpace, Facebook, and LinkedIn (all discussed in Chapter 10). A quick way to gather information on people from a variety of sources is the Pipl (pronounced like "people") site.

Pipl

www.pipl.com

Pipl is a specialized search engine that provides a simple search interface that quickly delivers basic contact and other information about individuals. As well as identifying phone numbers, Pipl searches databases that may include further information, such as birthdays, Amazon customer profiles, publications, etc. Altogether it covers more than 1,000 "Deep Web" sites, including social and professional networking sites such as MySpace, Facebook, and LinkedIn, newspapers, genealogical sites such as Ancestry.com, and Find A Grave, and others such as the Lycos People Search, Whitepages.com, ZabaSearch, BirthDatabase.com, Internet Movie Database, Flickr, Avvo, Hoover's, Google Blog Search, and Google Scholar.

LITERATURE DATABASES

As great as internet resources are, they still cover only a small portion of what we think of as the world's literature. The majority of journal articles (especially those more than a few years old) are not available on the web in full text. But just as even a very large library owns only a small portion of extant literature, both a library and the internet at least provide pointers to the broader corpus.

You will find a number of bibliographic databases on the web that let you identify at least portions of what has been published on a particular topic, by a particular author, and so on. Many of these databases are available only through subscription, but many are available free, particularly on some large government-sponsored databases. For books, you can go to major national libraries' catalogs, and for journal literature, go to databases such as Medline, ERIC, and others. Depending upon the subject area and other factors, for much "scholarly research," sites such as IngentaConnect and Google Scholar may not be an adequate substitute for searching the proprietary, subscription literature databases found in libraries. Those "library" databases may provide more comprehensive coverage, provide greater clarity about the extent of coverage, and are more definitively "scholarly" and more "searchable" because of better commands, structure, and indexing.

For researchers, it is extremely important to take care in choosing your tools when doing a literature search. If all you need to do is get one or two articles to read for background on a topic, either the free bibliographic tools available on the internet or the more high-powered "library" databases (such as PsycInfo, INSPEC, BIOSIS, SciFinder Scholar, etc.) will probably suffice. However, if you are doing in-depth research, consider carefully the tool's coverage in terms of time frame, language, number and type of publications covered, and quality of indexing.

To identify bibliographic databases on the web for a particular subject, use the resource guides (discussed in Chapter 2) for that area. A good resource guide for any subject will clearly identify important literature databases in that area. For single-site access to a broad range of scholarly journal literature, try IngentaConnect and Google Scholar. Other databases, such as Scirus (www.scirus.com), CiteSeer (citeseer.ist.psu.edu), and PubMed (www.ncbi.nlm.nih.gov/pubmed), provide similar access but to a smaller range of topics, such as science or business.

IngentaConnect

www.ingentaconnect.com

When you search the IngentaConnect site, you have access to more than 13,000 publications, mainly journals (from all fields) and more than 4 million articles. These publications include trade, scientific, and technical journals with coverage going back to 1988. Click on Search on the home page to get to the advanced search options. IngentaConnect is searchable by keyword, author, publication, volume, and issue. When searching, remember that you are usually searching titles, abstracts, and keywords, not the full text, so you may need to be a bit more imaginative in your choice of terms. Ingenta is in the business of selling articles, and though a few articles are free, in most cases you will need to purchase the item in order to get the full document.

HighBeam Research

www.highbeam.com

Like Ingenta, HighBeam Research is in the business of selling content and provides a database that will locate articles for you. In the case of HighBeam, it covers more than 80 million articles from 6,500 publications, from the areas of business, technology, science, news, hobbies, and personal interest. In addition, its Reference search includes a half-million articles from encyclopedias, dictionaries, thesauri, almanacs, and other reference tools. With HighBeam's advanced search, you can use simple Boolean and search by publication type (almanacs, books, encyclopedias, etc.), date, author, and article title.

Google Scholar

scholar.google.com

Google Scholar is a collection of "peer-reviewed papers, theses, books, preprints, abstracts and technical reports," made available by agreements with publishers, associations, universities, and others. For searching, you can take advantage of Google's OR capability, plus the *intitle:, allintitle:, site:,* and *author:* prefixes. An advanced search page lets you use simple Boolean; search by author, publication (i.e., journal), or date (or date range); and also narrow your search to one or more of seven broad subject areas. Clicking on a title on results pages will take you to an abstract of the article, and in some cases, the full article. In addition to basic bibliographic information, you may find a link to the library (or other database) from which Google indexed the item, and a link (for some books) that lets you find the book in a local library. Other links may lead you to articles that cite the article you retrieved and to sites where you may purchase the articles. Though what Google Scholar provides is impressive, keep in mind that its coverage and completeness are still less than that which may be available in more traditional bibliographic databases.

COLLEGES AND UNIVERSITIES

Peterson's

petersons.com

The Peterson's site offers a broad range of information for those looking for a school. From the main page, choose the level of education in which you are interested, and from there you can find categories such as Find a School, Pay for School, etc. In the Find a School section, you can successively narrow your search for schools by a broad range of criteria, such as location, major, tuition, size, GPA, type of college (e.g., four-year institution), religion, and dozens of other, more specific, criteria. If you have a specific school in mind, you can also search by the name of the school. You can sort results, create lists of schools in which you are interested, export results to a spreadsheet, and much more.

College Board

www.collegeboard.com

The College Board site provides a variety of resources relating to the Scholastic Aptitude Tests (SATs) and other tests, plus information on finding a college and financing an education. A tremendous amount of practical advice is included, on such things as writing essays for college applications, transitioning to college, etc. The site contains information on 3,800-plus colleges and presents a useful side-by-side comparison option. With the College MatchMaker section, you can narrow your search by dozens of criteria, create a list of your selections, and easily sort out your options.

TRAVEL

Travel is one area where you definitely need to know and use more than one website. Especially for travel reservation sites, don't count on any one always providing either the lowest cost flight or the itinerary that best suits your needs. On the other hand, loyalty to one site, and consequent heavier usage of that site, may get you special deals and discounts. Even if you don't book your own flights, it can be useful to visit these sites before you call your travel agent. If you use a travel site to select your flight first, you have more time to consider your itinerary than you would on the phone with the travel agent.

When using the web for travel planning, don't think only of reservation sites. Take advantage of travel guides, discussion groups, and thousands of other sites that provide information on your destination, how to get there, and what to do and how to get around while you are there. (For a broader sampling of what is available, look at the companion site for the author's book on using the internet for travel, *The Traveler's Web*, at www.extremesearcher.com/travel.)

Destination Guides

Fodor's

www.fodors.com

Fodor's, the print publisher, has a reputation for publishing what many travelers consider to be the best travel guides out there. Its website is an extremely rich resource with a useful collection of travel information, from what to see in a particular city to tipping practices worldwide.

Lonely Planet

www.lonelyplanet.com

The Lonely Planet site is a down-to-earth online guide to world travel from another well-known publisher of travel guides. For an excellent travelers' discussion group, try the Thorn Tree Forum on this site.

Reservation Sites

Travelocity

travelocity.com

As with most other travel reservation sites, Travelocity provides not just airfare, but rail fares, car rentals, hotel reservations, cruises, and more. It also provides travel guides and advice. On Travelocity, read the tips for identifying lowest fares.

Expedia

expedia.com

Expedia sometimes has lower prices than Travelocity (and vice versa). Some users will prefer the way in which Expedia lets them search for fares and itineraries, and the way in which the results are presented.

Orbitz

orbitz.com

The third of the "big three" reservation sites, Orbitz provides differences in navigation and display of results. Compare the three to see which best suits your needs, but if you want the lowest price and best itinerary, check all three. On this and other travel reservation sites, check out the deals and the savings available by booking combinations of travel, hotels, and car rentals.

FILM

Internet Movie Database (IMDb)

www.imdb.com

Whether you are looking for current show times or a list of all of the movies in which Kevin McCarthy appeared, IMDb is the place to go. It is not just a database of movies, but a movie portal with many resources, including commentary, movie and TV news, new releases, etc.

REFERENCE RESOURCE GUIDES

The sites discussed in this chapter only scratch the surface in terms of what is available. For other reference shelf sites, consult the general reference directories (resource guides) discussed in Chapter 2. For a good print reference tool covering the kinds of sites mentioned in this chapter, see *The Web Library: Building a World Class Personal Library with Free Web Resources* by Nicholas G. Tomaiuolo (CyberAge Books, 2004).

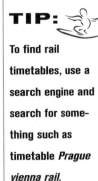

TIP:

To find rail timetables, use a search engine and search for something such as timetable *Prague vienna rail*.

CHAPTER 7

SIGHTS AND SOUNDS:
FINDING IMAGES, AUDIO, AND VIDEO

Even for someone with a lot of web experience, it is sometimes hard to believe how much is available in the way of multimedia (images, audio, and video) resources on the web. Images are not only available, but they are searchable—not as searchable as we would like, but still searchable. Whether you need a photo of the person you are about to meet, or of the streets of a specific town in a remote country, or of an obscure microorganism, you have a pretty good chance of finding it on the web. Audio and video files can be tremendously useful, whether you are using open sources for military intelligence purposes, for a discussion of Winston Churchill's "Finest Hour" speech in a history classroom, or for learning how to knit. This chapter summarizes what is available, provides some basic background and terminology for understanding and using these resources, points to the tools for finding what you need, and offers some techniques to do so most effectively.

THE COPYRIGHT ISSUE

Prior to using—or discussing—any of the resources here, the overarching issue of copyright must be considered. Although most people using the internet for research, teaching, and other professional applications already know about the issue and its implications, the importance of the copyright issue should be emphasized. The good news is that hundreds of millions of images, audio, and video files can be found easily on the web. The bad news is that you may not be able to use those images as you would like. Whenever you are using images (and any other original works) in any way, remember first of all that the vast majority of images on the web belong to someone: They are copyrighted. Some people (even some who should know better) still have the attitude that "I found it on the internet, so I can use it any way I want."

As most readers of this book know, that's simply not so. This does not mean that you cannot use these types of files in a variety of ways, but it does mean that you must use them within fair use guidelines and other provisions of copyright law.

If you have found an image of interest and want to use it in a report, on your own webpage, or for other purposes, in most cases you cannot legitimately do so without getting the permission of the copyright owner. First, look on the site where you found the image. You may be lucky and find a copyright statement that specifies when, where, and how you may use images from that site. (For a good example of such a statement, look at the NASA statement at www.nasa.gov/audience/formedia/features/MP_Photo_Guide lines.html, but don't expect most sites to have such a clear statement with such minimal conditions.) For people in companies, universities, school systems, and other organizations, your organization may have published copyright guidelines for your use. For the layperson who is trying to understand and interpret the actual laws, it may be somewhat of a challenge. For a very basic understanding of copyright issues, look at the articles on copyright in the Patents, Copyright & Art section of Nolo (www.nolo.com).

IMAGES
Some Technical Background

To view images on your screen, no technical knowledge is required. If, however, you plan to save images and use them (remember copyright!) on a webpage, or print the image you save, a few tips are in order.

Digital Image File Types

Web browsers can typically display only three image file formats: Joint Photographic Experts Group format (JPEG or JPG file extensions), Graphics Interchange Format (GIF file extension), or Portable Network Graphics format (PNG). The latter format is still relatively rare. Some search engines will allow you to narrow your image search by these file types, but it is unlikely that you will to need to do so.

Image Size

You will usually see image size referred to in pixels ("picture elements"), which are the space-related elements that make up a digital image. You can think of them as the "atomic" level of an image—the smallest unit of a digital image. An internet user can think of a typical monitor (with typical settings) as displaying about 72 or 96 pixels per inch (ppi). So depending on a number of factors, you can expect an image that has dimensions of 140 pixels by 140 pixels to take up about a 2″ square on a typical screen.

Capturing Images

An image file can be saved by doing the following:

1. Hold your cursor over the image you wish to capture.
2. Click the right mouse button.
3. From the menu that pops up, choose Save Image As (in Firefox and Safari) or Save Picture As (in Internet Explorer).
4. Select the folder where you want to save the image and rename the file if you want. Do not assign or change a file extension. It is important that the original file extension (.gif, .jpg, .jpeg, or .png) be retained.

Editing Images

A discussion of image editing is beyond the scope of this book. However, since the object of an image search is often to get a print copy of the image, searchers may need to do some minor editing of what they find. Operations such as cropping (trimming) and resizing are fairly common and easy to do. Anyone who has purchased a scanner or digital camera may have received software that offers these functions. Image editing programs are often packaged with scanners and digital cameras, and almost any photo editing software will provide the basics. Windows operating systems also often include an image editing program such as Paint. But some of these, surprisingly or not, may not offer some of the basic operations you might want to use. For the user who wants more high-powered image editing, three of the better-known choices are PaintShop Pro, PhotoShop, and PhotoShop Elements. (The latter is a lower-priced option offering all the PhotoShop features the amateur is likely to need.) Some substantial programs can be downloaded for free (Paint.NET and GIMP are among the most popular). Pixlr (pixlr.com) is another excellent online photo editor. The main problem with photo editing is that it quickly becomes addictive. When you have decided on a program to use, do a quick search in one of the search engines for the program AND the term *tutorial*. There are dozens of good photo-editing tutorials out there.

Types of Image Collections on the Web

The web offers many image collections. Some are collections of the images found on billions of webpages, such as the image collections found on Google and Yahoo!. Some are specialized by topic and represent the collections of specific organizations, such as the Australian National Botanic Gardens' National Plant Photographic Index (www.anbg.gov.au/anbg/photo-collection). Others are specialized by topic and represent the holdings of multiple institutions or sites, such as The Digital Scriptorium, which includes medieval and renaissance manuscripts (www.scriptorium.columbia.edu). Some collections are arranged by format or application, such as the numerous clip art collections. Increasingly popular are collections of photos shared by individuals, such as those on Flickr. Another category, especially important for those who need good images that they can safely (legally) reuse in publications or elsewhere, is the commercial collections, such as Corbis (corbis.com).

Searchability of Images

Though there are now billions of images that can be searched on the web, the search capabilities are fairly limited, and search results can be rather "approximate." This is primarily because the amount and quality of indexing that can currently be done by search programs is quite limited. Technologies are in development that will be able to see a picture of a tree, and without any text attached to the image, be able to tell that the tree is a tree, maybe even to identify it as a spruce and even as a blue spruce. Implementation of this image recognition on a large scale for web applications may take a while (though the ability to recognize images that contain faces has already been implemented in some search engines). Except for some relatively small collections, web search engines often do not have much to work with when identifying and indexing what a picture is showing. In most cases, the most that can be used for indexing is the name of the image file (e.g., sprucetree.jpg), an "alt" (alternative text) attribute that may be included in the HTML code, a caption if the image is in a table, and text that is near the photo. Indexing based on text near a photo becomes somewhat of a gamble and can account for many of the false hits that may occur in image search results. In some cases, image collections such as Flickr provide an opportunity for users to add "tags" to images that become part of the indexing, although this approach also carries with it some problems. That said, with a little imagination and a little patience and tolerance, the searcher can usually find a useful image quickly and easily using the collections and search techniques now available.

Directories of Image Resources on the Internet

As with almost any other type of internet content, there are specialized directories (resource guides) that offer easy identification of image collections. The two that follow are well-known and useful examples that can direct you to sites that contain collections of images. For both of these sites, the directory is displayed on one long page, so if you want to find a specific topic quickly, you may want to take advantage of your browser's Find in This Page option (under the Edit menu).

Digital Librarian: A Librarian's Choice of the Best of the Web—Images
www.digital-librarian.com/images.html

Here you will find more than 500 well-annotated links to image collections. For maps, check the companion Maps and Geography collection (www.digital-librarian.com/maps.html).

BUBL LINK—Image Collections
bubl.ac.uk/link/types/images.htm

BUBL LINK has links to more than 150 image collections, with good and often extensive descriptions of each site. In addition to the obvious usefulness of these annotations, this means that by using your browser's Find In This Page option, you can search the entire page easily for topics.

Search Engine Image Collections

With images from the billions of webpages covered in their web databases, the major general web search engines provide not only access to billions of images but also easy searchability (given the limitations on image searching previously discussed). As with a regular web search, use more than one engine. For any particular search, which images they retrieve will vary considerably as well as how many. Of the engines below, Google, Yahoo!, and Bing typically

TIP:

When searching for images, start by limiting your query to one or two words. Most images have very few words of indexing associated with them. If you search for *Boeing 747*, you will get substantially fewer good pictures of the plane than if you search for just *747*.

retrieve many more images than Ask.com. Keep in mind that the number of images retrieved does not necessarily reflect the relevance of the images to your specific search. (Google, for example, usually finds by far the largest number of images, but it may be identifying images where your search terms were simply somewhere on the same page as the image, not directly connected to the image.) Searchability and display of image results also differ among these engines.

Google's Image Search

Google says that it has the web's "most comprehensive image search," and there is a very good chance that the claim is true. To get to it, either click on the Images link on Google's main page or go directly to images.google.com. Once in Google Image Search, you can simply enter your terms in the search box, or you can click on Advanced Image Search to go to the advanced version. One feature to be sure to explore is the "faces" search option on the advanced image search page.

Image Searchability—Main Image Search Page

On Google's main image search page, all terms are automatically ANDed. If you enter *temple esna*, you will get only those images indexed under both terms. Quotation marks can be used for phrases, and a minus sign in front of a term can be used to eliminate items indexed under that term. You can also use the OR as with a regular Google web search. To retrieve all images indexed under the term *temple* and also under either *esna* or *khnum*, search for:

> *temple esna OR khnum*

You can also use any of the prefixes used in Google's web search. For images, the *site:* prefix will limit image retrieval to a particular website. This can be used in combination with other operations such as the OR. For example, images of either a corn or maize kernel from the U.S. Department of Agriculture site are available by searching for:

> *corn OR maize kernel site:usda.gov*

Advanced Image Search Page

Using Google's advanced image search page (Figure 7.1), you can:

- Use the Find Results boxes for simple Boolean ("all the words," "any of the words," or "not related to the words")
- Specify a phrase search by using "related to the exact phrase" (using quotation marks around the phrase in any of the boxes works just as well).
- Narrow by content type for any content, news content, faces, photo content, clip art, or line drawing. For "faces," Google is using a technology that enables it to identify images that are probably faces. Definitely try this when searching for people.
- Use the pull-down Size menu to specify images of the following sizes: any size, small, medium, large, or extra large.
- Specify the exact size, the width and/or height in pixels.
- Specify JPG, GIF, PNG, or BMP formats using the Filetypes menu (default is "any filetype").
- Specify "any colors," "black and white," or "full color" images.
- Retrieve images only from a specific domain (such as .gov or fda.gov).
- Use the SafeSearch option to set adult content filtering at No Filtering, Use Moderate Filtering (the default), or Use Strict Filtering (available only in the English version of Google).

Image Results Pages

As the result of a search, Google will return a page containing thumbnail images for the first 18 images retrieved (with links at the bottom of the page for additional results). Included with each thumbnail is a snippet of the text

Figure 7.1

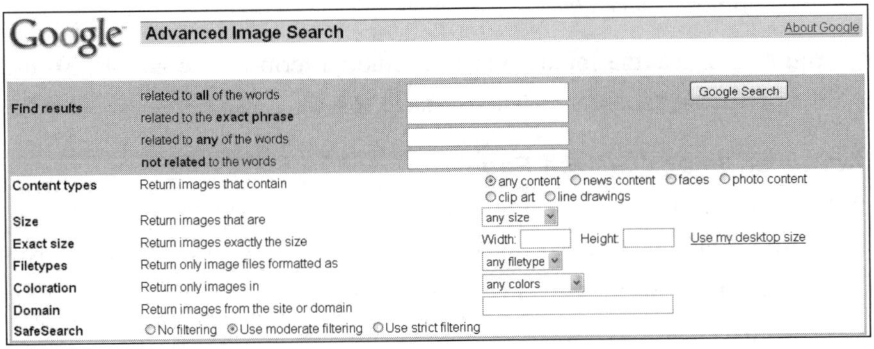

Google advanced image search page

around the word(s) that retrieved the image, the dimensions in pixels, the size of the file (e.g., 16k), the file type (e.g., .jpg), and the URL for the site on which it was found. The results pages also provide menus for further narrowing the results by size and content type. Click on the Show Options link to see the menus.

When you click on an image on a results page, it will take you to a split screen: In the top frame is a thumbnail of the image with links to See Full-Size Image, to Remove Frame (the upper part of the screen), and to go to the webpage where the image appeared; and in the bottom frame is the webpage where the image was found.

Yahoo!'s Image Search

Yahoo!'s image search database likewise contains images identified from webpages covered in its web database, plus images from Yahoo! News, Flickr, and "partner" sites that feed images (and often useful indexing data) to Yahoo!. To search, either click on the Images tab on the main Yahoo! Search page and then enter your search, or click on the Images tab after doing a web or other search. The latter will automatically search your terms in the Images database. You can also go directly to images.search.yahoo.com. For a bit more searchability, take advantage of the Advanced Image Search link.

Image Searchability—Main Image Search Page

In the search box, you can enter one or more terms and use quotation marks for phrases. Terms are automatically ANDed. You can use the *site:* prefix to limit your results either to a specific website or to a top-level domain, such as .gov.

Example: *"space shuttle" site:gov*

You cannot use the minus sign to exclude a term or use an OR. To use NOT or OR, use Yahoo!'s advanced image search.

Advanced Image Search Page

Yahoo!'s advanced image search page (Figure 7.2) lets you:

- Apply simple Boolean by entering your search terms in the boxes labeled "all of these words," "any of these words," or "none of these words"
- Search for an exact phrase

- Specify image size: any size, wallpaper, large, medium, small, or Custom (where you can specify the exact size in pixels)
- Choose coloration (Black & White or Color)
- Choose site/domain (use radio buttons for flicker.com, .com, .edu, .gov, .org, or enter a specific domain in a text box)
- Narrow to images with a Creative Commons license, allowing reuse of the image
- Use a SafeSearch option to filter out adult image results

Image Results Pages

Yahoo!'s image results pages show the number of images found and thumbnails of the first 18 or so images, with file names, dimensions in pixels, file

Figure 7.2

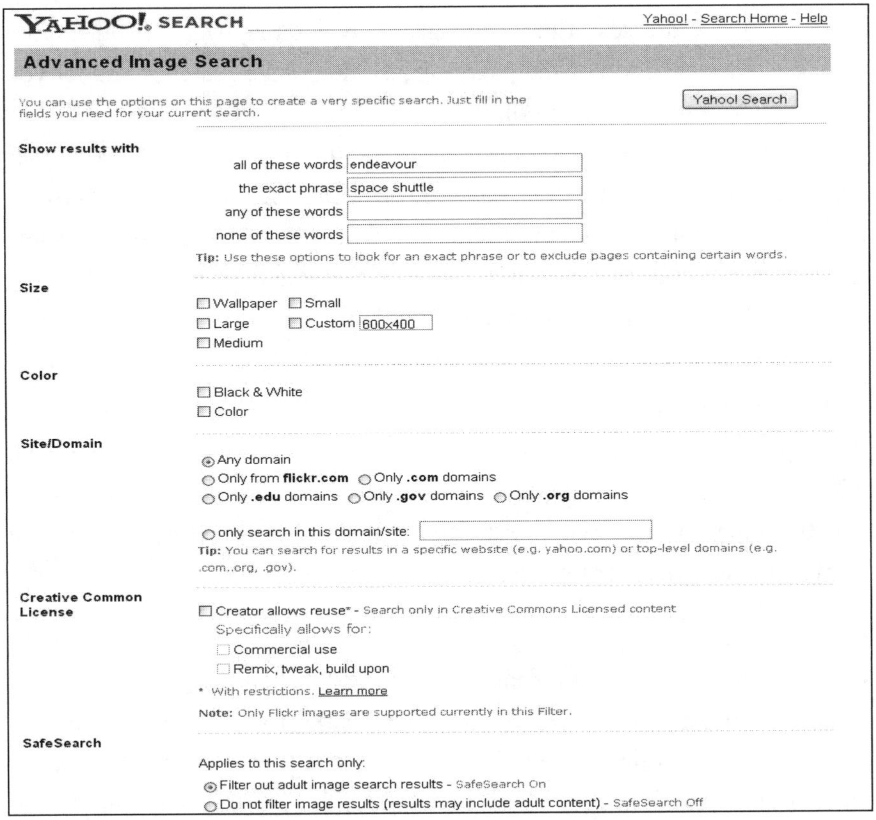

Yahoo! advanced image search page

Figure 7.3

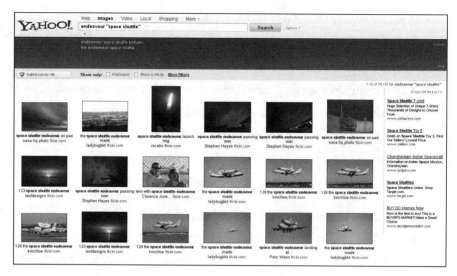

Yahoo! image search results page

sizes, and the addresses of the webpages on which they were found (Figure 7.3). Links near the top of the page suggest alternative searches and let you narrow the results by size or color.

Click on one of the thumbnails to go to a split screen with a larger thumbnail of the image in the top frame and the page on which the image was found in the bottom frame. In the top frame, you will also see a repetition of some of the other thumbnails and links found on the results page. An "X" in the upper right enables you to close the top frame.

Bing Search

Bing has a very substantial image database that competes well against the other general web search engines and also has a more innovative results page than the others. You can get to it using the Images link on Bing's main page or by going to bing.com/images.

Image Searchability

In the main search box for Bing's images search, terms are automatically ANDed, and you can use ORs, quotation marks for phrases, a minus to exclude terms, and the *site:* prefix to narrow to a specific site. When using ORs, be sure to enclose the ORed terms in parentheses. Bing does not have an advanced image search page, but on results pages, you can refine your current results by Size (small, medium, large, wallpaper), Layout (square, wide, tall), Color (color, black and white), Style (photograph, illustration), and People (faces, head and shoulders, other). As you see, Bing, like Google, has the "face" option, but takes it a step further and allows a head-and-shoulders option and an "other" option that identifies more distant images, groups, etc. For some searches, you will also see links for Related People, etc.

Image Results Pages

Unlike the other general web search results that give you 10 to 20 or so images per results page, with Bing you get continuous scrolling—you can just keep on going until you get to the end. There are other display differences as well. At first, just the thumbnails alone are shown, but when you hold your cursor over the image you get the image's file name, its dimensions and file size, the URL of the site on which it is found, and also a link to see similar images. There are also icons enabling you to see larger or smaller size thumbnails or to automatically see the details, not just the thumbnails. When you click on a thumbnail, a window opens on the right of the screen showing the page from which the image came.

Exalead

Exalead's image database size and its search features are more limited than the others just discussed. (Find it at exalead.com/image.) Search terms are automatically ANDed, and you can use quotation marks for phrases, but there is no OR or exclusion option available in the main search box. On results pages, however, you are given options to narrow results by choosing options shown beneath the search box or by clicking the Advanced Search link. Options include Size (small, medium, large), Content (face), Filetype (.jpg, .gif, .png), Color (color, black & white), Wallpaper (800 x 600), Realism (graphic, photo), and Orientation (portrait, landscape). On search results pages, by holding your cursor over a thumbnail, you will see the dimensions, file size, and URL, and a link to the page, plus a link to save the image on your computer or to your Favorite Images. If you make use of the latter, thereafter, when logged on to Exalead, you can click on the Your Favorite Images links and see all images you have saved. Clicking on a thumbnail will lead you to a view of only the image in full size.

Ask.com

When searching Ask.com's images database, the number of images you can expect to retrieve is about the same number as for Exalead. (Find it at ask.com/?tool=img.) In the main search box, the terms you enter will automatically be ANDed, and you can use quotation marks for phrases and a minus sign to exclude a term. There is no advanced search page, but on results pages, you can narrow results by Size (buddy icon, small, medium, large, wallpaper), File types (.jpg, .gif, .png, .bmp), and Color (all colors, color, black & white). Results pages show 36 thumbnails with URLs, dimensions, and file size. Click on a thumbnail to go to a split screen with image thumbnail and details at the top and page of origin at the bottom.

Other Searchable Collections

There are a number of other searchable collections that contain images from webpages. The general web search engines just discussed contain the largest collections by far, but you may want to examine the three directories of image resources listed earlier to identify searchable collections in specific subject areas. The following description of Picsearch highlights one of the best-known alternative web-image search engines.

Picsearch

www.picsearch.com

   Like the general web search engines, Picsearch, which only does images, gathers its image collection by crawling the web. Based on comparative searches, you can expect it to deliver fewer results than Google, Yahoo!, and Bing but more than Ask.com and Exalead. The terms you enter in Picsearch's main search box are automatically ANDed, and you can use a minus sign to eliminate a term and quotation marks for phrases, but Picsearch does not allow the use of an OR. The Picsearch advanced search page lets you limit by image type (Only Images, Only Animations, Images and Animations), color (Only Color, Only Black & White, Color and Black & White), orientation (Portrait, Landscape, Square, All), and size.

Getting Images You Can Use

If you are looking for a high-quality image for use in a publication or on a website and you don't want to worry about possibly violating copyright or tracking down an owner to ask permission, consider going to a commercial collection of images (stock image library) where you can buy the right to use an image. Corbis and Fotosearch are two examples of sites where you can do this. Other websites, such as Stock.XCHNG, provide a place where photographers display their works so others can use the images without charge. Another free option is the image collection searchable through the Creative Commons website.

Corbis

corbis.com

Drawing upon a range of collections—the Bettmann Collection, the Hermitage Museum, UPI, and 1,500 other collections—Corbis collects and sells a variety of photography, fine art, illustrations, etc. The collection contains 100 million images, with 5 million of them searchable online.

Fotosearch

www.fotosearch.com

Fotosearch lets you browse, search, and view images (for free), and then purchase usage rights for 5.6 million images (plus video and audio) from more than 100 image publishers.

Creative Commons

creativecommons.org

Creative Commons is a nonprofit organization that provides a registry of "some rights reserved" materials, including images, audio, video, text, and teaching materials. On the Creative Commons home page, click on the Find link, then on the next page, enter your search terms in the search box.

Stock.XCHNG

www.sxc.hu

With the SXC site, you can browse or search nearly 400,000 stock photos from more than 30,000 photographers. You must be signed up to download the full-size image, but if you want to use high-quality photos for free, signing up will be worth the couple minutes it takes.

Exemplary Individual Collections

By browsing through the directories of image resources discussed earlier, users can view hundreds or perhaps thousands of sites that contain useful collections of images. The following websites are just two examples of specific collections that demonstrate the possibilities.

American Memory Project

memory.loc.gov

From the Library of Congress, this collection contains more than 9 million digital items from more than 100 historical collections at the Library of Congress. It contains Maps, Motion Pictures, Photos & Prints, Sound Recordings, and Written Materials (Books & Other Printed Texts, Manuscripts, Sheet Music). Even though this is a government site, much of the material on the site is protected by copyright. Use the Browse button to browse by collection or topic, or use the Search page to search across collections.

WebMuseum (Paris)

www.ibiblio.org/wm (or more specifically, www.ibiblio.org/wm/paint)

This impressive collection of artwork is a collaborative project headed by Nicolas Pioch. It is searchable by artist (about 200 of them) and by theme/period (from Gothic to the 20th century, plus Japanese art from all periods).

Websites for Storing and Sharing Your Own Photos

A number of websites let you store your own photos online for free and share them with friends, or you can use the site as a place to keep your photo files. These include, among others, Flickr, Photobucket, SmugMug, Picasa, and others. Flickr is the best-known among these sites.

Flickr

flickr.com

Flickr (owned by Yahoo!) is one of many photo sharing (and storing) sites on the web. It is among the biggest (with hundreds of millions of photos), best-known, and most fully featured. With Flickr, you can upload and save your own photos, as well as arrange them in albums, organize them, tag them and describe them as you wish, share them online, and have them printed. You can browse, search, and view your own photos, and those of others who have made their photos public. There are at least a dozen other significant features to use for either finding pictures or managing your own photo collections on Flickr. Without a paid subscription, the number of photos you can load in any month and the total number of photos you can store is substantial, but there is a limit.

Flickr should be kept in mind not just for its storing, sharing, and organizing functions but also as a very effective image search engine for three reasons: (1) It provides images you won't find in other image search engines; (2) you may be able to get much better precision for your image searches; and (3) it is a good source for images for which you can easily obtain permission to use.

Flickr Content

In contrast to image searching in engines such as Google and Yahoo!, in Flickr a larger proportion of the images are going to be more recent photos of people, places, and events but also images probably not found on regular webpages. You may be surprised, though, as to how many images on Flickr are of such things as drawings, antique maps, etc. In addition to images, Flickr now also contains some videos, screencasts, and other formats.

Precision Searching

Image searching with Flickr can actually be much more precise than image searching in general search engines, since those may rather liberally decide which words to associate with an image. Searches on multiple words in general search engines often yield images where the words were associated with entirely different images located elsewhere on a webpage. In Flickr, the word association is for a single particular image. The tagging of images in Flickr by users can also provide for both better precision and better recall. On Flickr, images may now also be "geotagged" by the contributors.

Search Options

The main search box provides tabs for searching Photos, Groups (Group names and descriptions or group discussions), or People (name or email addresses of Flickr members or their interests). The advanced search page provides simple Boolean and phrase searching in combination with searching of either the full text associated with the image or just tags. It also provides searching by content type (photos, videos, etc.), date (date taken or date posted), a SafeSearch filter, and, for registered users, even a Search by Camera option (in Flickr's Camera Finder section).

Flickr for Redistributable Images

If you need an image for a webpage, blog, newsletter, etc., and don't want to incur the cost and time spent in buying stock images, you can easily use Flickr Mail to request permission. (Flickr also provides a Creative Commons search option.)

Clip Art

While still in the category of images, clip art serves a somewhat different function and requires different sources. In the web context, the term usually refers to artwork available on the web, usually but not always free, for use on websites or printed documents. Numerous collections and directories exist for these resources, three of which are listed here. Users should read the fine print carefully. Most of the artwork is free, but you may be required to give a specific acknowledgment of the source.

Free Graphics

www.freegraphics.com

Free Graphics is a resource guide with links to collections of free clip art, graphics, photos, webpage templates, and more. The site is searchable and browsable by more than a dozen categories.

Barry's Clipart

barrysclipart.com

This collection is both searchable and browsable by topic. The tabs at the top of the page lead to other large clip art collections.

Yahoo! Directory > Graphics > Clip Art

dir.yahoo.com/Computers_and_Internet/Graphics/Clip_Art

This section of Yahoo!'s Directory provides links to more than 100 collections of clip art, arranged alphabetically and by category.

Audio and Video

Although probably less frequently used by researchers than the image resources on the internet, audio and video files have a variety of applications beyond just entertainment (though all work and no play makes the extreme searcher a dull person). Accessing these resources is much easier than it was a few years ago, since most computers come with the necessary players, or they at least make it easy to identify and download the necessary player. For most types of files, the same players can be used for both audio and video. One of the greatest advances that made these files easy to use was the advent of "streaming" audio and video players that allow you to begin hearing or seeing the file without having to wait until the file downloads completely, and consequently, to make use of files of almost any length. The one remaining drawback to larger files is the slow transfer time for those users who still do not have a broadband connection. For them, many large files, especially videos, are still virtually inaccessible.

As with viewing images, hearing and viewing sound and video files is easy, but searching them has been the challenging part, mainly because of poor indexing. However, that situation is changing, with more indexing of transcripts and increased amounts of metadata.

Players

For virtually all of the sound and video file types you are likely to encounter (.wav, .au, .avi, .midi, .mp3, .mpeg, etc.), your computer probably came equipped with the software necessary to play them, including the more recent file types, such as the currently dominant, highly compressed, but high-quality sound and video file format MPEG (Moving Pictures Expert Group format, with .mpeg, .mpg, .mp2, and .mp3 file extensions). If you do encounter a file type not currently supported, there is a good chance that there will be a link on the page that leads you to an easy free download of the necessary player. Among the players that many users are likely to encounter are Windows Media Player (pre-installed with all recent Windows operating systems), RealPlayer (a free download for the basic version, with upgrades for a fee), Winamp, Musicmatch, QuickTime (essential for Apple users but also available in a Windows version), and DivX—"The Playa" (for DVD), among others.

Audio

Historic speeches, online radio stations, and other sound resources can be valuable for many reasons, but in terms of frequency of use, the most frequently accessed audio content type on the internet is music. Unfortunately, much of the accessing that is done is illegal due to the violation of copyright. However, there is ample opportunity for legal access to music and also access to other types of useful audio content.

Since unaware serious searchers (and their employers) could easily become the target of copyright infringement suits, the copyright issue should be prominent in the minds of those who download audio and video from the internet. File sharing (peer-to-peer or P2P) among computer users on the internet became very popular very quickly with the advent of the Napster program. (Napster's first life was short, 1999–ca. 2000, but it has now been rehabilitated and legally reincarnated.) The Napster file-sharing concept begat a number of other P2P programs, such as Kazaa, Grokster, Morpheus, and Gnutella, that have allowed listeners to continue to avoid paying for music. The intent of this book is neither to sermonize nor editorialize, but the serious searcher must be aware of the copyright issue.

The next several pages list directories of audio resources, sites that help you find the audio you are looking for, and sites that focus on specific types of audio resources (music, podcasts, radio, speeches, and movie sound clips).

Digital Librarian: A Librarian's Choice of the Best of the Web—Audio
www.digital-librarian.com/audio.html

The Audio section of the Digital Librarian site features more than 500 links—annotated and arranged alphabetically—mostly to sites containing collections of various kinds of audio.

Audio Search Engines

Other than for music searching, the number of sites that provide searches specifically of audio has actually declined in the last few years. The following search engines vary significantly in the content they cover, their searchability, and the added services they provide (such as music sales). Some cover video as well as audio.

PAV–Play Audio Video

www.playaudiovideo.com

PAV, Play Audio Video Multimedia Search, which bills itself as "The World's first Multimedia search engine," has indexed more than 12 million audio files, 18 million videos, and 600 million images. A single search of PAV retrieves all three media in one shot. Though PAV often refers to all of its audio content as *music*, very importantly for the researcher, the audio actually contains a good collection of other audio, such as interviews, speeches, and lectures, both historical and current.

In PAV's homepage search box, an AND operator is implied, you can search for phrases using quotation marks, and you can NOT a term by using a minus sign immediately in front of the term. There is no advanced search link on the main page, but on results pages, you can (a) narrow your results to audio, video, or images, (b) specify that images be small, medium, or large (c) rank results by either relevance or date, and (d) filter what PAV identifies potentially as "pornography." (The PAV folks don't hide behind typical euphemisms such as "adult content.") With the latter menu, you can specify Maybe, Avoid, Put Last, or Allow.

Results pages typically show a ranked selection of audio results, followed by video results and image results. For each individual result, you will see a title, an "I" (Information) icon for which a mouseover will show a date and the site, and a "home" icon, which when clicked takes you to the page containing the file. Depending upon the kind of file (audio, video, image), you may see the file size and format (e.g., mp3), icons to play a preview clip of the full file or see a cached version of the original document, and a "down-arrow" icon that provides instructions for saving the file. For audio and some video, a "Transcoding" icon (a wrench) may be present, which takes you to a page to convert the format of the file (e.g. to mp3 or other format).

Be aware that PAV very knowingly and intentionally indexes a lot of P2P files such as "torrent" (BitTorrent) files that, by their nature, include vast quantities of copyrighted material that may have been copied illegally. The user may be legally liable for downloading such material.

FindSounds

www.findsounds.com

This site is included here as an example of a more specialized audio site. FindSounds specializes in sound effects (and similar sounds such as musical instrument samples). The main page lets you search by topic, file formats, number of channels, minimum resolution, minimum sample rate, and maximum file size. Click on the Types of Sounds You Can Find link for a directory of sounds (categories for animals, birds, holidays, etc.). The results pages show a waveform display, indicating not only loudness (amplitude), but also, by use of color, frequency content. Here you can hear a hippo and also the sounds of a siren, a sapsucker, a shotgun, a storm, a snare drum, and even a snore.

Internet Archive—Audio Archive
www.archive.org

The Internet Archive has stored more than 400,000 recordings including 70,000 recordings from concerts (with the agreement of the artists). The rest is a variety of other music and sounds including recordings from 78-rpm records, presidential speeches, lectures, Creative Commons materials, radio programs, and conference proceedings. The advanced search page can be used to search by title, creator, description, collection, date, and other specific criteria.

Audio Resources: Radio Stations (Real and Virtual)

With thousands of radio stations now providing audio archives of their programs and/or streaming audio of their current broadcasts, great possibilities are open to internet users. Besides the recreational possibilities, these radio resources not only provide another channel for news (see Chapter 8), but they can supply answers for "Who said what and when?" "Did so-and-so really say what she was quoted as having said?" and "What have people been saying about a particular topic?" Although recent interviews may not be available in transcribed form, the audio may be there, whether on a well-known source such as the BBC or on a local radio station. These radio stations can also be valuable to those who are learning a foreign language. The Radio-Locator site will be useful in locating a specific station.

In addition to "real" radio stations, the internet also provides "virtual" radio stations so you can tune in on your computer and listen to your own choice of musical genres. Some of this on-demand music is free, and some requires a subscription. If you subscribe to satellite radio for your car, check with your provider for the possible added capability of accessing their services on your computer as part of your subscription.

Radio-Locator (formerly the MIT List of Radio Stations on the Internet)

www.radio-locator.com

Radio-Locator provides links to more than 10,000 radio station sites worldwide and includes 2,500 with live, streaming audio (for continuous listening). From this site, you can search for radio stations by country, U.S. state or ZIP code, Canadian province, call letters, and station format (classical, rock, etc.). The advanced search page provides searching by multiple criteria, but it limits your results to only the U.S. or Canada.

CBS Radio

www.cbsradio.com/streaming/index.html

The CBS Radio site provides a directory of links to streaming video from more than 150 CBS stations throughout the U.S. It now also powers more than 150 stations on Yahoo! Music (music.yahoo.com) and 200 stations on AOL Radio (music.aol.com/radioguide/bb).

Podcasts

Podcasts are downloadable audio recordings (broadcasts), analogous to blog postings, that have become a source for valuable information and commentary for internet users. Podcasts are "published" using feeds (e.g., RSS) that can be downloaded via the web and transferred to an mp3 player (or to your computer) so you can listen at your convenience. There are a number of programs that will periodically check for new downloads and download them automatically, including, among others, iTunes, Juice, Doppler, and BlogMatrix Sparks.

For locating podcasts of interest, there are several podcast directories and search engines, including the three following podcast search engines and directories. Other sites, such as blinkx, cover podcasts as well as other audio formats. Another good source for podcasts is iTunes, coming up in a few paragraphs.

For users of the podcast search and directory sites, the most important difference among them may be the categories under which the podcasts are organized and whether those particular categories match your needs.

Podscope

www.podscope.com

Podscope bridges three of the main topics discussed in this chapter—audio search, podcasts, and video search. It also exemplifies one of the important technological directions for audio and video: the ability to search for the spoken word, not just by the indexing of transcripts, but through voice recognition technology. The aim of the Podscope creator (TVEyes) is ultimately to cover a broad range of multimedia content, beginning with podcasts.

On the main page, you can search for audio, video, or both, or you can search by clicking on one of the more popular tags that you see on the main page. Search capabilities are quite limited (to a single word or phrase) and results can be pretty far off (largely because every word spoken in a podcast episode can be indexed). Search results show the episode title, the date, and the source (the podcast). Links beside each result take you to the webpage of the podcast and allow you to play the episode. Results are sorted by date, but there is also a link that sorts them by ranking score. Though the initial search functions are limited, the voice recognition and indexing technology is very promising, and Podscope is a good place to explore some of the possibilities.

Podcast Alley

www.podcastalley.com

Podcast Alley provides a directory of podcasts, arranged into 19 genres. Click on a category to see the list, then click on a specific title to see a description plus links for more details, to subscribe, or to vote for the podcast. If you click on the Details link, you will be shown descriptions of recent episodes with a link to download the episodes. Podcast Alley also provides a search box that enables you to search the titles and descriptions of podcasts (but not the episodes). Terms you enter in the search box are ORed. Podcast Alley also provides a useful forum about podcasts and links to information on podcast software.

Podcastdirectory.com

www.podcastdirectory.com

Podcastdirectory.com provides a search option but emphasizes browsing by category. You can browse for podcasts by country, region, city, state, genre, language, popularity, and "buzz" (what people are looking for on the directory today), and on a Google Map. The latter is a Google mashup that shows the location of the podcasters on a map. Each of the browsing options provides extensive subcategories. A keyword search is also available on the main page. The terms you enter there are automatically ANDed, and you can use ORs, a minus in front of terms for a NOT, and quotation marks for phrases.

Browsing results usually show the podcast's logo, its name, and a brief description. Click on the name to get to a fuller description and a list of episodes, each with its own description. Search results show similar information and also provide, at the top of results pages, links to search episodes, search internet radio, and search video podcasts.

A Sampling of Other Audio Resources
The History Channel: Speeches & Video

www.historychannel.com/video

A search in this section of The History Channel site will deliver links to a variety of audio and video resources on the site. On the main page, you can browse by show and by topic. The Speeches link at the top of the page is a starting point for access to a great collection of historical speeches. Even if you are not a history buff or scholar, you are at great risk of being captivated by what this site provides.

The Movie Sounds Page

www.moviesounds.com

This is a source for sound clips from more than 80 major movies. The Sound Tools page has a very good collection of links to audio editing tools.

Music Search and Sales

Some of the sites already mentioned provide a way to search for music and serve as "music stores." More and more companies have gotten into the online music sales competition, including "stores" such as Amazon. The following two sites are among the current leaders in legal music downloads; their descriptions will provide a glimpse of the possibilities.

Apple: iPod & iTunes

www.apple.com/itunes

On the iPod and iTunes website, you can download iTunes, a combination of digital jukebox, music download store, music manager, CD burner, general player for other audio files, and more. Early on, and especially because of the iPod connection, iTunes took the leadership among online music stores, allowing you to not just purchase songs legally, but also to create your own library of music and video, both by purchasing music online and by importing music and videos from your own digital music library. From there, you can organize your library, "sync" to your iPod, listen on your computer, create your own CDs, and do several other tasks. On the "store" side, you can use the iTunes software to go online and download any of more than 10 million songs, plus music videos, TV shows, audiobooks, and podcasts (the latter usually free).

When you select the iTunes Store option on iTunes, you can use the search box near the top of the window to search by keyword (artists, song, etc.). On search results pages, you will see a button where you can narrow your results by Music, Movies, TV Shows, Applications, Music Videos, Audio Books, Podcasts, or iTunes U (educational materials). The Radio option in the iTunes Source section provides access to hundreds of radio stations (both internet and "real") arranged by genre.

iTunes also provides a podcast directory (Figure 7.4). Click on Podcasts from the iTunes Library list, and toward the bottom of the resulting screen, you will see a Podcast Directory link that will take you to the Podcasts section of the Music Store. From there, you can either search or browse for podcasts of interest to download.

Figure 7.4

iTunes podcast directory

Video

In terms of usefulness and applications, most of what can be said about audio resources on the internet is also true for video resources. In most cases, the same players that can be used for audio are used for video (although you may find that your computer is not equipped with Apple's QuickTime Movie Player, available also for PCs, which is worthwhile to download if you run across a file that requires it).

To look for video, try the following places:

- For news video, try news services such as BBC, CNN, and MSNBC, plus local radio and TV station websites.
- Use the video search capabilities of Yahoo! or Google.
- Look around on subject-specific sites such as The History Channel and American Memory (discussed previously under Audio).
- Use the BUBL LINK video resource guide that follows.

Directory of Video Resources on the Internet
BUBL LINK: Catalogue of Internet Resources—Video
bubl.ac.uk/link/v/video.htm

The BUBL LINK page is actually a directory of directories, providing annotated descriptions and links to more than a dozen sites, each of which, in turn, provides collections of links to video resources for a variety of subject areas.

Video Search Engines

Watching videos has become a major activity on the web and finding videos has become very easy with video search offerings from all of the major search engines, as well as on video sites themselves, such as YouTube. Along with the opportunities provided by the vast quantity of video available, video indexing and search technologies have expanded, including the use of enhanced RSS to provide additional metadata that can be attached to a video or audio file, the tagging of videos by individuals, and the use of voice recognition technologies to create transcripts of news and TV shows.

As mentioned previously, all of the major web search engines provide a video search. They differ primarily in terms of the sources for the video they index and in the search features they provide. As with web search, if you want to be exhaustive or want to find something very obscure, you may want to try at least two or three of the video search sites.

Google's Video Search

video.google.com

Google claims that its video search index is the most comprehensive on the web. A large proportion of its content comes from YouTube (owned by Google), with other content obtained from the crawling of other websites across the web. In the main search box, you can do the same types of searches as with a Google Web search, including the use of ORs, a minus in front of a term for a NOT, and quotation marks for phrases. You may also want make use of the *title:* and *site:* prefixes, for example, *market OR marche intitle:montmartre site:youtube.com*

Using the advanced video search page, you can search by simple Boolean, duration (less than 4 minutes, 4–20 minutes, more than 20 minutes), language, when uploaded (today, past week, past month), availability of "closed captioning" (subtitles, as in "movie subtitles"), domain (e.g., youtube.com, myspace.com), and file type (.avi, .mov, etc.), and narrow results to those videos that are playable directly on the Google site. Search results can be sorted by relevance, date added, number of times the video has been viewed, or user ratings.

Yahoo!'s Video Search

video.yahoo.com

Yahoo!'s video collection contains video gathered by crawling the web, video gathered directly from video publishers, and video uploaded by users. As with some other Yahoo! offerings, the sophistication of Yahoo!'s Video Search has declined in the last few years, but it still offers one of the most substantial collections of crawled web video content.

In the search box on the Yahoo! Video Search main page, all terms you enter are automatically ANDed, and you can use quotation marks for a specific phrase. You cannot use the OR. The advanced video search permits you to use simple Boolean, specify format (avi, mpeg, QuickTime, Windows Media, Real, Flash), specify duration (all lengths, less than 1 minute, 1–4 minutes, longer than 4 minutes), and site/domain (.com, .edu, .gov, .org, or a specific domain). You can also apply a SafeSearch filter.

Figure 7.5

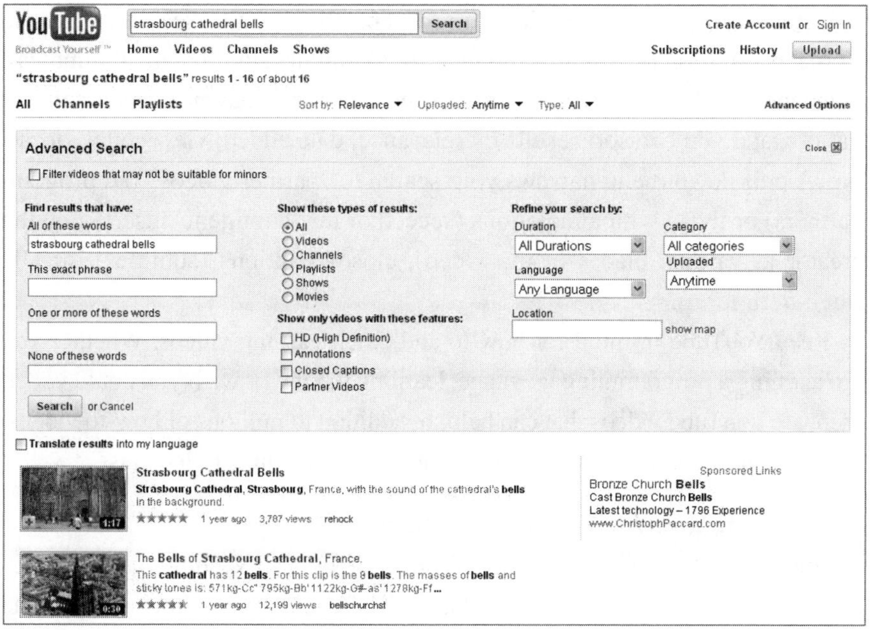

YouTube advanced search page

YouTube

youtube.com

YouTube, owned by Google, has become not just an entertainment site and a place to share one's own videos, but it is also becoming a significant research tool. As you have undoubtedly noticed, YouTube's popularity has grown astoundingly, as has its size (13 hours of video is uploaded every minute). Unlike the video search engines just discussed, which index video found on other sites, all of the YouTube video is stored on the YouTube site. Individuals or organizations can upload a video in as little as a couple of minutes.

YouTube is both browsable and searchable. For browsing, the main page offers some suggestions (Videos Being Watched Now, Most Popular), but for a more extensive browsing experience, click on the Videos link beneath the search box, which will take you to a list of 15 categories (Comedy, Education, How-To, News & Politics, etc.) and Movies, Contests, Events, etc.

YouTube's powerful searching options are a bit hidden—you don't see the Advanced Options link until you've clicked the search button. Once you've found and clicked on the Advanced Options link (Figure 7.5) though, you will find several video search features, permitting you to search by simple Boolean, duration (less than 4 minutes, 4–20 minutes, more than 20 minutes), language, and location. You can filter out videos that may not be suitable for minors, and you can sort results by relevance, date added, view count, or rating. A pull-down menu narrows your search to "partner videos" (ad program partners) or those with annotations (speech or text comments inserted by the creator at various places in the video), closed captions (subtitles), or HD (high-definition).

Keep YouTube in mind for how-to and other learning videos. Whether you are learning a programming language, learning to knit, or wish you could yodel, there are YouTube videos that can help. In addition to millions of how-to videos, there are more than 130,000 YouTube videos indexed under "lectures."

Search Engines for Video—TV-Specific

If you are looking for video of TV news or other TV shows and want to search for it easily and effectively, take advantage of the following sites. The first one, blinkx, is free (and includes more than just TV), while the other two that follow require a fee.

blinkx

www.blinkx.tv

At blinkx, you can get more than 35 million hours of video including lots of TV footage. With a number of major news suppliers, you will be taking advantage of full-text searching of every word spoken on the video, made possible through advanced voice recognition and speech-to-text technology, which lets blinkx automatically create transcripts of the audio and video content and index it. The search function, though, also extends to metadata beyond just the content of those transcripts. On top of that, it's free.

Click on the Partners link on the main page to see the impressive list of participants, including almost all major TV networks, newspapers such as the *New York Times* and the *Washington Post*, plus other sources such as *Forbes*, Public Radio, the Discovery Channel, the Biography Channel, and the Comedy Channel. Search terms you enter are automatically ANDed, and you can use ORs and NOTs in your search statements. You can also browse videos by category.

On results pages, you will find an RSS button that will quickly set up an RSS feed for you on the topic you searched. Look around the site for a number of other features, such as Wall It, which provides a 5x5 "wall" of videos (on any topic) that you can put on a blog or website.

ShadowTV

www.shadowtv.com

ShadowTV is a fee-based service that monitors major networks, cable stations, and local affiliates and serves as a clipping service with automatic notification. At present, it just covers U.S. stations. It makes video available within a few minutes of when it was broadcast and also includes an archive dating back further.

TVEyes

www.tveyes.com

TVEyes is a fee-based search of radio and TV content from stations in the U.S., the U.K., the Middle East, Canada, Greece, and China. It indexes the audio feeds from these by means of voice-recognition technology and provides alerts and a searchable archive. Though it is fee-based, take a look at either the samples you can get online for free or sign up for a full demo.

CHAPTER 8

NEWS RESOURCES

Once more, the word "amazing" has to be used. To be able to read the headline stories from a newspaper 10,000 miles away, sometimes before the paper appears on local residents' doorsteps, is indeed amazing. This chapter covers the range of news resources available (news services and newswires, newspapers, news aggregation services, etc.) and how to most effectively find and use them. Importantly, this chapter emphasizes some limitations with which the researcher is faced, particularly in regard to archival and exhaustivity (comprehensiveness) issues.

TYPES OF NEWS SITES ON THE INTERNET

Understanding news resources on the web is challenging not just because there is such a broad and rich expanse of news available, but because almost every news site is designed differently from the next, with differing functions and missions. In "ancient" times, it was relatively easy to group news resources into categories such as newspapers, magazines and journals, radio, and TV. Today, it is harder to definitively categorize the types of places to go on the web for news. Although many typologies of news sources are possible, the following categories can prove to be helpful in sorting things out (while recognizing that there is considerable overlap and that many sites fit in more than one category):

- Major news networks and newswire sites – Sites that are original sources for news stories but may also gather and provide stories from other sources
- Aggregation sites – Sites that serve primarily to gather news stories from multiple sources
- Newspaper and magazine sites – Sites that serve as the online version for a printed newspaper or magazine

- Radio and TV sites
- Multi-source news search engines – Sites that provide extensive search capabilities for a broad range of news sources
- Specialized news services – Sites that focus on news in a particular subject area
- Email (or RSS) alert services – Sites that provide a personalized selection of current news stories on a regular basis

FINDING NEWS—A GENERAL STRATEGY

A good starting point for finding news on the web is to ask the question, What kind of news are you looking for?

1. Are you interested in breaking news (today's headlines)?
2. Do you need older news stories?
3. Do you want to be kept up-to-date automatically on a topic?

For breaking news, you might start with virtually any of the categories listed earlier, depending upon the breadth of your interests, both with regard to subject and with regard to the local, national, or international perspective needed. If you want to browse headlines, consider bookmarking and personalizing a general portal (such as My Yahoo! or iGoogle) and perhaps using it as the start page for your browser. Headlines in categories of your choice will show up every time you open your browser (or click Home). Alternatively, you might choose a news network site (BBC, MSNBC, etc.) or your favorite newspaper as your start page.

For older news stories, the choice is much more limited. If you are interested in the last few weeks, one of the general search engines may serve best. For international or high-profile news going back a few years, BBC may be a good choice because it provides searching of all stories covered on its site back to 1997. If your interest is more local, check to see if the local paper has searchable archives. To search the most retrospective collection of news on the web, take advantage of Google News' archive search, with some sources going back to the 18th century.

If you need to keep up-to-date on a particular topic, definitely take advantage of one of the news alert services and have headlines relating to your interests delivered to you by email.

Characteristics to Look for When Accessing News Resources

For a research project or question, particularly when it is important that you know what you have and have not covered in your research, it is imperative that you be aware of exactly the kinds of items and time frames particular news sites include. You certainly do not need to know this for every search, but the following factors are among the major content variables encountered among news sources on the web:

- Time frame covered – Some sites cover only today; others go back weeks, months, or years.

- Portion of the original publication actually included – Particularly for newspapers and magazines, there is great variation as to how much of the print version is available online.

- Sources covered – Some sites may draw only from a single newswire service; others may include thousands of sources. Some go beyond the more traditional news sources and also cover blogs.

- Currency – Although "old news" can be tremendously valuable, *news* often implies *new*. Depending on the site, the stories may be only minutes old, whereas for other sites, the delay in posting stories may be considerably more.

- Searchability – Some sites only allow you to get to stories by browsing through a list or by category. Other sites allow searching by keyword, date, and other criteria. Look around on any news site for a search box.

- Availability of alert services – Although the service may not be emphasized, on many sites, if you dig around a bit, you may find that a free email alert service is available. Some sites exist specifically as alert services.

- Availability of RSS feeds – RSS as a concept is discussed near the end of the chapter. However, until you get there, RSS stands for Really Simple Syndication and, briefly, is a mechanism whereby a website, such as a news source, can code its pages so that stories are automatically distributed ("syndicated") to any website (or web user) that chooses to automatically receive those stories.

- Personalization capabilities – Some sites may allow you to personalize the site, so that when you sign in to your account, headlines in categories of your choice are displayed, along with your local news, weather, and sports.

NEWS RESOURCE GUIDES

With thousands of news sites out there, this chapter can only include a few selected sites. To find out about other sites, take advantage of one of the several good news resource guides. The guides listed here are among the more highly regarded. Each provides somewhat different options in terms of coverage and searchability or browsability. One of the most important uses of the first five sites listed here is the easy identification of newspapers and other news resources for virtually any country or large city in the world. If you need to know the website for the local newspaper in Kathmandu, these resource guides will lead you there. You will find it worthwhile to go to one of these guides, choose a country, and spend a few minutes browsing through the sites for that country. The other guides mentioned here focus on finding specific news features—political cartoons and "news in pictures" sites.

Kidon Media-Link

www.kidon.com/media-link

Kidon Media-Link is arranged to let you browse nearly 20,000 media sites by continent and country, but it also has a search section where you can search by a combination of media types (newspaper, radio station, etc.) and either by city or by words in the title of the site. It will also display sites by language (English, Spanish, French, German, Italian, Portuguese, Arabic, Russian, Chinese, and Dutch). Symbols indicate whether streaming audio and video are available on the sites (Figure 8.1).

ABYZ News Links

www.abyznewslinks.com

ABYZ News Links contains mostly newspapers, but it also includes many broadcast stations, web services, magazines, and press agencies. For some countries and localities, ABYZ offers more links than Kidon Media-Link (and for some, fewer links). The search page on the site does a Google site search. You can browse by continent and country.

Figure 8.1

Kidon Media-Link continent page

Metagrid

www.metagrid.com

Metagrid covers not just newspapers but also magazines, for which it provides a nice browsable directory by subject. It covers altogether 8,000 sites.

NewsLink

newslink.org

In addition to browsing newspapers worldwide by continent and country, NewsLink allows you to browse U.S. newspapers by the following categories: National Papers, Most-linked-to (state or type), Major Metros,

Dailies, Non-dailies, Business, Alternative, Specialty, or Campus papers by state. It also has a collection of magazines and radio and stations (U.S. only). You can search for sources by city and state, and specify All, Newspaper, TV, or Radio. It covers considerably fewer sites than Kidon Media-Link, and dead links are frequently a problem.

NewsWealth
www.newswealth.com

NewsWealth has a respectable number of links to newspapers around the world, but its strength is in the other kinds of browsable news resource categories it provides. These include Magazines, Columnists, Blogs, Cartoons, Celeb Gossip, Sports, Business, Weather, Live Cams, Scanners Live, and Lotto Results.

News Resource Guides—Specialty Content
News in Pictures
www.newsinpictures.com

News in Pictures is a collection of links to more than 100 sites, with sections such as Photos of the Day and News in Pictures. Links are arranged according to the following categories: News, Sports, Disaster, Entertainment, History, Science, Miscellaneous, News in Video, USA Local News, and World News.

Daryl Cagle's Professional Cartoonists Index
www.cagle.com

Daryl Cagle's Professional Cartoonists Index is more than a resource guide with links to other sites; it actually contains the political cartoons from almost 200 cartoonists dating back to late-2000. You can browse and search for free, and you can purchase rights to reprint a cartoon from the site. On the home page, you can browse by topic, and if you click on the Search for a Cartoon link, you can search by keyword, date, coloration, and artist.

MAJOR NEWS NETWORKS AND NEWSWIRES

Major news networks and newswires have sites that provide news items that they themselves have produced, although they may use and incorporate other sources as well. Sites such as BBC, CNN, and MSNBC are the choice of many web users for breaking news, because the headlines are updated continually. They also typically provide a number of other items of information beyond news headlines, such as weather. These are sites for which the "click everywhere" principle emphatically applies. By spending some time clicking around on the page, clicking through the index links at the bottom of the main page, and browsing through the site index, you can get an idea of the true richness of these sites.

Newswire services such as Reuters, UPI, AP, and Agence France Presse are primarily in the business of providing stories to other news outlets. Their sites contain current headlines and perhaps substantially more, but they may also be more a brochure for the service.

BBC

news.bbc.co.uk

A large portion of searchers throughout the world consider BBC (Figure 8.2) the best news site on the web. It is particularly noted for its international coverage (BBC "International Version"). In the international section of some U.S. services, "international" seems to be defined as "news from abroad that is of particular interest to the U.S." BBC's international coverage, though, is much more truly international.

Among the site's strengths are its easy browsability, its search capability, and the availability of free searchable archives going back to November 1997. The BBC news site is only one small portion of what the overall BBC site offers. If you go to the U.K. version, you will find a link to Explore the BBC. Browse through that page to find content ranging from Adult Learning to Zimbabwe. (Speaking of adult learning, check out the BBC's Languages section.) On the news home page, look for the Video and Audio section, the Country Profiles, and the free email and newsfeed services.

All content comes from BBC writers, though they may utilize other sources such as Reuters in writing their stories.

The search box allows searching by multiple keywords, and all the terms you enter are automatically ANDed. You can also make use of quotation marks for phrase searching. On the results pages, you can use tabs near the top of the page to narrow your results to BBC News & Sport or TV & Radio Programmes. On the right side of the results pages, the first few audio and video records are displayed along with links to play them.

Figure 8.2

BBC News home page (International Version)

CNN

www.cnn.com

CNN.com, a Time Warner company, has been displaying an increasingly international perspective, partly in connection with CNN's strong presence on European TV. It has U.S. and international editions as well as interfaces in several languages (Arabic, English, Japanese, Korean, Spanish, and Turkish). The site, which is particularly rich in video, features a Video section of the home page that makes it easy to browse recent videos. Click on the Video link, and you can easily move to other videos and search for video. Use the links at the bottom of pages to sign up to receive audio and video podcasts, daily or weekly email news alerts, RSS feeds, desktop alerts, and mobile access.

MSNBC

www.msnbc.com

The MSNBC site has an excellent fly-out menu (under Categories on the main page) for browsing through headlines by category and subcategory. The front page also provides lead stories, a stock market overview, video, and a search box. In addition to MSNBC's own stories, you will find stories from local NBC stations, AP, *Newsweek*, and other sources. Most stories remain available online for a few weeks, some for many months. U.S. users can sign in and personalize this site by entering their ZIP code; they will then see local news, weather, and sports headlines at the bottom of the main page. There is a free email option and a number of RSS and podcast feed options available.

Reuters

reuters.com

Reuters.com provides content from Reuters journalists around the world. The site lets you browse through general, financial, and investment news for the last day or so, and the search box allows retrieval of stories going back to 2006. The site is searchable by keyword, company name, or stock symbol, and you can browse current stories using 10 main news categories on the home page. Searching by company name or ticker symbol leads to stock quotes for the company and company profiles, news, and other enterprise information. Reuters also provides free email newsletters and alerts.

Aljazeera.net

english.aljazeera.net

There is definitely some truth to Aljazeera's motto that "now when Aljazeera speaks, the world listens and 'reads'." The content on this site is aimed primarily at the Arab world and is presented from an Arab perspective. The Arabic version is available at www.aljazeera.net, and it is important to note that the content there is not identical to the English version.

NEWSPAPERS

Thousands of sites for individual newspapers are available on the web. There may still be a few newspaper sites that contain an insignificant number of actual stories, but most contain at least the major stories for the current day, and most contain an archive covering a few days, a few months, or even several years. Most online versions of newspapers do not contain sections such as the classified ads (or display ads) that appear in the print version. Some online versions contain things that are not in the print version, such as profiles of local companies.

Although most people are not likely to completely desert the print version of their favorite newspaper for a while to come, the online versions do provide some obvious advantages, such as searchability and archives. Some also provide greater currency, with updates during the day. Perhaps the most obvious advantage is simply availability—the fact that newspapers from around the world are available at your fingertips almost instantly. Take advantage of the availability of distant papers particularly when doing research on issues, industries, companies, and people. For industries, take advantage of specialized coverage in newspapers dependent upon their location. For example, the *San Jose Mercury News* (online version, MercuryNews.com) is strong on technology because of its location in Silicon Valley, the *Washington Post* is strong on coverage of U.S. government, and Detroit papers are strong on the auto industry. In any geographic area, for companies and for people, the local paper is likely to give more coverage than larger papers.

More and more newspaper archives are available online. In some cases, you can get recent stories for free, but you have to pay for earlier stories. The price is usually quite reasonable, especially considering the cost to obtain them through alternative document-delivery channels.

Use the news resource guides mentioned earlier to find the names and websites for papers throughout the world. For availability of newspaper archives, check the site for the particular paper. Keep in mind that commercial services such as NewsLibrary, Factiva, LexisNexis, and Dialog have newspaper archives that may predate what is available on the newspaper's website. If you are not in an organization that has a library that provides access to some of these, your local public library may.

Newspapers—Front Pages

The following two sites provide a look at the actual pages of newspapers.

Today's Front Pages

www.newseum.org/todaysfrontpages

Brought to you by the Newseum, this site offers a look at the actual front pages of more than 700 newspapers from more than 70 countries. On the front page, the thumbnails of the pages are listed alphabetically (by U.S. state and city, and then by other countries and cities). Tabs at the top of the page let you choose a location on a map or regional list. Click on a thumbnail to see a larger view, and from there, you can click on a link that gives you a PDF version that can be enlarged further.

PressDisplay.com

www.pressdisplay.com

The main page of the PressDisplay.com site at first looks like many other news sites, with news headlines and images. Either the Select Title button at the top of the main page or the Titles by Country menu on the left of the page will lead you to thumbnails of the front pages of newspapers, more than 1,000 newspapers from more than 80 countries. When you click on one of the images of a newspaper front page, you will go to images of the full front page. From there you can go to images of all of the news pages of the paper, but to get beyond the front page, you will need to pay, either for a single issue or for a subscription. The window by the search box at the top of the main page permits you to search by time frame, or you can go to an advanced search page and search (within the papers) by newspaper, date, language, and author, and limit to headline.

Radio and TV

Sites for radio and TV stations are excellent sources for breaking news and may also contain audio (and sometimes video) archives of older programs. The next two sites make it easy to locate radio stations from around the world. The third site, NPR, is particularly valuable for its archives of National Public Radio shows.

Radio-Locator (formerly the MIT List of Radio Stations on the Internet)

www.radio-locator.com

Radio-Locator's site offers links to more than 10,000 radio station sites (and 2,500 audio streams) worldwide and allows you to search for radio stations by country, U.S. state or ZIP code, Canadian province, call letters, and station format (classical, rock, etc.).

RadioStationWorld

radiostationworld.com

RadioStationWorld is a directory of thousands of radio stations worldwide organized first by continent, then by country, and then by type of station within the country.

NPR

www.npr.org

This site provides easy access to National Public Radio stations throughout the U.S., and also provides a searchable audio archive of NPR stories and a facility for ordering transcripts. Using the pull-down menu at the top of the page, you can find a list of programs ("All Things Considered," "Car Talk," etc.) and from there, schedules, summaries, and audio files for individual programs.

AGGREGATION SITES

There are a number of sites that have a main function of gathering news stories from a variety of newswires, newspapers, and other news outlets. Also, two of the largest general search engines (Google and Yahoo!) provide extensive news searches of thousands of news sources. (As for the other major search engines' news searches, Ask.com's news search is rather limited in terms of searchability, and Bing utilizes MSNBC's news database and technology, which was discussed earlier.) Among the following sites are the two search engine sites with greatest news search capability and three of the most prominent sites that focus specifically on news aggregation. (See Table 8.1 for a comparison of the numbers of sources, types of sources, language coverage, and retrospectiveness of these sites. Be aware that the numbers will tend to change.) These are all good places to go to make sure you are covering a wide range of sources, and each does the job in a somewhat different way, with differing content and differing browsing and searching capabilities. Another aggregation site, EIN News, is included because of its international coverage and extensive categorization of news

News Search Engine Comparison Chart

Table 8.1

News Search Engine	No. of Sources	Main Types of Sources	Languages	Retrospective
Google	25,000	Newspapers, newswires, TV, radio, selected blogs	Main site in English, retrieves multiple languages 64 regional (country) editions	30 days and Archive Search (with some content going back 200+ years)
Yahoo!	7,000	Newspapers, newswires, TV, radio	35 languages	30 days
NewsNow	37,000	Newspapers, newswires, TV, radio, RSS, blogs	15+ languages	30 days
EIN News	35,000	Newspapers and online sources	Multiple languages	12 days
World News Network	20,000	Newspapers, newswires, TV, radio	53 languages	6 months

stories. The final site covered is World News Network, an international network of news sites.

Google News

news.google.com

In 2009, Google's main news search went from covering 4,500 English language sources (and about 3,000 sources in other languages) to covering 25,000 sources, the additional number primarily representing blogs. It crawls the sites continually, which means that you may be able to find some things on Google only minutes after they appear in the original source. Items are retained in Google's news database for 30 days, and Google provides a powerful free alert service, along with a news search in many of its country-specific news sections. You can access these by means of the pull-down menu on the main news search page. For the 72 regional (country/language) versions, Google will retrieve the same records as in the U.S. version, but the local (country/language) results will appear first on the results pages.

On Google's news page, you will find headlines arranged in nine categories (Top Stories, World, U.S. Business, etc.) with three leading stories for each (Figure 8.3). If you have a Google account, you can personalize the page by changing the order of appearance of the sections, adding additional sections from the non-U.S. Google News versions. You can also add a local section based on your own location, add a custom section that identifies stories based on keywords you choose, and add a Recommended section that displays headlines related to earlier news searches you have done (if you have enabled Google's Web History option).

Each news story record has the title, an indication of how long ago the story was indexed, a 25 to 40 word excerpt, and links to related stories from other sources. Sources for each story are chosen algorithmically, rather than by human editors. If the story has a photo, a thumbnail appears beside the story summary. The small In the News section provides links to 10 hot topics.

On the left side of the page, links for each of the news categories will take you to a full page of 20 top stories for that category. Below that is a link for an image version of the page.

Figure 8.3

Google News

In the search box, you can use prefixes such as *intitle:* and *inurl:*. (However, for narrowing down to a specific news source, the *source:* prefix will probably work best, e.g., *inflation source:"wall street journal."*) Google has an advanced news search that allows you to use simple Boolean, search by source, location, and date, and narrow by limiting to occurrence of your terms in the headline, the body, or the URL of the record. Search results look very similar to web search results, but you will also find a Sort by Date link that conveniently arranges results with the most recent first as well as links that allow you to select various timeframes.

Although news records are retained on Google for 30 days, for some sources, the article may not be there when you click, especially for newspapers that have dynamic pages that change frequently or that keep older articles in a separate archive database (mainly for fee-based access). Unlike Google web search, Google News does not offer a cached copy of news pages.

Even though the main Google News search only includes content going back 30 days, retrospectiveness does not end there. Google's news archive search allows searching of news content that goes back over 200 years. This includes content provided directly by publishers (Google "partners") and archived news content that Google has found by crawling the web. The search is free, but for most articles, you will need to pay the provider to see the full article. With the advanced archive search, you can search by date, language, source, and price. The results page shows a very handy timeline that enables you to narrow your search to a particular time frame. (This is a great resource for genealogists, as well as historians and other researchers.)

Yahoo! News

news.yahoo.com

For years, Yahoo! News has been a favorite place on the web for newsseekers. It covers more than 7,000 news sources in 35 languages. The content comes from news providers such as AP, Reuters, Agence France Presse, the *Washington Post*, *USA Today*, *LA Times*, *Chicago Tribune*, and NPR, plus news found from crawling thousands of other news sites on the web. Most stories are retained for 30 days.

The main page displays a featured article (usually with links to video and a photo slideshow) and five headlines from each of 15 news categories (U.S.,

Business, World, Entertainment, etc.). Links to a full news page for each section plus to content such as videos, photos, blogs and comics are located across the top of the main page (Figure 8.4). The Site Index link there leads to a clickable display listing each of the major news sources (AP, NPR, Politico, etc.) covered in each category. On the Site Index page, you will also find a link for Local News and menus for Comics and Editorial Cartoons.

Figure 8.4

Yahoo! News

The main page also contains links to video news, photo slideshows, obituaries, RSS feeds, and weather alerts.

With the search box on the main page, you can search All News, Yahoo! News Only (the news from partner sources), News Photos, or Video/Audio. In the search box, you can use most of the same techniques you use in a Yahoo! web search (OR, *intitle:, inurl:,* etc.) plus two other prefixes, *headline:* for headlines and *author:* for author or photographer (to search both first and last name, you must use curly braces around the name, for example, *korea author:{mark smith}*).

If you use the Advanced Search link next to the News Search box, you can use simple Boolean; sort results by relevance or date; narrow your search by date, source, location, categories, and language; and specify the number of results to be shown on each results page. (Yahoo! News used to cover all languages automatically. Now to get languages other than English, you must search specifically for the desired language.)

News search results look much the same as web search results, with the story title, date, and first line of the story, source, and when it was retrieved but without a cache link. For crawled, non-partner sources, clicking on a story takes you to the page on which it was found. Click on the link for a story from a Yahoo! news partner (indicated by a notation such as *AFP via Yahoo! News)* for access to many additional features, such as links to video, RSS feeds, a link to add that source automatically to your My Yahoo! page, a link to create an alert on the topic, a link to email the story, and more.

NewsNow

newsnow.co.uk

NewsNow is in the business of providing newsfeeds to other organizations and sites, and it was the first major news aggregation site dedicated to a U.K. audience (but actual coverage is very international). It covers more than 37,000 sources and updates from them every few minutes. From the NewsNow home page you can either search or browse by category. The categories are a major strength of the site, and the 11 main categories are broken down into hundreds of subcategories. Using these categories, you can quickly and easily focus in on news relevant to your specific areas of interest. In the search box, you can use multiple words (they are automatically ANDed), and you can use quotation marks for phrases.

EIN News

www.einnews.com

EIN is a business information and online news service that draws from 5,000 newspapers and online publications, designed "for all who need to, or want to, think globally." Its major strength is signaled by the more than 300 browsable categories you see on the main page (and by the 200,000 news feeds organized within 50 individual news sites that it generates). The categories include countries, regions, U.S. states, and topics. The categories enable the user to easily browse within a country to the topics of interest or within a topic to the locality of interest. For example, if you click on Slovenia, you will see current headlines relating to Slovenia, but you will also see subject categories there that allow you to find, for example, Oil & Gas News specifically related to Slovenia. This ability to quickly sort out the news in such way is outstanding. The bad news is that to see the text of the stories you have identified, you will need a subscription or will need to track down the story elsewhere. In EIN's search box, terms you enter are automatically ANDed, and you can use ORs, quotation marks for phrases, parentheses for nesting terms, and an asterisk at the end of the word to search variant endings.

World News Network
wn.com

World News Network is an impressive network that aggregates more than 20,000 news sources packaging them into more than 1,000 sub-sites by country, industry, region, and more. The main page provides headlines and a list of categories for Regions, Politics, Entertainment, Science, Health, Technology, Sport, Business, Cities, and Photographers, with subcategories for most of those. The regional categories lead to individual country news sites; the subject categories lead to news for a tremendous variety of subjects ranging from nuclear waste to cocoa. Stories are held for six months.

The search options on the main page offer a search by a combination of keywords and language, and the advanced search lets you search by keywords, simple Boolean, and language, and sort your results by relevance or date. Consider taking advantage of the free email alert services found within the various sections.

SPECIALIZED NEWS SERVICES

Having a site for specialized news for a particular industry, area of technology, and so on can be not just useful, but sometimes critical for those who need to make sure they are not missing important developments in that area. Such sites exist for a tremendous variety of subjects. In some cases, they are news-only sites, but in some cases, specialized news is just one function of the site. For a good idea of the possibilities, go to the World News Network (just discussed) and click on the WN Sitemap link (found at the bottom of the main page). There alone, you will find more than 1,000 specialized news sites. One very simple yet effective approach to finding a specialized news site is to use a web search engine and search for the industry or topic and the word *news*, for example, *paper industry news*. A good example of a more specialized news aggregator site is Silobreaker, which focuses on national security-type issues and presents the news in a very innovative way.

SiloBreaker

www.silobreaker.com

Silobreaker is a news aggregator with its main focus on issues related to national security. By means of relational analysis, visualization tools, and identification of entities, connections, trends, and related topics, it provides a really easy way to not just get to news stories but also to better understand the context of the stories. It covers more than 10,000 news, blog, research, video, and other sources.

At the top of Silobreaker's main page, you will see six browsable news categories. Above that, you will find a search box, and on the left side of the page, current major stories. The uniqueness of the site begins to be seen on right side of the page, where you will see, among other things, snapshots of what is provided by Silobreaker's visualization tools (Trends, In Focus, Hotspots, Network). Do a search on a specific topic and you will see in the In Focus box a list of "entities" that match your term. (Hold your cursor over one and you will see facts about that entity, usually with a link to a more detailed, frequently updated fact sheet). This time the visualization displays will be specific to your topic.

Silobreaker tools include:

- Network – A graphic showing connections between related topics (entities). Click on the graph for a larger, more detailed view and to reconfigure the view for emphasis on companies, organizations, persons, cities, and key phrases.
- In Focus – A list of searchable entities related to your topic.
- Hot Spots – A map showing locations of current news stories.
- Trends – A graph showing the recent frequencies of stories on related entities. With the "360° Search," you will see more of an "overview" for your topic, including snapshots of all of the relevant graphics and other tools.

In the main search box, you can enter one or more terms connected with AND, OR, or NOT, use quotation marks for phrases, and use several search prefixes. The Advanced Search link beneath the search box enables you to narrow by content type, specific sources, and date. There's much more, including personalization of your pages, search suggestions, and creating automatic topic filters to apply to subsequent searches.

BLOGS

Fitting, somewhat, into the category of specialty news sites are blogs. These sites (originally known as weblogs) began to appear in very large numbers around 2001. Blogs are, according to blog pioneer Dave Winer, "often-updated sites that point to articles elsewhere on the web, often with comments and to on-site articles." They often focus on topics of very specialized interest and are a good way of keeping up-to-date on such specialized topics. They can range from very useful sites that gather news and provide well-informed commentary to pages of inane ramblings. In any case, they have become a significant part of the "news" content available on the web, and being able to locate either blog sites or individual blog items is now a part of news searching, as indicated by the fact that many of the news sources already discussed in this chapter include blog content. If you find a blogger whose interests closely match yours and the blogger tracks the news in that particular area, you can think of the blogger as your "agent in the field," doing the work of helping to gather your information for you.

Blog Search Engines and Directories

The popularity, usefulness, and proliferation of blogs provides web searchers with the inevitable challenge of finding useful blog sites, and, among the billions of postings, those individual postings that discuss a specific topic. Fortunately, there are a number of sites that provide some substantial search capabilities, often in addition to other blog-related functions such as readers, blog publishing services, and directories.

Be aware though that blog searching presents some unique search problems. Many blog search sites cover only blogs that provide an RSS feed (thereby leaving out some blogs), and exactly what gets indexed for a particular posting will vary, depending upon how much of the blog posting was included in the RSS feed (title, summary, full text, etc.). As with news search engines, how many sources these blog searches cover and how retrospective they are will vary greatly. You will also notice a lot of variability in what search features are provided.

Among the dozens of blog search engines, the following are among the most popular, fully featured (for searching), and/or extensive in terms of retrospective coverage. Because of the problems mentioned, if you really don't want to miss something, use more than one of these engines.

Bloglines

bloglines.com

Bloglines covers both blogs and newsfeeds, has content that goes back to January 2004, and with its advanced search (found under the "more options" link near the search box), you can use simple Boolean and limit results to blogs or news, to where the term occurs (title, author, subject, body, or URL), to language (20 options), and to date posted. You can sort results by popularity or date or relevance. In addition to searching All Blogs, if you use the Bloglines "reader," you can narrow your search to—or exclude—those blogs to which you have subscribed.

Technorati

technorati.com

With content dating back to late 2004, Technorati indexes tens of millions of sites and billions of blog postings. Its advanced search lets you search using simple Boolean and phrases, search blog sites that focus on a specific topic, search a specific blog URL, or search by user-applied tags.

IceRocket

www.icerocket.com

Also going back to late 2003, IceRocket's advanced search (available from results pages) enables searching by simple Boolean, title, tag, author, site, date, posts "from" a blog site, and posts that link to a specific blog page. The following prefixes can also be used in the main search box: *title:, author:,* and *tag:.*

RSS

Depending on who you ask, RSS stands for either Really Simple Syndication or Rich Site Summary, though the former definition seems to have considerably overshadowed the latter. RSS is a format that lets news providers (and others) easily syndicate (distribute) their content. It makes use of XML language, which is a cousin of HTML (on its mother's side). The "product" is an RSS "feed," which is basically a specially coded webpage that feeds the information to those who request it. Using RSS feeds, sites can gather the headlines from a broad range of sources and create simple links on their own pages that lead to the stories. RSS has been increasingly used by a broad range of news sites, from networks such as BBC and MSNBC on down to individual newspapers. It is also used extensively by blogs, though not all blogs (nor all news sites for that matter) offer an RSS feed.

On the slightly more technical side, there are actually a number of formats that provide these kinds of feeds, and feeds may be referred to as RSS, RDF, OPML, Atom, etc. For the user, they are all essentially the same, so unless you are producing a feed yourself, don't worry about the differences.

To make use of these feeds you need an RSS reader—software, or a website, that goes out and gathers the feeds that you request. To request a feed, click on the orange RSS or XML button (or similar button or link) on a news site or blog. For someone who has not yet gotten into RSS, that is where the surprise may come. Sometimes when you click on one of those buttons, what you may see is a page of code that makes little sense to the average web user. The secret: Ignore the code, look at the address bar, and copy the URL of the page. It is the URL of that page that you need in order to sign up for an RSS feed. Take that URL to your RSS reader. More and more, sites providing feeds have made the process easier and often list several readers from which you can choose and in one or two clicks will get your subscribed.

If you see a My Yahoo! link, click it and, if you are signed up for My Yahoo!, another click or two and that feed will show up on your My Yahoo! page.

RSS Readers

The following tools, most of which have already been mentioned, can be used for locating RSS feeds of interest and reading them. These are just a few of many RSS readers available. Most allow you to not just add and read feeds but also to organize them into folders or groups and perform other functions.

Bloglines

bloglines.com

If you click the My Feeds link in Bloglines, you will see links to RSS feeds you have already signed up for and a link to add new feeds (Figure 8.5). For the former, just click on the name of the feed to see the new items.

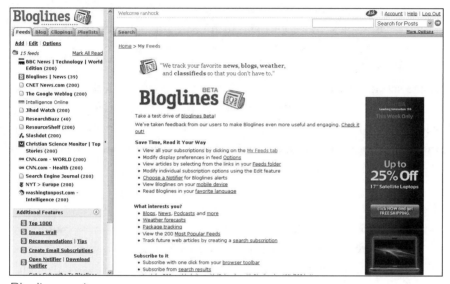

Bloglines main page

Figure 8.5

My Yahoo!

my.yahoo.com

Almost all of the readers are easy to use, but with a My Yahoo! account, when you see an Add to My Yahoo! link on a news site, you can have the feed appear on your My Yahoo! page with just a couple of clicks. If you find a news site with an RSS button, but no Add to My Yahoo! button, you can still add it to My Yahoo! by copying the URL. In My Yahoo!, click the Add Content link and then the Add RSS Feed link.

ALERT SERVICES

Among the most underused news offerings on the web are the numerous, valuable, and easy-to-use news alert services. These are services that automatically provide you with a listing of news stories, usually delivered by email and that are sometimes very personalizable according to your interests. You don't have to go to the news; it comes to you. Although the concept has been around for decades, it has gone through many incarnations, ranging from mailings of 3 x 5 cards in the 1960s to the overhyped "push" services in the mid-1990s to the more typical (free) email mailings that have now stood the test of web time. If you are not familiar with this concept, the way it works is that you find a site that provides such a service, you register and, in most cases, pick your topic, and thereafter, you will receive emails regularly that list news items on that topic. Many newspapers provide alert services, some allowing you to receive just selected categories of headlines. Some services cover a number of sources and allow you to be very specific with regard to the topic. The best way to find out about these is simply to keep an eye out as you visit sites. Several of the sites already mentioned in this chapter provide alert services. The following are two sites that epitomize the possibilities presented by this kind of service.

Google Alerts

www.google.com/newsalerts

Google offers a free alerting service for its 25,000 news sources. You can enter your search and then specify the delivery frequency (once a day, once a week, or as-it-happens). Multiple alerts can be established. With Google Alerts, you can choose to have them cover news, blogs, video, Google Groups, or a comprehensive search including all of those.

Yahoo! Alerts

alerts.yahoo.com

From Yahoo! News pages, click the News Alerts link to set up keyword alerts on any topic you wish, using the Yahoo! Keyword Alerts option. The Yahoo! Alerts page also provides other alert options, including delivery of alerts by email, Yahoo! IM, or mobile devices.

CHAPTER 9

FINDING PRODUCTS ONLINE

Whether for one's own purchase, for one's organization's purchase, or for competitive analysis purposes, many searchers frequently find themselves searching for and comparing products online. The internet is a rich resource of product pages, company catalogs, product directories, evaluations, and comparisons. From the rather mundane purchase of a pair of slippers to finding vendors of programmable "servo motion" controllers, the internet can make the job quicker and easier. This chapter takes a look at where to look and how to do it efficiently and effectively. As with other chapters, the intent is not to be exhaustive, but rather to provide readers with a bit of orientation and some tips, point them in a useful direction, and provide examples of some leading sites.

CATEGORIES OF SHOPPING SITES ON THE INTERNET

A wide variety of types of "shopping" sites on the internet serve a wide variety of functions. Most sites could fall into one (or more) of the following categories:

- Company catalogs
- Online shopping malls
- Classifieds
- Price comparison sites
- Auction sites
- Product and merchant evaluation sites
- Consumer rights sites

Used in combination, these types of sites enable the user to find the desired product, check on the quality of both the product and the vendor, and feel confident and safe in making a purchase. ShoppingSpot.com, the first site listed here, is a good place to start if you want to explore, in an organized way, the variety of shopping resources available on the web. Many of the sites covered in this chapter serve multiple functions. They are placed in the category that seems to best fit the site's primary function.

ShoppingSpot.com

shoppingspot.com

ShoppingSpot.com will not only point you in a good direction as to *where* to shop, but it also has a lot of links related to *how* to shop, with review sites, price comparison sites, consumer protection sites, coupon sites, and other resources. It has an excellent directory of specialized sites, from Antiques to Travel.

LOOKING FOR PRODUCTS— A GENERAL STRATEGY

The all-purpose rule "keep it simple" works very well when looking for products online. If you already know who you want to buy from, start out with that site. If you have in mind a specific brand, product, or set of specifications or criteria, jump into a general web search engine and get a quick (and perhaps a bit random) feel for what information is out there about the product. In the first 20 or so records, there is a good chance that you may get some links to vendors, some pages on specific models, some reviews, and often, for popular items (for example, photo printers), links to sites about selecting that kind of product.

Then move on to a more systematic approach. For a business-related purchase, you might next go to ThomasNet to identify vendors and specific products. For consumer products, you might go to one of the online shopping malls such as Yahoo! Shopping or eBay. Once you begin to focus on a likely choice, you can check out some reviews of the product itself at one of the review sites, do a search engine search on the specific model or product (ANDing the word *review* to your search), use one of the merchant rating sites, and look around in newsgroups to see what other buyers have said about it.

COMPANY/PRODUCT CATALOGS

If you know the name of the company you might want to buy from and don't know its web address, put the name in a search engine, and you usually will be at their site in seconds. If you don't know who manufactures or sells a certain product, go to one of the following company/product directories. Each will lead you to companies that produce a product, with a brief description of the company, how to contact the company, and usually a link to the company's webpage.

ThomasNet

www.thomasnet.com

ThomasNet, which was also discussed in Chapter 6, is the online replacement for the former *Thomas Register* and *Thomas Regional*—what library users and librarians in the U.S. may recognize as that shelf full of thick green books that for decades was the starting place in many libraries for identifying industrial products and manufacturers. ThomasNet contains millions of industrial product listings from 600,000 U.S. and Canadian distributors, manufacturers, and service companies, with products listed under 67,000 headings. You can either browse through the categories or make use of the search box (Figure 9.1). If you prefer to search, the tabs near the top of the page will direct your search toward Products/Services, Company Names, Brand, CAD Drawings, or Industrial Web (information from supplier websites, catalogs, etc.), White Papers, or More. Browsing is probably the best way to get a feel for what the site has to offer, and the breadth and detail of the categories. (There are 30 categories just for fuel cell types and components.) Another Thomas site, Thomas Global (www.thomasglobal.com), provides information from suppliers in 28 countries and is available in nine languages.

Kompass

www.kompass.com

The Kompass directory includes products from 2.3 million companies in 70 countries. Products are searchable by 57,000 product/service keywords and 860,000 trade names; 4.6 million executive names are also included and searchable. On the Kompass main page, you can search by Products/Services or by Companies and search worldwide, by region, by country, or by U.S. state. The More Search Criteria link provides a search by trade names and executives as well. The advanced search requires a subscription, but there is also a pay-as-you-go option. The specificity of the categories and the searchability by location make it easy to precisely and thoroughly locate providers (for example, the 113 companies in Western Europe that provide velvet

Figure 9.1

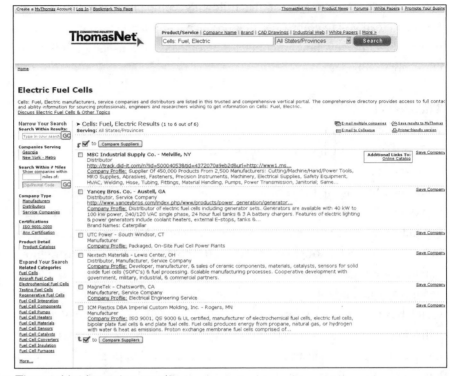

ThomasNet browsing results

gloves). The site also has sections for Public Tenders (free to advertisers) and Requests for Quotations (free, but requires registration).

Kellysearch

www.kellysearch.com

From a company that goes back to 1790, Kellysearch covers products from 2 million companies in 13 countries. From the main page, you can browse through 200,000 product headings. You will also find alphabetic indexes to companies and products. Using the advanced search page, you can search by either Product or Company and specify a country, region, or city. A search covers product headings, trade names, and brand names.

SHOPPING MALLS

You don't have to look hard to find sites that enable you to purchase an item online from hundreds or thousands of online stores through a single site.

Amazon and Overstock.com are among the most widely used of these online malls, but there are many, many more that serve the same function or may be specialized for a particular category of product (see ShoppingSpot.com, mentioned earlier). All the sites included in this section are ones where you can purchase items directly from the site, paying the site easily, securely, and confidently, without having to go to other merchant sites to make the purchase. This feature distinguishes online malls from the price comparison sites, where the site sends you to the websites of the individual merchants to complete your transactions. Most shopping mall sites use Shopping Cart technology, enabling you to gather multiple items and then check out all items at once.

Shopping mall and price comparison sites have many features in common. A third category covered in this chapter, auction sites, likewise demonstrates a lot of similarities. Pretty obviously, they all give basic information about products (name, brand, model, price, pictures, and a brief description). All of the sites discussed here also provide a search box in which you can search multiple terms (the terms are automatically ANDed). With the exception of Google Product Search, all of the shopping sites listed here have a directory where you can browse by category and subcategories. And (also with the exception of Google Product Search) all of these sites allow you to perform a search in a specific category as well as across all categories.

The following descriptions focus on the ways in which these sites differ from one another.

Amazon

amazon.com

Initially just an online bookstore, Amazon has expanded to a full shopping mall, where you can buy almost anything, from rare books to sweaters and software. As well as a search box, the main page provides a detailed directory for browsing. (Hold your cursor over any of the categories to get a useful fly-out menu with subcategories.) As you browse through the subcategories, look on the left side of the pages for more detailed subcategories. When you get down to the level where you are seeing actual products displayed, you will usually find a section on the left that allows you to narrow your results by category, brand, or price range, and in some cases, additional criteria related to the kind of product. Because of the richness of the site, both in terms of shopping breadth and shopping features, you will find it worthwhile to try the "click everywhere" approach to exploring the Amazon site. Among the other things you will find are: personalized recommendations based on your previous purchases; sites for Canada, the U.K., Germany, Japan, China, and France; shipment tracking; gift registries; selling options; personal lists where you can store items of interest; and the ability to Look Inside a book and view selected actual pages from the book.

Overstock.com
www.overstock.com

Overstock.com, as hinted by its name, is an online close-out retailer, an "outlet mall" with an emphasis on discounts. It also has auctions, cars, and real estate sections. On search results pages, you can narrow your search by category, price, and brand, and buttons there enable you to identify items that are on Clearance, have special promotions, etc. For some items, you will find product ratings and reviews.

PRICE COMPARISON SITES

Basically any time you look at the same product from two different suppliers, you are doing a price comparison. In that sense, most of the sites discussed in this chapter are price comparison sites. The following sites discussed, however, put emphasis on the comparison aspect. Those that emphasize consumers' own reviews and opinions are grouped together as a separate subcategory. This division is somewhat arbitrary and reflects more a matter of emphasis of the site than a definitive distinction. The sites that follow cover the broad range of shopping. Although the interfaces are all different, you will notice a number of commonalties. For most, expect to find the obvious product information (name of the product, make, model, a brief description, and price); name of the merchant; product and merchant ratings and reviews; links to compare prices for the same product from multiple merchants; links to do side-by-side comparisons for items that you select from the results page; and links on results pages that allow you to further narrow your selection by brand, store, price range, category, etc. Most have a directory that allows you to browse by category, and all have a search function. There are also sites on the web that do such comparisons for particular types of products or services, such as computers or travel. (For links to sites that do comparisons for travel, see www.extremesearcher.com/travel.)

For a good list of price comparison sites, check out the Compare Prices section of ShoppingSpot.com (shoppingspot.com) discussed at the beginning of this chapter.

Yahoo! Shopping
shopping.yahoo.com

Yahoo! Shopping contains millions of products and provides a wide range of shopping features. Whether you get to a products page by browsing or searching, you will find there the following options:

- Links to save the item to your list of saved items and to see your list
- Link to more items of that type from that merchant (Yahoo! Shopping only displays one item from each store on the initial product page)
- Merchant rating (ratings of that merchant by buyers)
- Compare Prices button (when the specific brand and model is found in other stores, clicking this button will produce a page showing a grid that compares prices, etc. from the various merchants)
- Compare Side-by-Side button (use the checkboxes by each item to select those you wish to compare, and then click this button to see a comparison chart of the various brands/models)

On product pages, you will also see a link to Show Grid View and view the products in a grid rather than a list and another link to sort the results by such things as product rating and price (Figure 9.2). With the Narrow Results section on the left side of the page, you can narrow by such things as price range, brand, etc. For some types of items, such as computers, cell phones, and cameras, when you are browsing through the categories, you will find Buying Guides, "Top 10" lists, and more.

mySimon
www.mysimon.com

mySimon, one of the earliest comparison shopping sites, gathers price and product information from thousands of merchants. On the home page, take advantage of the Shopping Guides and Consumer Reports sections for advice on a range of popular products. To get to what mySimon can tell you about specific products, use the category tabs or the search box near the top of the

Figure 9.2

Yahoo! Shopping product page

page. When searching, use the categories menu to the right to narrow to a specific category. On the results pages, you can narrow your search by price range, brand, or other criteria specific to the product. The See More Prices button for a product will give you a table that provides a price comparison chart for the various stores that sell that item. The table also includes the store rating, the availability of the item from the store, and a link to take you to the corresponding page from the store's site. Depending upon the product, you may also find links for product ratings, user reviews, and product specifications. On the See More Prices (Compare Prices) page, you can sort results by best matches, price, store name, store rating, or total price.

PriceGrabber.com
www.pricegrabber.com

PriceGrabber.com has a very clean, easily navigable interface, with emphasis on its search function and its 26 product categories, each of which is further divided into additional levels of categories. Product pages are likewise

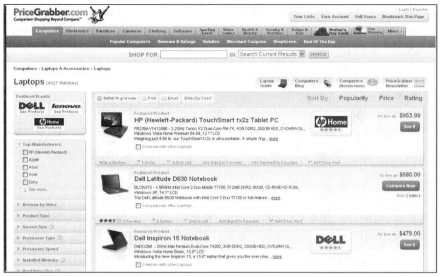

Figure 9.3

PriceGrabber.com product page

easy to use, but rich in functionality (Figure 9.3). On the left is a panel where you can narrow your results by brand, price range, etc., often with a wide range of additional criteria depending on the product (for laptops, there are 20 criteria). Whether you get there by searching or browsing, you can sort results lists by price, popularity, or rating. Check boxes and the accompanying "Compare with other …" links enable you to select products from the results list and then see a side-by-side comparison chart. With the Compare Now button, for an individual product, you can see prices and other comparisons for the stores that sell the product. On PriceGrabber.com, you will also find product guides and discussion groups for categories of products.

Shopping.com
www.shopping.com

Shopping.com, owned by eBay, has websites in the U.S., the U.K., Australia, France, and Germany. It has millions of reviews from the affiliated consumer review site Epinions as well as millions of products and thousands of merchants. Get to a product listing either by browsing the categories on the home page or by using the search box. Once on a product page, you will find options to further narrow your results by category, price range, brand, keyword, and often a wide range of other product-specific criteria. As with both

Yahoo! Shopping and PriceGrabber.com, you will find buttons to get charts comparing selected products from the list, or prices for a particular product from different merchants.

Shopzilla
www.shopzilla.com

Shopzilla provides information on more than 30 million products from more than 92,000 stores. Either Shopzilla's search box or its categories will lead you to a product page where you can narrow your search by price range, brand, and other criteria. Results can be sorted by popularity, price (high–low or low–high), or product rating. On the pages for individual products, you can sort by price, store, or store rating. With the Compare Prices button, you can compare prices for the particular product from various stores.

Become.com
www.become.com

Become.com has features similar to most comparison sites (browsing, searching, etc.) but also has some that are unique and/or particularly useful. Try the Research button next to the search box to find articles, news, reviews, product guides, etc. relating to your product that Become.com has identified by crawling the web. As you enter terms in the search box, note the search suggestions that automatically appear, and on pages for a specific product, look for the link to "Email me when the price drops."

Google Product Search
www.google.com/products

Google Product Search (formerly Froogle, a much more clever name) includes content that (1) is the result of Google's crawling of the web to iden-tify product sites, or (2) was submitted by merchants (but Google accepts no payment for this). On the home page, you will see a search box, a link to the Advanced Product Search page, and a sampling of product headings. Google Product Search does not provide an option to browse by product category, so you are limited to searching.

The advanced search page allows you to search by simple Boolean and price range and limit your search to product name or description. On the search results pages, you can choose to view results in a list or grid, and sort results by relevance, price, product rating, or seller rating. Though some searches will take you to a results list that will individually show products from each separate store, most searches will take you to a listing by product (as available from multiple stores). There, beside each result, look for a Compare Prices button and links to reviews that Google has found by crawling the web. Also on the search results page, you can add items to your Shopping List. Clicking either on the product name or the Compare Prices button will take you to the page for the specific product, where you will see pricing details from the various stores where the product is available and links or tabs for details on seller ratings, reviews, technical specifications, and related items.

Items cannot be purchased through Google, but for some sellers, you can take advantage of Google Checkout for easy payment.

AUCTIONS

Auction sites on the web have a lot in common with the shopping malls and price comparison sites, but differ, of course, in the "bidding" approach. The best-known auction site is eBay, though there are a number of others and some shopping sites, such as Overstock.com, that have an auctions option.

eBay

ebay.com

Although many people think of eBay as an auction site where almost anything but body parts are auctioned off, it is also a shopping mall where you can buy things outright, avoiding either the fun or effort (however you see it) of having to go through the auction process. When you do a search or browse through the categories, you will see tabs that take you to All Items, Auctions, or Buy It Now Only. The Buy It Now Only option is for those items that don't have the auction option. eBay has one of the most sophisticated sets of search features of any of the shopping sites. Look for the Advanced Search links on the main page and other pages. eBay's advanced search allows you to search by simple Boolean ("all of these words," "any of these words," "exclude these words") and by "exact phrase," "exact match only," category, price range, buying formats (auction, buy it now, classifieds), location, seller, etc.

On search results or browsing pages (Figure 9.4), you will find a section that contains links to categories that match your search terms and a number

Figure 9.4

eBay product page

of narrowing criteria such as price and condition and criteria that relate particularly to the "auction" side of eBay, such as location of the seller, payment methods accepted, etc. Also on the results pages, you will find suggested related searches and options to sort your results by auction times (newly listed, ending soonest, etc.), price, distance, payment, and product category. Click on the name of an item to find full details about the item, the seller, and the auction status. If you are new to auctions, the Help section is an excellent place to find out how it all works.

CLASSIFIEDS

Most of the shopping sites just discussed are designed to lead to a transaction between a purchaser and a merchant. eBay, in addition to connecting a potential purchaser with "stores," makes it possible for anyone to become a "store" and sell items. What about people who only have one or two things to sell or who don't want to sell things on an on-going basis? Just as with newspapers, this is where "classifieds" come in. Classifieds make it possible for individuals to sell to individuals and to buy and sell "locally." craigslist is by far the best-known site for classifieds.

craigslist
www.craigslist.org

craigslist has a very plain-looking home page, but one that indeed gets the job done—providing easy-to-use and primarily free classified listings for more than 570 cities in 50 countries. Except for job postings, some apartment rental postings, and erotic services, all ads are posted for free. The main page is arranged geographically (county/continent, state, city) and after choosing a locality, you can browse through or search the classified sections. On most pages, you will find a search box with an attached menu by which you can narrow your search to "for sale," community, events, gigs, housing, jobs, personals, resumes, or services. Whether searching or browsing, the listings to which you are led are shown most recent first. craigslist makes both buying and selling a really easy experience, attested to by the fact that it serves up more than 20 billion page views a month.

PRODUCT AND MERCHANT EVALUATIONS

Some of the sites just discussed may build both product and merchant reviews into their results. Other sites on the internet specialize in reviews and evaluations, including consumer opinion sites and merchant rating sites. Among these are Epinions, Consumer Reports, ConsumerREVIEW.com, and ConsumerSearch.

In addition to using these sites, you can use web search engines effectively to find reviews and evaluations by simply doing a search on the name of the product (e.g., *Nikon D60*) or the type of product (e.g., *digital cameras*), in combination with the term *evaluations* or *reviews*.

Example: *"digital cameras" (reviews OR evaluations)*

Going one step further, especially if you are tracking your own or competitors' products, you can take advantage of the frequent comments regarding products that appear in newsgroups. Look at Google Groups (groups.google.com),

Yahoo! Groups (groups.yahoo.com), and other group sites discussed in Chapter 5.

Epinions
epinions.com

On the surface, Epinions looks much like other shopping sites, with a search box and browsable categories that include millions of products and services. What differs is that the emphasis in Epinions is on the reviews. For each product, you will find links to further details about the product and to reviews written by Epinions users. To provide reliable reviews, even the reviewers can be reviewed through Epinions' "Web of Trust" system. For various products, you will also find advanced search options, buyer's guides, and store ratings.

Consumer Reports
consumerreports.org

Consumer Reports, the publisher of the well-known product review journal, has its evaluations available online but only to paid subscribers. There are some parts, such as buying guides, that you can read (or view videos) without a subscription.

ConsumerREVIEW.com
consumerreview.com

ConsumerREVIEW.com, one of the specialized product review sites, focuses on reviews of outdoor, sporting, and consumer electronics products.

ConsumerSearch
consumersearch.com

ConsumerSearch takes a different approach to providing reviews by having its editors "scour the Internet and print publications for comparative reviews and other information sources relevant to the topic." The reviews on the site are based on those sources and a set of criteria developed by ConsumerSearch.

BUYING SAFELY

Although many internet users quickly began to take advantage of the benefits of online purchasing, some users are still quite shy about giving up their credit card numbers to a machine. Having a healthy skepticism is indeed a reasonable approach. Knowing where caution ends and paranoia begins is the problem. In general, following a few basic rules should keep the online purchaser fairly safe. There are few guarantees, but there are also few guarantees that the waiter to whom you gave your credit card in the restaurant did not do something illegal with it. If the following precautions are kept in mind, online purchasers should feel reasonably secure:

1. Consider who the seller is. If it is a well-known company, there is some security in that. (Yes, we *do* remember Enron.) If you don't recognize the seller, do you know the site? Sites such as Amazon and Barnes & Noble are respected and want to protect their reputations. If you are buying through an intermediary such as eBay, it likewise has a reputation to protect and builds in some protections, such as providing access to feedback about sellers from other customers. On some merchant sites, you will see symbols displayed that indicate the merchant is registered with organizations that are in the business of assuring that member merchants meet high standards. The best known of these organizations is BBBOnline (from the Better Business Bureau, www.bbbonline.org). On its site, you can search to see if a company is a member. For various legitimate reasons, even large and reputable sites may not necessarily participate in programs such as these, so the lack of a seal of approval alone should certainly not keep you from buying.

2. When you get to the point of putting in payment information, check to see that the site is secure. Look for the closed padlock icon on the status bar at the bottom of your browser, or the *https:* (instead of *http:*) at the beginning of the URL in the address bar of the browser.

3. As with traditional purchases, read the fine print. Look for information on the payment methods, terms, and return policy. Also look around for seller contact points, such as phone number and address.

4. Print and keep a copy of the purchase confirmation message you receive when you complete the purchase.

5. When possible, pay by credit card to be able to take advantage of the protections the card issuer provides regarding unauthorized billings. Some sites, such as eBay, will also provide services that help protect your payments. These services charge the seller a fee and may cause a

slight delay but hold the money until the product is received. Payment services such as PayPal also build in some safeguards.

If you encounter problems with an online purchase, you may want to consult the Online Shopping & E-Payments page of the Federal Trade Commission's site (www.ftc.gov/bcp/menus/consumer/tech/online.shtm). For cross-border complaints, consult eConsumer.gov (www.econsumer.gov).

CHAPTER 10

YOUR OWN PLACE ON THE WEB: PARTICIPATING AND PUBLISHING

The internet is, obviously, a two-way street. So far, this book has primarily discussed using the internet to *find* information. The other direction is providing information to be found. Creating and participating in groups (discussion groups, etc.), which were discussed in Chapter 5, is one way of contributing to the content on the internet, but there are numerous other ways of participating, providing information to others, and having your own presence on the web—something that tens, maybe hundreds, of millions of web users are already doing. Achieving a presence on the web can be as simple as sending a Twitter message or as intensive as maintaining a full-fledged website with many pages and a broad range of features.

Indeed, the major change in the nature of the web in the last few years is the phenomenon that is often referred to as Web 2.0. The term refers not to an actual "version" of the web, but to the fact that by the middle of the first decade of the 21st century, the web had changed from being primarily a place to go to find information to being a place that was much more personalized and interactive, with collaboration, sharing, desktop-type programs, and social networking. Chances are that, perhaps not even realizing it, most readers of this book are themselves already a part of the Web 2.0 phenomenon.

A "PLACE" ON THE WEB

There are numerous ways to be a part of this, to make a place for yourself on the web, ways that provide varying levels of simplicity, exposure, and impact. One way already mentioned in Chapter 5 is participation in groups and forums, but there are a lot more ways. These include such things as collaborative web-based software, networking sites, "sharing" sites, microblogs, blogs, podcasts, and full-fledged websites. As with the rest of this book, the sites that follow are just a sampling, but they are leading sites in their category and/or are representative of their type.

WEB-BASED SOFTWARE

"The web as platform," meaning making use of software that resides on the web rather than on your own computer, is often cited as one of the manifestations of the new web. Web-based applications provide an easy way to be a "producer" of web-based content as well as a user. Like many other things that are part of recent trends, web-based software is not a new concept. Many people have been using web-based email programs such as Yahoo! Mail and Hotmail for well over a decade. Some newer examples, though, not only reside on the web but by doing so provide a very useful means of sharing and collaboration. Among the best examples of these are Google Docs and PBworks, and the sites in the later section on "sharing" can also be considered web-based software.

Google Docs
docs.google.com

Google Docs is a combination of word processor, spreadsheet, presentations program (very similar to PowerPoint), and HTML forms processor. With it, you can create, import, export, work with, and share these kinds of documents online. It is the sharing and collaborative aspect that is most powerful. For example, a number of people can be working with the same report at the same time and see changes made by others almost instantaneously. You can allow the world at large to see it or only those to whom you have given permission. Likewise, you can choose for an individual to see it but not be able to edit it. Documents can be imported from or saved in a variety of formats, making them compatible with a variety of software (for example, a word processing document can be downloaded in Word, HTML, RTF, Open Office, or PDF formats).

PBworks
pbworks.com

PBworks allows anyone, without programming experience, to set up either a private or public wiki, for free. (In case you've forgotten, a wiki is a site created and maintained as a collaborative project of internet users that allows fast and easy input and online editing by users. To see an example, look at Wikipedia.) PBworks, whose name derives from its slogan that it is as easy to make as a peanut butter sandwich, can be used for just about any situation where multiple people need to have collaborative access to a document or documents. As with Google Docs, reading, writing, and editing permissions can be selective. Like in many other situations, there is both a free version of PBwiki and a more-robust version available for a fee.

NETWORKING SITES

Social networking sites are one of the easiest ways to make oneself known on the web, to allow people to find you and connect with you, and to keep in touch with others in your "network." The more "social" sites such as MySpace and Facebook have expanded rapidly and now include a much broader demographic. They include not just people, but organizations, causes, etc. Professionally oriented networking sites, such as LinkedIn, allow for similar connections but with a professional, "workplace" slant.

MySpace

myspace.com

MySpace, one of the first very successful social networking sites, was in the beginning at least, primarily populated with teens, 20-somethings, bands, and celebrities (or, more likely, their publicists). It is about socializing, it is about the "personal."

Facebook

facebook.com

Facebook started in 2004 as a social networking site with membership limited to those associated with particular colleges, etc., but once it opened up its membership to anyone, it took off and quickly began to overtake MySpace. By 2009, Facebook had more than 300 million users. It has some-what fewer "bells and whistles" than does MySpace, but it also has a more "adult" aura.

LinkedIn

linkedin.com

LinkedIn provides networking with an emphasis on business connections. Content is primarily business-oriented (with members' profiles often resembling resumes), and communications and network connections usually have a business purpose. LinkedIn, like the other social networking sites, can also serve as a research tool. If your research involves identifying individuals and finding more about them, these sites are a good resource, since they contain useful information and also have a search function. LinkedIn particularly has become a site of interest to researchers who are doing company intelligence, since people often post information that provides clues as to what their companies are up to.

"SHARING" SITES

Sharing tends to be a very human trait, and the internet provides ample opportunities and platforms where things can be shared. There are a variety of sites where such sharing is the essence of the site, including sites for sharing photos, videos, slideshows, bookmarks, news, opinions, and much more. As with the social networking sites, because of the kind of content on these sharing sites, they are also of interest for searching purposes. Among the most popular sites are those that enable sharing of photos and videos. YouTube, the best-known video sharing site, was discussed in Chapter 7. Two of the best-known image sharing sites, Flickr and Picasa Web albums, plus Delicious, a site for sharing bookmarks, are discussed in this section.

Flickr

flickr.com

Flickr was discussed in Chapter 7, primarily in terms of its usefulness as a search engine for images. Its initial intent though is a photo sharing site where users can share with family and friends the photos (and now short videos) they have taken. On Flickr, images can be edited, tagged, organized, and stored and viewed as groups and as a slideshow. A photo, or a group of photos, or all of your photos can be shared with everyone, or you can choose to restrict access to "friends" or "family." As well as tagging your pictures with words and phrases, you can "geo-tag'" photos and access them by location, from a map. You can even get statistics as to which photos are being viewed and where the people viewing them are coming from. Flickr allows you to store up to 200 images for free, but for an annual fee, you can have unlimited storage. The next time you are planning a trip, check out photos of the place that other people have shared through Flickr.

Picasa Web Albums

picasaweb.google.com

Picasa is a free downloadable photo editing and organizing program from Google that provides a site on the web where you can store and share your photos. The Picasa program is nicely integrated with the online Picasa web albums, enabling a large number of images to be uploaded at once. Images you have stored can be arranged and viewed by album or in a slideshow, and you can tag them, email them, order prints, and do lots more.

You can upload a total of 1024 MB (upwards of 4,000 pictures if you use the uploaded image size recommended by Picasa), and you can designate them as Public, Unlisted, or as Sign-in required to view. (With the latter option, only the people you list will have access.) As well as adding regular tags ("captions"), you can geo-tag the images; and when you create an album, if you name a place, Picasa automatically finds that place on the map and tags your images for that location. A unique and particularly interesting tagging option is Picasa Web Album's "name tagging," which uses technology that automatically identifies pictures with similar faces and allows you to apply name tags to them. You can then organize images or search them based on the name tags. The name tags are private by default, but you can choose to make them visible to others. Like Flickr, public photos on Picasa Web Albums can be searched, but Flickr has a big head start in terms of the number of searchable images.

Delicious

delicious.com

Delicious is a social bookmarking site on which you can store your bookmarks, share them with others (if you wish), and see other's bookmarks (if they wish). Keep Delicious in mind for the following reasons: (1) It allows you to have access to your bookmarks from any internet-connected computer anywhere; (2) it allows you to add bookmarks regardless of where you are; (3) it allows you to easily organize your bookmarks by the tags you apply to them; (4) it allows you to be able to search for bookmarks by tags you assign or for bookmarks from others who have used that tag; and (5) it allows you to see bookmarks of people who have similar interests. You can also see those users who have linked to one of your saved sites and what other sites those users have bookmarked. One of the best ways to get a feel for the possibilities Delicious offers is to do a search on a term of interest, and then from that results list, explore the tags associated with the sites and the users who have bookmarked the sites (links to both the user names and the tags are shown next to each bookmark on your search results list). Sign up and practice adding some sites to your own list.

MICROBLOGS

Working our way generally from the simpler to the more complicated tools, we should talk about microblogs before we talk about blogs (weblogs). Blogs, as you will recall, are frequently updated pages that provide commentary, news, etc.—usually, though not always, from individuals. Microblogs are simpler, consisting just of very brief messages, updating "followers" with news, comments, etc. from the microblogger. They can actually be thought of as a hybrid of blog, email, mailing list, and newsfeed—but very simple and very short. Though there are a number of sites that provide a microblogging capability (including Facebook and MySpace), the site that made microblogging famous is Twitter.

Twitter
twitter.com

Twitter, one of those websites whose name we suddenly began seeing numerous times every day, provides a quick and easy way to send very short messages to everyone who has chosen to "follow" you. It is a way of staying connected and letting family, friends, and colleagues know where you are and what you are up to, but it is also a way to send short messages to a TV commentator, to share ideas with colleagues, and to ask for and get advice.

Posts (Twitter updates) are called "tweets" and are limited to 140 characters (including spaces). When you post them, they appear on your page of the Twitter site, but more importantly, they are sent to followers (people who have signed up to receive your tweets automatically on their Twitter pages, or for that matter, on their cell phone). Tweets can be searched at search.twitter.com, and there you will find a link to an advanced search page where you can search for tweets by words, people, places, dates, and attitudes (positive or negative), and for tweets containing links.

Blogs

If you have something you wish to say and/or information that you feel should be shared not just with friends and Twitter followers, there is really no easier way to make a place for yourself on the web than to get yourself a blog. Blogging has found much favor and publicity over the last decade and getting started requires little effort. Discussed earlier in Chapter 8 from the news content perspective, blogs provide an easy means to gather and distribute news, commentary, advice, and so forth (Figure 10.1). The main intent of blogs is to provide a place for short and frequently updated postings. Although blogs may lack the fancier graphics and other capabilities of a website, their ease of use has been a major factor in their popularity.

Software and Sites for Creating Blogs

There are a number of sites and software programs (blogging tools) that allow you to create blogs, some that you can use through your browser, and some that you download and install on your server. Those that allow you to

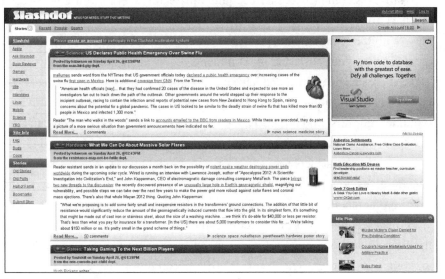

Figure 10.1

Example of a blog

do your blogging online, through your browser, typically will also host your blog on their sites. The following are some of the more well-known places where you can go to create a blog.

Blogger

blogger.com

Blogger is a free blogging tool and hosting service. It is one of the best known and is both simple to use and powerful. On the Blogger site, you can create your blog, and Blogger will host the site for you on its hosting site, blogspot.com. Indeed, in the five minutes or less that Blogger advertises, you really can get your blog created and up on the web. You can choose from several templates for your page or, with some HTML skills, you can modify one as you wish. Posts can be made from the Blogger site (using a WYSIWYG interface), by email, or from your mobile device. You cannot categorize your posts on Blogger, but among the other features that Blogger provides, you can moderate and otherwise control visitor comments, block spam robots, post photos from your computer or your camera phone, post audio blogs, and easily create a newsfeed.

WordPress.com

wordpress.com

WordPress.com provides a free, quite full-featured, easy-to-use web-based interface for creating and hosting blogs, and you can get a blog set up in minutes. With the features WordPress.com offers, you can categorize posts; RSS feeds for both your posts and for comments received are automatically set up; you can create a site index and have multiple pages; you can import posts you have posted on another blog service; statistics are automatically provided (volume, referrers, and top posts, for both the blog and feeds); you can control spam with your own list of spam words and your own blacklist; and you can create bookmarklets for each post, and conduct polls. WordPress.com in general gives you quite good control both over how posts are displayed and over comments. Posting images, audio, and video is quite easy.

Blogs created on WordPress.com can be hosted elsewhere, as well as on the WordPress.com site, and if you wish, you can download the program to your own server. The basic WordPress.com service is free, but for advanced services such as extra storage and domain hosting, there is a fee.

WordPress.com can get a beginner going quickly, easily, and free, yet it allows users to take advantage of features that should keep even experienced bloggers happy.

Moveable Type

www.movabletype.com

Moveable Type, a pioneer in blogging software, is client software that you download to your own computer or server (rather than using online software such as Blogger). It is very full-featured and because of that it is the favorite of many professional bloggers, even though it is less easy to use than Blogger and some other programs. It is designed to allow management of many blogs from many people. There is a free downloadable version, but for a supported version, you must pay. Moveable Type does not itself provide hosting of blogs. The installation of the program is best handled by someone with some technical expertise.

LiveJournal

www.livejournal.com

LiveJournal is a community-focused blogging tool. When you are signed up with LiveJournal, you can create a journal and you can join its Communities, which are interest-specific or region-specific. LiveJournal has two levels of free service and a paid version. By allowing ads, you get access to more features. The paid version gives you additional control over the style of your journal, more room for pictures, polling capabilities, and more.

PODCASTS

Podcasts, which were discussed in Chapter 8 from the perspective of finding them, are also a way for anyone to publish on the internet. For messages that are best conveyed aurally, for genres such as storytelling, or as an avenue for reaching a sight-impaired audience, podcasts present a very viable publishing option.

To create a podcast of your own, you need the following, some of which should be pretty obvious: (1) something to say; (2) a microphone; (3) a computer with an internet connection; (4) sound recording software; (5) an MP3 encoder to convert what you record into MP3 format; and (6) a place on the web to host your podcast. For hosting, a blog or other personal website can work fine. For more detail, visit the following site.

Podcasting Tools

www.podcasting-tools.com

Podcasting Tools contains all the information you need to know to get started podcasting: tutorials for getting started, directories of podcasting software and places where you can host podcasts online, and a variety of other resources.

YOUR OWN FULL-FLEDGED WEBSITE

Beyond the ways of achieving a web presence that were already discussed, for the full experience and the greatest level of exposure, versatility, variety, and communications power (plus self-esteem and social standing), you can set up an actual website of your own, with, as you wish, your own design, photos, links, images, audio, video, and much more.

As for why you would wish to do any of this, there are many reasons to consider publishing a website: You may wish to provide a "personal" space for yourself, or a space for an organization to which you belong, a committee of which you are a member, a course you teach, a "cause," your own business …

Whatever your reasons, as you move into publishing, keep two words in mind: *content* and *style*. It is a truism that on the web "Content is king." You must have useful content to make visitors to your place feel it was worth the trip and to make them come back. Have something to say! What you say may be as simple as family news, family photos, your resume, or a syllabus for a course. As for style, the term in this context has two aspects: personal style and presentation style. For the first, don't put yourself on the web unless you can do so with "style." You don't need to come across as suave, sophisticated, sexy, or debonair, but what you put on your website should reflect the best you have to offer.

The other aspect of style is your writing style and the design of your page. You want the look of your place to convey neatness, thoughtfulness, and organization. If you are going the blog route or are creating a website using a template, the style of the page itself will pretty much take care of itself. As for what you write, do it correctly. Poor grammar and other writing problems definitely communicate something, but not what you want. (Think about your own reaction when you encounter a page with multiple spelling errors.) Though it is written primarily for people building webpages, the following site can be useful for most people who want to have any form of effective web presence.

Web Style Guide

www.webstyleguide.com

Written for people who are creating websites, the well-known Web Style Guide presents, in an easy-to-read, non-technical way, the basic principles of design that should be considered for any website. Even for those who are using templates, or who are just involved in some way in the management of a website, this time-tested guide is worthwhile and interesting reading. (Though the Web Style Guide website is great, the inexpensive, beautifully presented book version is slicker and perhaps more convenient to read. Sometimes "books are better.")

On "Personal" Web Places

We are all our own "company," even if we work for someone else. As Tom Peters said, "To be in business today, our most important job is to be head marketer for the brand called You" (www.fastcompany.com/magazine/10/brandyou.html). This is true not just for executives and aspiring executives, but very true for academics, artists, writers, entrepreneurs, and others. Having a personal place on the web, where you can send people or where people can find you, is both easy and (for many but not all people) important. If you choose to have a personal website, do it with style. Make sure it conveys the degree of professionalism you want it to convey. Then advertise it. Submit it to search engines. Put the URL in your automatic email signatures. Put in on your business cards.

WEBSITES

In addition to the reasons previously mentioned, having a website of your own is also useful for another reason. For those who are involved in contributing input to their organization's site or to someone else's site, having done your own website can provide a healthy perspective. It can, on one hand, take away a lot of the mystique (you will no longer be unnecessarily awed by some of the cute little things you see), and on the other hand, you will have a better appreciation for the more sophisticated things you see. Also, if your time and inclinations permit such, building your own site can be enjoyable and fulfilling.

What follows is not intended to teach you how to build a website, but rather to provide an overview of what is involved in order to help answer the questions: Can I do it (build my own website)? What is involved? What will it cost?

If you go for a website, you have a range of options and levels of sophistication. You can have, or not have, your own domain name; you can use templates or a webpage editor, or if you are (or want to be) in the techie category, you can build pages from scratch by writing HTML.

What's Needed

The main tools needed for building a website of your own are a purpose, time, software, skills, and a place to publish. Depending on what you want to produce, each of these components can either be minimal or extensive.

Purpose

The introductory paragraphs to this chapter mentioned some of the reasons for creating your own place on the web. Before you start with a website, though, it is advisable to give a fair amount of consideration to why you are doing it and what you want to accomplish. Though those things may seem very obvious, a focus on those two considerations is important for all website designers, from beginner to the most experienced. Your aims may change continually, but the more direction you have established to begin with, the less you may have to go back and change later. Write down your purpose. The main purpose of almost any page is "communication." What do you want to communicate and why?

Tied in closely to your statement of purpose will be an analysis of your intended audience. Who are you addressing? What background are they likely to have in connection with your topic? What age level are you addressing? How skilled are they likely to be in using and navigating through webpages? What is their level of interest? If your site is for a course you are teaching, users have a high level of interest in that they may be required to use the site. If you are selling something, you need to design a page that will do a good job of attracting and keeping the readers' attention.

Time

If you are using a free website service such as Tripod (discussed later in this chapter) and you take advantage of their templates, and if you already know what information you want to put on the site, you can have a website created and available for use in an hour or so. The time required to build and maintain a site goes up from there, depending upon how fancy you want to get, how much content you want to include, and how much maintenance the site will require (updating, etc.).

Software

If you are building a site using one of the free website services, you can get by with no software other than your browser. These sites provide what you need to make a basic but at the same time very attractive site, with room for lots of content and many pages. Beyond that, unless you decide to learn how to write HTML (HyperText Markup Language) code, you will need a webpage editing program such as Dreamweaver, KompoZer, or Microsoft Expression Web (there are many, many more). These are basically word-processor-like programs that convert what you enter, and the features you choose, into HTML code.

The cost of these programs ranges from free (e.g., KompoZer) to several hundred dollars. If you are using the editor for educational purposes, you may be able to find an educator's rate for some programs that is substantially less than the full price.

KompoZer provides the basics of what you need to build a webpage. Parts of the program can be a bit clunky, and it does not provide the more sophisticated features, such as image maps capability and integration of various web developer languages. It does, however, provide what most beginners need, and the fact that it is free is significant.

If you think you are going to want a more sophisticated site, have many pages on your site, and make it interactive, you may want to start with a sophisticated but still relatively easy-to-use program such as Dreamweaver (Figure 10.2).

Uploading your finished pages to a web server will require file transfer software. HTML editors usually build in this feature.

Graphics Software

It is likely that you will want some images on your site, and unlikely that you will want to put them on your page without making some modifications to the images, such as cropping and some other easy changes that can improve the image. If you have a scanner or a digital camera, it may have come with a program for editing photos that will perform most operations needed to prepare

Figure 10.2

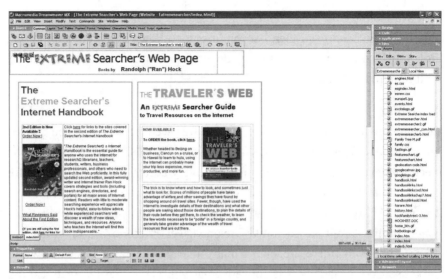

Example of page built in Dreamweaver

images for inclusion on a webpage. An excellent free photo editing program is Paint.NET. If you want to move up a step, consider Adobe PhotoShop Elements, a program that does the vast majority of things that the well-known and more expensive PhotoShop does.

Skills

To build a website with the minimalist approach (using templates on a free website service) requires only the ability to follow step-by-step instructions. Beyond that, the ability to use (or learn how to use) an HTML editor will be necessary, and the ability to work with graphics will be useful. Be aware that the use of graphics software can be addictive—as well as using it for your website, you may find yourself up at 3 AM fixing the cracks and tears in that photo of your great-grandfather and adding feathered edges, drop-shadows, and other special effects to your pictures.

If you are new to using web editors and graphics software, there are a number of ways to learn. Your choice will probably depend upon your own learning style. Most programs you purchase will have a built-in tutorial, and if you commit an hour or so, you can be on your way. If you are willing to commit several hours, you will probably find yourself in quite good control of the program. There are also tutorials available on the web for most popular programs, and they sometimes provide a more simplified, yet effective, approach to page editing and graphics software. Do a web search for the name of your program and the word *tutorial,* and you will probably find several. YouTube is an excellent place to find video tutorials. (It has hundreds of Dreamweaver tutorials!) There are also numerous books and classes available for the more popular programs.

The alternative to using an HTML editor is to learn to write all the HTML code yourself. Most people would probably consider this the hard way, but it can actually be fun. (Then again, some people also consider jumping into an icy river on New Year's Day "fun.") For most, starting with a webpage editing program makes the most sense, but as you get more heavily into webpage building, you eventually will want to learn the basics of HTML because of the added control it can give you. (In the interest of full disclosure, the author admits to having had fun writing HTML code.) Knowing some HTML code can make the use of an editor such as Dreamweaver easier, quicker, and more flexible.

Domain Names

If you make use of one of the free website hosts, your site will have an address that looks something like *yourname.tripod.com.* If you go with a paid hosting service, you will need to get a domain name of your own. For someone who has a company and/or needs to make the most professional impression, having one's own domain name is the way to go. The cost of purchasing (registering) a domain name has come down tremendously, and when you sign up for a web-hosting service, the service will usually bundle the process and cost of getting the name of your choice registered into the hosting.

Related to that last point is the issue of whether you would prefer to sign up through a domain registration service and then, separately, choose a host; or whether you want to just have your chosen hosting service do the registration process for you. The latter is easier, but if you decide later to switch hosts, some extra steps will be involved.

Even if you aren't ready to build a site, you may want to get a domain name for your own name (*yourname.com*) or reserve a name for the company you dream of having. (This is called "domain parking" and is a way of protecting some of your "intellectual property.") Some domain name registration services will not only register and "park" your name for you, but they will throw in an email service so you can use your domain name for your email even if you do not yet have a website. These services can be very inexpensive (less than $15 per year). Regarding the email service, as long as you keep your name registered, your address will always be there. If you change jobs, you will still have your personal email address, and it also provides that backup email address you can use when you don't want to use (or shouldn't be using) your employer's email system. (For that purpose, you can, of course, just use a free email service such as Yahoo! Mail or Gmail, but an address from a free webmail provider does not convey the same "importance" as an address from your own domain name.) The following is one example of a registration service that specializes in providing these added services. (For an excellent book that addresses what's involved in getting and implementing a domain name, see *I've Got a Domain Name—Now What???* by Jean Bedord, HappyAbout. info, Silicon Valley, CA, 2008.)

000Domains.com
www.000domains.com

000Domains.com provides registration services for more than 25 top-level domains, including the usual general domains (.com, .net, etc.), plus several country domains such as .us, .uk, and .de. In addition to domain registration, 000Domains.com includes, among other services: domain parking; email forwarding; domain forwarding (from multiple addresses to an existing site); and unlimited ownership changes (you can assign your domains to someone else).

Where to Publish Your Website

Among the main options for places where an individual website builder may place a webpage are the following: on a web-hosting service with your own domain name, on your organization's server, or on one of the "free website" sites.

Web-Hosting Services

Once you have decided that you want to have a website of your own with your own domain name, you will need to choose a web-hosting company (service) where your webpages will reside. These kinds of companies can easily be located through their ads in computer magazines, a yellow pages directory, or a web search. There are numerous directories specifically of web-hosting services. To locate these directories, you can use the following Open Directory category (at dmoz.org):

Computers > Internet > Web Design and Development >
Hosting > Directories

Web-host services will host your site for as little as $5 per month or even less for basic service and will also guide you through the process of getting your own domain name. One of the big advantages of these services is that they handle most of the paperwork of the domain name registration. Compare their ads, call their toll-free numbers, and talk to two or three of them, partly to get a feel for their degree of customer service orientation.

As you explore these, you will get a feel for the various levels of service provided and be able to decide which you need. (If, for example, you aren't selling a product, it is unlikely that you will need a Shopping Cart service as part of your hosting contract.) Be sure to check the reviews of web-hosting services. The following site will help.

Upperhost

www.upperhost.com

Upperhost is an independent web-host reviewing service. It provides up-to-date benchmarking and reviews, done by webmasters, on a very wide range of web-hosting companies. You will also find user comments and a useful collection of articles on web hosting.

Putting Your Site on Your Organization's Server

If you are in an academic institution, there is a good chance that your institution will provide some free web space for you. For other organizations, there may be similar possibilities, depending on your purpose and the nature of the organization. Do not be surprised if you are presented with a list of criteria that must be met, with regard to both content and format. If you are a faculty member at a university, you may easily be assigned web space with minimal restrictions and permission to upload your pages when and as you like. At the K–12 level, there is a very good chance that there will be cooperation and enthusiasm for teachers or others to create school and classroom sites (or, at least, pages). In other situations, it may not be as easy, and there are situations where you will encounter institutional web administrators who impose requirements that make little sense. Fortunately, a larger proportion of those in charge of organizational sites are realistic and helpful.

Free Webpage Sites

For many people who want to get started, using a free website service is an excellent starting place. Even if you are planning to eventually place your site on your organization's server, or to have your own domain name on a hosting service, free website services provide a good initiation. Free websites are available from a variety of sources. The ISP (Internet Service Provider) you use at home may provide free site hosting for subscribers. There are also commercial sites that specialize in providing free space. You pay for these by putting up with the ads that will come along when your page is displayed, but it is often a good bargain. They usually also offer upgrades (that avoid the ads) for a relatively small monthly fee. Among the leading free website services are Tripod (www.tripod.lycos.com) (see Figure 10.3) and Angelfire (www.angelfire.lycos.com).

Figure 10.3

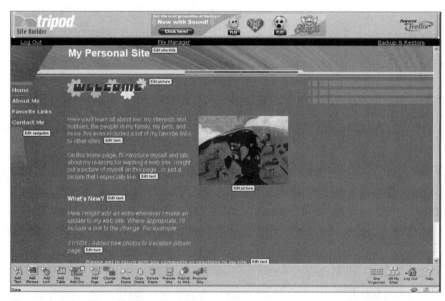

Example of a Tripod "Site Builder" template

Free website services provide at least 15 megabytes of storage (often much more), which is enough for a very substantial website. They also provide templates that can be used, web editors, and uploading capabilities, as well as allowing you to upload pages you have created elsewhere, such as in another web editor. These sites also make it easy to place features such as the following on the pages you create: photo albums, a counter, news headlines, weather (for places you choose), online messages, and guest books. In most cases, you will have at least a little control over the kinds of ads that appear by your choice of interests or communities that you may select as part of the sign-up procedure.

Google, of course, has gotten into the free website game with Google Sites (sites.google.com), which offers extensive storage and easy incorporation of other Google services such as the Google Calendar, Google Docs., etc. With Google Sites, you cannot, however, upload pages created elsewhere.

Sites to Help You Build Your Websites

There are thousands of websites that provide help in building webpages, ranging from the tutorials already mentioned to sites that provide specific features you can place on your pages (such as graphics and JavaScript scripts) to sites that bring together a large collection of a variety of tools. The following representative site, Webmonkey, is one that the beginner may want to explore, particularly to get a feel for the kind of help that is out there.

Webmonkey

www.webmonkey.com

Webmonkey is especially strong on tutorials for a variety of things you might want to place on your page (Figure 10.4). Webmonkey's content is pre-

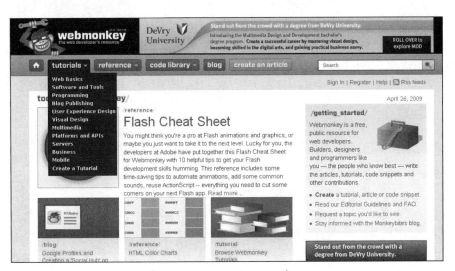

Figure 10.4

Webmonkey main page (showing tutorials menu)

sented and arranged in such a way that you can, at your own speed, build up your webmaster skills one step at a time.

Though it wasn't emphasized in the discussion of reasons for creating blogs and websites, if you are the kind of person who is inclined to try out the publishing side of the web, an added benefit that will almost undoubtedly accrue is that you will have some fun, probably a lot of fun, doing it.

Conclusion

It is hoped that the preceding chapters have provided some new and useful ideas, information, and sites, even for the very experienced internet user. My final bit of advice is: "Explore!" As you use the sites I've mentioned, or any site, take a few extra seconds to look around. Poke into the corners of a site, and if it looks very promising, "click everywhere."

—*Ran Hock*

GLOSSARY

The following words are defined in the context of the internet and are not necessarily intended to be applied generally.

Ajax. Asynchronous JavaScript And XML. A technique for creating interactive web applications. It increases the interactivity of a page by making it unnecessary to reload the entire page when only a portion of the page needs to be changed.

algorithm. A step-by-step procedure for solving a problem or achieving a task. In the context of search engines, this is the part of the service's program that performs a task, such as identifying which pages should be retrieved or ranking retrieved pages.

ALT attribute. Text associated with an image, in the HTML code of a page, that can be used to identify the content of the image or for other purposes. Standing for "alternate text," the ALT initially provided a description while waiting for the image to load, but it is now used more for other purposes, such as providing a description of the image that can be read by screen readers for sight-impaired users. In some browsers, you will see the ALT text pop up when you hold your cursor over an image.

AND. The Boolean operator (or connector) that specifies the "intersection" of sets. When used between words in a search engine query, it specifies that only those records are to be retrieved that contain both words (the words preceding and following the "AND"). For example, *stomach AND growling* would only retrieve records containing both of those words. For major search engines, you do not actually type AND since it is implied (automatically applied). (See **Boolean.**)

API. Application Program Interface. An interface that one program provides to allow requests for services or interchange of data from another program.

applet. A small Java program used on a webpage to perform certain display, computational, or other functions. The origin of the term refers to "small applications programs."

blog. Originally called weblogs, websites, or pages, most typically created by individuals that are updated frequently and usually provide commentary, news, links to news items elsewhere on the web, etc., usually on a specific topic.

bookmark. A feature in web browsers, analogous to bookmarks in a book, that remembers the location of a particular webpage and adds it to a list so a user can return to the page easily. Firefox and others refer to these as *bookmarks*, while Internet Explorer uses the term *favorites*.

Boolean. Mathematical system of notation created by 19th-century mathematician George Boole that symbolically represents relationships between sets (entities). For information retrieval, it uses AND, OR, and NOT (or their equivalents) to identify those records that meet the criteria of having both of two terms within the same record (AND), having either of two terms within the records (OR), or will eliminate records that contain a particular term (NOT).

broadband. High-speed data transmission capability. In the home or office context, it usually refers to DSL (Digital Subscriber Line), cable, high-speed fiber-optic access, or T1 (or higher) internet access.

browser. Software that enables display of webpages by interpreting HTML code, translating it, and performing related tasks. The first widely used browser was Mosaic, which evolved into Netscape. Internet Explorer is the browser developed by Microsoft. Among the several others are Firefox, Opera, and Safari.

browsing. Examining the contents of a database or website by scanning lists or categories and subcategories. When a site provides this capability, it is referred to as having *browsability*.

case-sensitivity. The ability to recognize the difference between upper- and lowercase letters in text. In information retrieval, it means the difference between being able to recognize *White* as a name versus *white* as a color, or *AIDS* as the disease versus *aids* as something that provides assistance.

classification. Arrangement of items (such as websites) by subject area, often using a hierarchical scheme with several levels of categories and subcategories. In some cases, alphanumeric codes are used instead of words (for example, the Library of Congress or Dewey Decimal classifications).

concept-based retrieval. Retrieval based on finding records that contain words related to the concept searched for, not necessarily the specific word(s).

co-occurrence. Occurrence of specific other terms in the same records. Analyzing the frequency of co-occurrence is one technique used to find records that are similar to a selected record.

cookies. Small files of information generated by a web server and stored on the user's computer, used for personalization of sites, etc.

crawler. See **spiders**.

Deep Web. Those pages that are not indexed by web search engines and therefore cannot be retrieved by means of a search on those engines. (Also referred to as the "Invisible Web" and the "Hidden Web.")

diacritical marks. Marks such as accents that are applied to a letter to indicate a different phonetic value.

directory (web). Collection of webpage records classified by subject to allow easy browsing of the collection.

domain name. The part of a URL (web address) that usually specifies the organization (computer) and type of organization where the webpage is located (e.g., in www.microsoft.com, "microsoft.com" is the domain name). Domain names always have at least two parts: The first part usually identifies the organization or specific machine; the second part (e.g., ".com") identifies the kind of organization. In some cases, there will be a two-letter code indicating the country of origin. All domain names have a corresponding numeric address, such as 207.158.227.228.

domain name server. A computer that converts the URL you enter into the numeric address of a domain and identifies the location of the requested computer.

field. A specific portion of a record or webpage, such as title, metatags, URL, etc.

file extension. In a file name, such as *letter.doc* or *house.gif*, the part of the file name that follows the period, usually indicating the type of file.

folksonomy. A process whereby users of a site, such as one that contains photos, can "tag" items with their own choice of descriptive terms. Theoretically, this is an aid to help other users locate items of interest.

FTP. File Transfer Protocol. Computer protocol (set of instructions) for uploading and downloading files.

gopher. A menu-based directory that allows access to files from a remote computer. Gophers were supplanted in the mid-1990s by web tools such as directories and search engines.

Hidden Web. *See* **Deep Web**.

home page. The main page of a website. It also refers to the page designated by a user to automatically display when the user's browser is loaded.

HTML. HyperText Markup Language. The coding language used to create webpages. It tells a browser how to display a record, including specifications for fonts, colors, location of images, identification of hypertext links, etc.

Internet. Worldwide network of networks based on the TCP/IP protocol.

Invisible Web. *See* **Deep Web.**

Java. A programming language designed for use on networks, particularly the internet, which allows programs to be downloaded and run on a variety of platforms. Java is incorporated into webpages with small applications programs called *applets* that provide features such as animation, calculators, games, etc.

JavaScript. A computer language used to write "scripts" for use in web browsers to allow creation of features such as scrolling marquees, navigation buttons that change appearance when you hold your mouse over them, etc.

mashup. In the web context, a product (web application, webpage, etc.) that combines data from two or more sources, such as map data provided by a source such as Google or Yahoo! and descriptive information provided by a user or other party.

metadata. Data about data. Words, phrases, etc. that describe the content and nature of information resources such as books, articles, webpages, images, videos, etc.

metasearch engines. Search services that search several individual search engines and then combine the results.

metasites. See **resource guides.**

metatags. The portion (field) of the HTML coding for a webpage that allows the person creating the page to enter text describing the content of the page (see **metadata**). The content of metatags is not shown on the page itself when the page is viewed in a browser window.

NEAR. A "proximity" connector that is used between two words in a search query to specify that a page should be retrieved only when those words are near each other in the page. (See **proximity**.)

nesting. The use of parentheses to specify the way terms in a Boolean expression should be grouped (i.e., the order of the operations). For example, *landmines (detection OR disarming)*.

newsgroup. An online discussion group. A group of people and the messages they communicate on a specific topic of interest. The term also refers more narrowly to such a discussion group on Usenet.

NOT. The Boolean operator (connector) that when used with a term eliminates the records containing that term. (See **Boolean.**)

OR. The Boolean operator (connector) that is used between two terms to retrieve all those records that contain either term. (See **Boolean.**)

podcasts. Downloadable audio recordings (broadcasts), analogous to blog postings. Podcasts are usually published using feeds (e.g., RSS) that can be downloaded via the web and transferred to an MP3 player (or to a CD) so the user can listen to the broadcast at his or her convenience.

portal. A site that serves as a gateway or starting point for a collection of web resources. Portals typically have a variety of tools (such as a search engine, directory, news, etc.) on a single page, so users can use that page as the start page for their browsers. Portals are often personalizable for content, layout, etc.

precision. In information retrieval, the degree to which a group of retrieved records actually match the searcher's needs. More technically, precision is the ratio of the number of retrieved relevant items to the total number of retrieved items (multiplied by 100 percent to express the ratio as a percentage). For example, if a query produced 10 records and six of them were judged relevant, the precision would be 60 percent. Precision is sometimes referred to as *relevance*.

proximity. The nearness of two terms. Some search engines provide proximity operators, such as NEAR, which allow a user to specify how close two terms must be for a record containing those terms to be retrieved.

ranking. The process for determining in what order records retrieved by a search engine should be displayed. Search engines use algorithms that evaluate records to assign a score that is meant to indicate the relative "relevance" of each record. The retrieved records can then be ranked and listed on the basis of those scores.

recall. In information retrieval, the degree to which a search has actually managed to find all the relevant records in the database. More technically, it is the ratio of the number of relevant records that were retrieved to the total number of relevant records in the database (multiplied by 100 percent to express the ratio as a percentage). For example, if a query retrieved four relevant records, but there were 10 relevant records in the database, the recall for that search would be 40 percent. Recall is usually difficult to measure since the number of relevant records in a database is often subjective and difficult to determine.

record. The unit of information in a database that contains items of related data. In an address book database, for example, each single record might be the collection of information about an individual person, such as name, address, ZIP code, phone number, etc. In the databases of web search engines, each record is the collection of information that describes a single webpage.

relevance. The degree to which a record matches the user's query (or the user's needs as expressed in a query). Search engines may assign relevance scores to each retrieved record, with the scores representing an estimate of the relevance of that record.

resource guides. Small, specialized web directories that provide a collection of related links on a specific topic. Also known as metasites, cyberguides, resource guides, specialized directories, webliographies, etc.

RSS. Acronym for Really Simple Syndication or Rich Site Summary. This is an HTML format by which news providers (and others sources such as blogs) can easily syndicate (distribute) their content over the internet.

screencast. A recording of a series of steps or events that take place on a computer screen, often used for providing instruction as to how to perform a certain task.

search engines. Programs that accept a user's query, search a database, and return to the user those records matching the query. The term is often used more broadly to refer not just to the information retrieval program itself, but also to the interface and associated features, programs, and services.

social software. Though definitions vary depending upon the context, in relation to general usage of the internet, social software encompasses those web-based programs that allow people to easily interact with one another, network, share, and collaborate.

spiders. Programs that search the World Wide Web to identify new (or changed) pages for the purpose of adding those pages to a search service's (search engine's) database. Also known as *crawlers*.

start page. The page that loads automatically when you open your browser, sometimes called your *home page*. You select what you want your start page to be by using the "Edit > Preferences" or "Tools > Internet Options" choices on your browser's menu.

stopwords. Small or frequently occurring words that an information retrieval program does not bother to index (ostensibly because the words are "insignificant," but more likely because the indexing of those words would take up too much storage space or require too much processing).

submitted URLs. URLs (internet addresses) that a person directly submits to a search engine service to have that address and its associated webpage added to the service's database.

syntax. The specific order of elements, notations, etc., by which instructions must be submitted to a computer system.

tagging. The process of attaching descriptive terms by users to pictures and other items found on the web. In its most typical application, tagging refers to the capability of any user of a site to add their own terms to help other users search for items on a particular topic.

TCP/IP. Transfer Control Protocol/Internet Protocol. The collection of data transfer protocols (set of instructions) used on the internet.

telnet. A program that lets a user log onto and access a remote computer using a text-based interface.

thesaurus. Listing of terms usually displaying the relationship between the terms, such as whether one term is narrower or broader than another. Thesauri are used in information retrieval to identify related terms to be searched.

thread. Within a group (newsgroup, discussion group, etc.), a series of messages on a specific topic, consisting of the original message, replies to that message, replies to those replies, etc.

timeout. The amount of time a system will work on a task or wait for results before either stopping the task or the waiting.

truncation. Feature in information retrieval systems that lets a user search with the stem or root of a word and automatically retrieve records with all terms that begin with that string of characters. Truncation is usually specified using a symbol such as an asterisk. For example, in some search engines, *town** would retrieve town, towns, township, etc.

URL. Uniform Resource Locator. The address by which a webpage can be located on the World Wide Web. URLs consist of several parts separated by periods and sometimes slashes. URLs may have various parts such as the domain name, subdomains, paths (directories), and file names.

Usenet. The world's largest system of internet discussion groups (newsgroups).

videotext. Systems, developed beginning in the 1970s, that allow for interactive delivery of text and images on television or computer screens. One of the first applications was the delivery of newspaper content.

Web (World Wide Web, WWW). That portion of the internet that uses HTTP (HyperText Transfer Protocol) and its variations to transmit files. The files involved are typically written in some version of HTML (HyperText Markup Language), thereby viewable using browser software, allowing a GUI (Graphical User Interface), incorporation of hypertext point-and-click navigation of text, and extensive incorporation of images and other types of media and formats.

Web 2.0. A term for a "second generation" of the web that provides a much greater focus on, and use of, desktop applications on the web, and collaboration and sharing by users. Forerunners of this include wikis, blogs, RSS, and podcasts. Though there is no precise definition, some people also define Web 2.0 in terms of the programs used, including APIs (Application Programming Interfaces), social software, and Ajax.

wiki (or WikiWiki). A site created and maintained as a collaborative project of internet users that allows fast and easy input and online editing by multiple users.

WYSIWYG. What You See Is What You Get. Refers to interfaces, such as in word processors, where the way something looks as you input the content is basically what it will look like when it is displayed in its final form (e.g., on a printer, website, or blog).

URL List

Links to all of the sites covered in this book can be found at www.extreme searcher.com.

CHAPTER 1
A Brief History of the Internet, version 3.1
www.isoc.org/internet/history/brief.shtml

Internet History and Growth
www.isoc.org/internet/history/2002_0918_Internet_History_and_Growth.ppt

Hobbes' Internet Timeline
www.zakon.org/robert/internet/timeline

Internet World Stats
www.internetworldstats.com/stats.htm

Network Solutions' WHOIS Search
www.networksolutions.com/whois

DomainTools
www.domaintools.com

Internet Assigned Numbers Authority—Roots Zone Database
www.iana.org/domains/root/db

The Virtual Chase: Evaluating the Quality of Information on the Internet
www.virtualchase.com/quality

Evaluating the Quality of WWW Resources
www.valpo.edu/library/user/evaluation.html

Wayback Machine—Internet Archive
www.archive.org

CompletePlanet
completeplanet.com

U.S. Copyright Office
www.copyright.gov

The U.K. Intellectual Property Office—Copyright
www.ipo.gov.uk/copy

Canadian Intellectual Property Office—A Guide to Copyrights
www.cipo.ic.gc.ca/eic/site/cipointernet-internetopic.nsf/eng/wr00037.html

Copyright Website
www.benedict.com

Copyright and Fair Use in the Classroom, on the Internet, and the World Wide Web
www.umuc.edu/library/copy.html

Journalism Resources—Guide to Citation Style Guides
bailiwick.lib.uiowa.edu/journalism/cite.html

Citation Styles, Style Guides, and Avoiding Plagiarism: Citing Your Sources
www.lib.berkeley.edu/instruct/guides/citations.html

ResourceShelf
www.resourceshelf.com

FreePint
www.freepint.com

ResearchBuzz
www.researchbuzz.org/wp

Internet Resources Newsletter
www.hw.ac.uk/libwww/irn

The Internet Scout Project
scout.wisc.edu

CHAPTER 2

Yahoo! Directory
dir.yahoo.com

Yahoo! Kids
kids.yahoo.com

Open Directory Project
dmoz.org

ipl²: Information You Can Trust
www.ipl.org

Search Engine Colossus
www.searchenginecolossus.com

The WWW Virtual Library
www.vlib.org

Search Engine Guide—Search Engines Directory
www.searchengineguide.com/searchengines.html

Refdesk
refdesk.com

INFOMINE
infomine.ucr.edu

BUBL LINK

bubl.ac.uk/link

Intute

www.intute.ac.uk

Library of Congress Gateway to Library Catalogs

lcweb.loc.gov/z3950/gateway.html

Best of History Web Sites

www.besthistorysites.net

Virtual Religion Index

virtualreligion.net/vri

ChemDex

www.chemdex.org

healthfinder

www.healthfinder.gov

MedlinePlus

www.nlm.nih.gov/medlineplus

Rutgers University—Subject Research Guides: Business

www.libraries.rutgers.edu/rul/rr_gateway/research_guides/busi/business.shtml

New York Times > Business > A Web Guide: Business Navigator

www.nytimes.com/ref/business/business-navigator.html

CEOExpress

ceoexpress.com

globalEDGE

globaledge.msu.edu

Resources for Economists on the Internet
rfe.org

Governments on the WWW
www.gksoft.com/govt

Explore GovDocs
www.lib.umich.edu/government-documents-center/explore

USA.gov
www.usa.gov

Directgov (U.K. Online)
www.direct.gov.uk

Government of Canada Official Website
canada.gc.ca

Political Resources on the Net
www.politicalresources.net

FindLaw
www.findlaw.com

GlobaLex
www.nyulawglobal.org/globalex

Kathy Schrock's Guide for Educators
school.discoveryeducation.com/schrockguide

Education World
www.education-world.com

Education Atlas
www.educationatlas.com

Kidon Media-Link
www.kidon.com/media-link

Cyndi's List of Genealogy Sites on the Internet
www.cyndislist.com

Traveler's Web
extremesearcher.com/travel

iGoogle
google.com/ig

AOL
aol.com

Excite
excite.com

Voila!
www.voila.fr

My Yahoo!
my.yahoo.com

Open Directory—World
dmoz.org/world

MSN
msn.com

Traffick: Frequently Asked Questions about Portals
www.traffick.com/article.asp?aID=9#what

CHAPTER 3
Open Directory—Computers > Internet > Searching > Search Engines > Specialized
dmoz.org

CHAPTER 4

Google
google.com

Yahoo!
yahoo.com

Bing
bing.com

Ask.com
ask.com

Exalead
www.exalead.com/search

HotBot
hotbot.com

Lycos
lycos.com

AltaVista
altavista.com

AllTheWeb
alltheweb.com

KartOO
kartoo.com

TouchGraph
touchgraph.com

Quintura
quintura.com

Zuula
zuula.com

TurboScout
turboscout.com

CHAPTER 5
Omgili
www.omgili.com

BoardTracker
www.boardtracker.com

BoardReader
www.boardreader.com

Google Group
groups.google.com

Yahoo! Groups
groups.yahoo.com

Delphi Forums
www.delphiforums.com

Yuku
www.yuku.com

Big Boards
www.big-boards.com

Topica
lists.topica.com

L-Soft CataList, the Official Catalog of LISTSERV Lists
www.lsoft.com/lists/listref.html

CHAPTER 6

Encyclopedia.com

www.encyclopedia.com

Encyclopedia Britannica Online

britannica.com

Wikipedia

wikipedia.org

HowStuffWorks

www.howstuffworks.com

yourDictionary.com

www.yourdictionary.com

Merriam-Webster Online

www.merriam-webster.com

Diccionarios.com

www.diccionarios.com

LEO (Link Everything Online)

dict.leo.org

Answers.com

answers.com

InfoPlease

www.infoplease.com

Infobel

www.infobel.com

Wayp International White and Yellow Pages

www.wayp.com

Yahoo! People Search
people.yahoo.com

AnyWho
www.anywho.com

Superpages.com
superpages.com

The Quotations Page
www.quotationspage.com

Bartleby.com
www.bartleby.com

Yahoo! Finance—Currency Converter
finance.yahoo.com/currency-converter

Weather Underground
wunderground.com

Perry-Castañeda Library Map Collection
www.lib.utexas.edu/maps

David Rumsey Historical Map Collection
www.davidrumsey.com

Global Gazetteer
www.fallingrain.com/world

World Gazetteer
www.world-gazetteer.com

U.S. Postal Service ZIP Code Lookup
www.usps.com/zip4

CNNMoney
money.cnn.com

BEOnline—Statistics
www.loc.gov/rr/business/beonline/subjects.php?SubjectID=56

Intute: SocialSciences—Statistics and Data
www.intute.ac.uk/socialsciences/statistics

USA Statistics in Brief
www.census.gov/compendia/statab/brief.html

FedStats
www.fedstats.gov

Amazon
amazon.com

Barnes & Noble
barnesandnoble.com

Library of Congress Online Catalog
catalog.loc.gov

The British Library
blpc.bl.uk

Google Book Search
books.google.com

Library of Congress Gateway to Library Catalogs
lcweb.loc.gov/z3950/gateway.html

The Online Books Page
digital.library.upenn.edu/books

Project Gutenberg
www.gutenberg.org

Bartleby.com
www.bartleby.com

EuroDocs: Online Sources for European History
eudocs.lib.byu.edu

A Chronology of U.S. Historical Documents
www.law.ou.edu/hist

University of Virginia Hypertext Collection
xroads.virginia.edu/~HYPER/hypertex.html

Governments on the WWW
www.gksoft.com/govt

CIA—The World Factbook
www.cia.gov/library/publications/the-world-factbook

U.K. Foreign & Commonwealth Office—Country Profiles
www.fco.gov.uk/en/travel-and-living-abroad/travel-advice-by-country/
country-profiles

USA.gov
www.usa.gov

GPO Access
www.gpoaccess.gov

THOMAS: Legislative Information on the Internet
thomas.loc.gov

Open CRS
www.opencrs.com

Library of Congress—State and Local Government Information

www.loc.gov/rr/news/stategov/stategov.html

Directgov—Web Site of the U.K. Government

www.direct.gov.uk

CorporateInformation

www.corporateinformation.com

Hoover's

www.hoovers.com

ThomasNet

www.thomasnet.com

Kompass

www.kompass.com

Kellysearch

www.kellysearch.com

American Society of Association Executives Gateway to Associations

www.asaecenter.org/Directories/AssociationSearch.cfm

AMA DoctorFinder

webapps.ama-assn.org/doctorfinder

Lawyers.com

lawyers.com

Pipl

www.pipl.com

Scirus

www.scirus.com

CiteSeer

citeseer.ist.psu.edu

PubMed

www.ncbi.nlm.nih.gov/pubmed

IngentaConnect

www.ingentaconnect.com

HighBeam Research

www.highbeam.com

Google Scholar

scholar.google.com

Peterson's

petersons.com

College Board

www.collegeboard.com

Fodor's

www.fodors.com

Lonely Planet

www.lonelyplanet.com

Travelocity

travelocity.com

Expedia

expedia.com

Orbitz

orbitz.com

Internet Movie Database (IMDb)
www.imdb.com

CHAPTER 7
Nolo—Patents, Copyright & Art
www.nolo.com

Pixlr
pixlr.com

The Digital Scriptorium
www.scriptorium.columbia.edu

Australian National Botanic Gardens'
National Plant Photographic Index
www.anbg.gov.au/anbg/photo-collection

Digital Librarian: A Librarian's Choice of the Best of the Web—Images
www.digital-librarian.com/images.html

BUBL LINK—Image Collections
bubl.ac.uk/link/types/images.htm

Google's Image Search
images.google.com

Yahoo!'s Image Search
images.search.yahoo.com

Bing's Image Search
bing.com/images

Exalead's Image Search
exalead.com/image

Ask.com's Image Search
ask.com/?tool=img

Picsearch
www.picsearch.com

Corbis
corbis.com

Fotosearch
www.fotosearch.com

Creative Commons
creativecommons.org

Stock.XCHNG
www.sxc.hu

American Memory Project
memory.loc.gov

WebMuseum(Paris)
www.ibiblio.org/wm (or more specifically, www.ibiblio.org/wm/paint)

Flickr
flickr.com

Free Graphics
www.freegraphics.com

Barry's Clipart
barrysclipart.com

Yahoo! Directory > Graphics > Clip Art
dir.yahoo.com/Computers_and_Internet/Graphics/Clip_Art

Digital Librarian: A Librarian's Choice of the Best of the Web—Audio

www.digital-librarian.com/audio.html

PAV—Play Audio Video

www.playaudiovideo.com

FindSounds

www.findsounds.com

Internet Archive—Audio Archive

www.archive.org

Radio-Locator (formerly the MIT List of Radio Stations on the Internet)

www.radio-locator.com

CBS Radio

www.cbsradio.com/streaming/index.html

Podscope

www.podscope.com

Podcast Alley

www.podcastalley.com

Podcastdirectory.com

www.podcastdirectory.com

The History Channel: Speeches & Video

www.historychannel.com/video

The Movie Sounds Page

www.moviesounds.com

Apple: iPod & iTunes

www.apple.com/itunes

BUBL LINK: Catalogue of Internet Resources—Video
bubl.ac.uk/link/v/video.htm

Google's Video Search
video.google.com

Yahoo!'s Video Search
video.yahoo.com

YouTube
youtube.com

blinkx
www.blinkx.tv

ShadowTV
www.shadowtv.com

TVEyes
www.tveyes.com

CHAPTER 8

Kidon Media-Link
www.kidon.com/media-link

ABYZ News Links
www.abyznewslinks.com

Metagrid
www.metagrid.com

NewsLink
newslink.org

NewsWealth
www.newswealth.com

News in Pictures

www.newsinpictures.com

Daryl Cagle's Professional Cartoonists Index

www.cagle.com

BBC

news.bbc.co.uk

CNN

www.cnn.com

MSNBC

www.msnbc.com

Reuters

reuters.com

Aljazeera.net

english.aljazeera.net

Today's Front Pages

www.newseum.org/todaysfrontpages

PressDisplay.com

www.pressdisplay.com

Radio-Locator (formerly the MIT List of Radio Stations on the Internet)

www.radio-locator.com

RadioStationWorld

radiostationworld.com

NPR

www.npr.org

Google News
news.google.com

Yahoo! News
news.yahoo.com

NewsNow
newsnow.co.uk

EIN News
www.einnews.com

World News Network
wn.com

SiloBreaker
www.silobreaker.com

Bloglines
bloglines.com

Technorati
technorati.com

IceRocket
www.icerocket.com

Bloglines
bloglines.com

My Yahoo!
my.yahoo.com

Google Alerts
www.google.com/newsalerts

Yahoo! Alerts

alerts.yahoo.com

CHAPTER 9

ShoppingSpot.com

shoppingspot.com

ThomasNet

www.thomasnet.com

Kompass

www.kompass.com

Kellysearch

www.kellysearch.com

Amazon

amazon.com

Overstock.com

www.overstock.com

Yahoo! Shopping

shopping.yahoo.com

mySimon

www.mysimon.com

PriceGrabber.com

www.pricegrabber.com

Shopping.com

www.shopping.com

Shopzilla

www.shopzilla.com

Become.com
www.become.com

Google Product Search
www.google.com/products

eBay
ebay.com

craigslist
www.craigslist.org

Epinions
epinions.com

Consumer Reports
consumerreports.org

ConsumerREVIEW.com
consumerreview.com

ConsumerSearch
consumersearch.com

CHAPTER 10

Google Docs
docs.google.com

PBworks
pbworks.com

MySpace
myspace.com

Facebook
facebook.com

LinkedIn
linkedin.com

Flickr
flickr.com

Picasa Web Albums
picasaweb.google.com

Delicious
delicious.com

Twitter
twitter.com

Blogger
blogger.com

WordPress.com
wordpress.com

Moveable Type
www.movabletype.com

LiveJournal
www.livejournal.com

Podcasting Tools
www.podcasting-tools.com

Web Style Guide
www.webstyleguide.com

000Domains.com
www.000domains.com

Upperhost

www.upperhost.com

Tripod

www.tripod.lycos.com

Angelfire

www.angelfire.lycos.com

Google Sites

sites.google.com

Webmonkey

www.webmonkey.com

ABOUT THE AUTHOR

Randolph Hock, Ph.D.

Ran Hock divides his work time between writing and teaching. On the teaching side, he specializes in customized courses teaching people how to use the internet effectively (through his one-person company, Online Strategies). His courses have been offered—in the U.S. and 11 other countries—to companies, government agencies, nongovernmental organizations, schools, universities, and associations. On the writing side, in addition to this book, he has written *The Extreme Searcher's Guide to Web Search Engines* (CyberAge Books, 1999, 2001), *Yahoo! to the Max* (CyberAge Books, 2005), and *The Traveler's Web* (CyberAge Books, 2007). He has also been a chemistry teacher and a librarian at two universities, as well as having held training and management positions with Dialog Information Services and Knight-Ridder Information. He lives in Vienna, Virginia, with his wife, Pamela, and they have two sons, Matthew and Stephen, and one daughter, Elizabeth. One of Ran's passions is travel, and he hopes to someday also have time to return to his hobby of genealogy.

Z

More Great Books
from Information Today, Inc.

Building & Running a Successful Research Business, 2nd Edition
A Guide for the Independent Information Professional

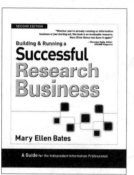

By Mary Ellen Bates

This is the handbook every aspiring independent information professional needs to launch, manage, and build a research business. Organized into four sections, "Getting Started," "Running the Business," "Marketing," and "Researching," the book walks you through every step of the process. Author and long-time independent researcher Mary Ellen Bates covers everything from "is this right for you?" to closing the sale, managing clients, promoting your business, and tapping into powerful information sources.

488 pp/softbound/ISBN 978-0-910965-85-9 $34.95

The Mobile Marketing Handbook
A Step-by-Step Guide to Creating Dynamic Mobile Marketing Campaigns

By Kim Dushinski

In this practical handbook, Kim Dushinski offers easy-to-follow advice for firms that want to interact with mobile users, build stronger customer relationships, reach a virtually unlimited number of prospects, and gain competitive advantage by making the move to mobile device users. *The Mobile Marketing Handbook* will help you put your message in the palms of their hands.

256 pp/softbound/ISBN 978-0-910965-82-8 $29.95